John Clarke
and His Legacies

John Clarke and His Legacies

✤

Religion and Law in Colonial
Rhode Island 1638-1750

Sydney V. James

Edited by Theodore Dwight Bozeman

The Pennsylvania State University Press
University Park, Pennsylvania

Publication was made possible by a generous grant from the University of Iowa Foundation

Library of Congress Cataloging-in-Publication Data

James, Sydney V., 1929–1993.
    John Clarke and his legacies : religion and law in colonial Rhode Island, 1638–1750 / Sydney V. James ; edited by Theodore Dwight Bozeman.
       p.   cm.
    Includes bibliographical references and index.
    ISBN 978-0-271-02815-6
    1. Clarke, John, 1609–1676. 2. Baptists—Rhode Island—Clergy—Biography. 3. Church and state—Rhode Island—History—17th century. 4. Freedom of religion—Rhode Island—History—17th century. 5. Clarke, John, 1609–1676—Will. I. Bozeman, Theodore Dwight, 1942– . II. Title.
BX6495.C5526J36   1998
974.5'02'092—dc21
[b]
                                                                                              98-16950
                                                                                                  CIP

Copyright © 1999 The Pennsylvania State University

All rights reserved
Printed in the United States of America
Published by The Pennsylvania State University Press,
University Park, PA 16802–1003

It is the policy of The Pennsylvania State University Press to use acid-free paper for the first printing of all clothbound books. Publications on uncoated stock satisfy the minimum requirements of American National Standard for Information Sciences—Permanence of Paper for Printed Library Materials, ANSI Z39.48-1992.

Contents

Editor's Acknowledgments		vii
Introduction		xi
1	John Clarke, from Suffolk Through the Antinomian Storm to Rhode Island, 1609–1649	1
2	"A Teacher: I will not say an Elder": Guiding an Antinomian Baptist Church, 1641–1649	21
3	"New Baptisme" and "the prophecies Concerning the rising of Christs Kingdome": Clarke as Evangelist and Visionary, 1649–1661	43
4	In Caesar's Court: The Royal Charter	59
5	Waning Years in Newport	85
6	Clarke's Estate, His Church, and His Colony, 1676–1717	107
7	The Dispute over the Clarke Trust	123
Epilogue		147
Appendix: Will of Dr. John Clarke		159
Notes		167
About the Author		199
Index		201

Editor's Acknowledgments

Early in 1993 I learned that Sydney James would not live to bring his study of John Clarke to publication. In last-minute conversations, he informed me that the scholarly work was virtually completed save for a few details, but that the writing did not yet have the "liveliness"—to use a term of Clarke's—he wanted it to have. With a view to leaving James's own voice and interpretation as intact as possible and yet respond to concerns of the publisher's referees, my own work has been limited to checking, completing, and updating documentation, preparing new introductory passages for Chapters 4 and 6 and a substantial revision of the Introduction, and various touches of light editing.

In preparation of this study the author incurred many debts. He owed a debt of thanks to the staffs of the Main Library at the University of Iowa, the Iowa State Historical Society in Iowa City, the Rhode Island Historical Society, and the Newport (Rhode Island) Historical Society, which were unfailingly efficient and helpful. Virginia DeJohn Anderson, Barbara A. Black, Jeffrey Cox, Richard Gildrie, Bruce H. Mann, Edwin S. Gaustad, and the late William G. McLoughlin supplied critical comment on all or part of the manuscript. Work on the project was speeded by a research appointment to the Charles Austin Warren Center for Studies in American History at Harvard University in 1979–80 and by faculty development awards from the University of Iowa in 1985 and 1991. Jean James, Linda K. Kerber, Albert T. Klyberg, and Peter Potter of Penn State Press offered counsel to the editor on many details of the project in its last stages.

Theodore Dwight Bozeman

Rhode Island, 1636–1659
Courtesy, The Rhode Island Historical Society

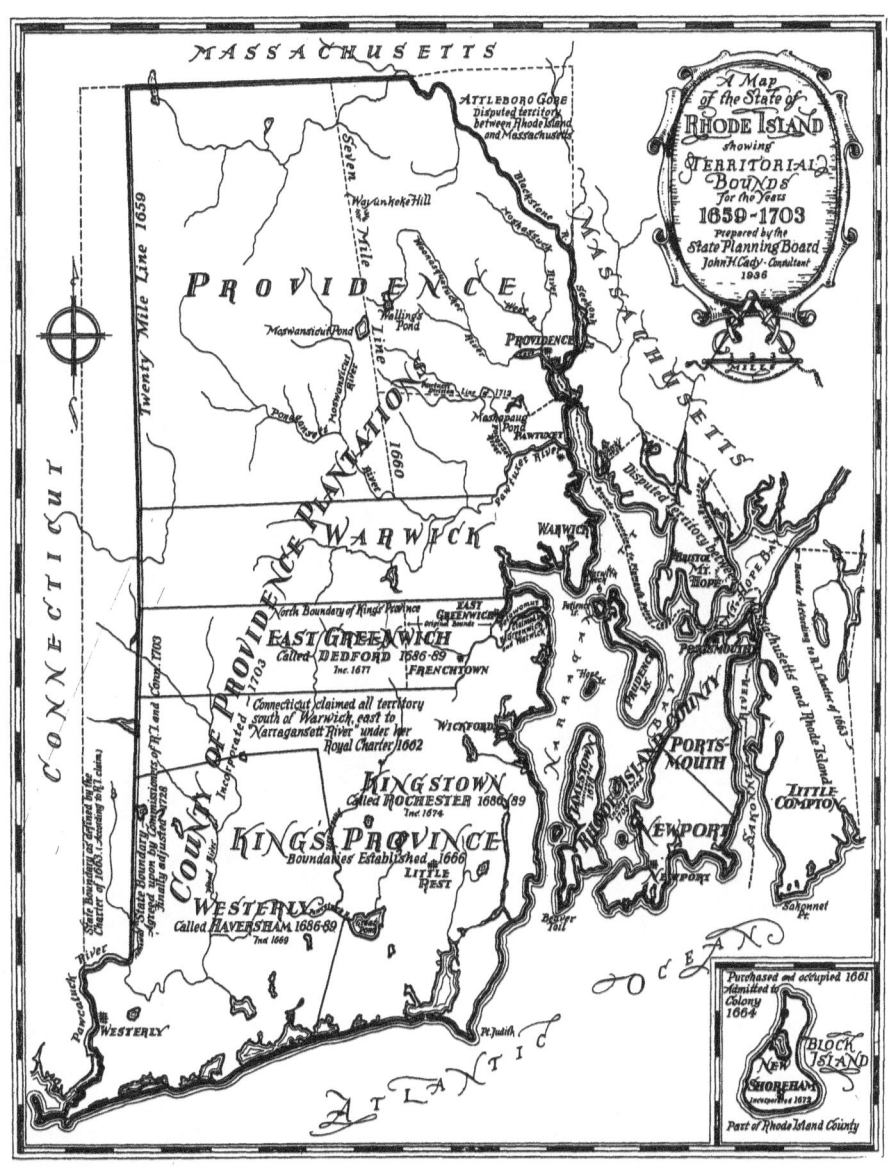

Rhode Island, 1653–1703
Courtesy, The Rhode Island Historical Society

Introduction

Dr. John Clarke led a life that took him through some of the great scenes of the seventeenth century. He had his moments of glory, although much of what he tried to do resulted in less than he hoped for, and he left a lasting imprint on his town and colony. Yet historians have written little about him except to tell that he was the agent who negotiated Rhode Island's royal charter and sometimes to mention that he was an early Baptist leader. Clarke became a Puritan of some sort in southeast England, went to Boston and became an Antinomian, and then, as an exile, helped found Rhode Island and launch the first Baptist church in Newport. Like other New England Puritans, he keenly favored the revolution against Charles I, and like a few he went back to England and joined in the vigorous public life of the Interregnum. He championed the Baptist cause and became a Fifth Monarchist. He negotiated the colony's royal charter and returned to Newport and a modest role in the new government. Along with other men in public office, he struggled rather ineffectually with the procession of difficulties that beset his colony in the ensuing years. He tried with diminishing success to keep his church a shelter for Baptists of all kinds. He died in 1676, nearly unnoticed amid the turmoil of King Philip's War.

Clarke's was no provincial life. Closely tied to Rhode Island beginnings, it intersected repeatedly with major events in the larger Anglo-American world. The chapters that follow illuminate important developments in old and New England, placing formative Baptist experience in a transatlantic context and clarifying many details of social, political, and legal history. They will reveal as well that Clarke, through the disposition of property in his will, continued to influence events in his town and church for nearly half a century after his death.

The relative tameness of Clarke's religious convictions has subdued interest in him in modern times. He had no equivalents to the dizzying and esoteric teachings of Samuel Gorton, no wild ideas to entertain the modern mind. He wrote little that survives and had little to say that stirs up intricate dissections of theology. He was a capable but not a brilliant writer. He could tell a story effectively but also wrote in a diffuse and rhapsodic manner that probably matched the style in which he preached and exhorted extemporaneously.

Nevertheless, his central conceptions deserve another look. In his most careful writing on the church, the distinctive word was "livelie." He used the word to mean something alive in the sense of actual as against speculative, to mean full of life and assertiveness and spontaneity (even in the kinetic sense) rather than studied formalities, to mean incandescent belief. His devotion to liveliness did much to define the special kind of radicalism that he espoused. He wanted a congregation that rejected infant baptism and required adult baptism by total immersion but that held no other rigid tenets. He favored a dignified, if simple, order of public worship. At the same time he favored another mode of association, the church meeting. There, echoing General Baptist practice in the parent country, the pastor's view and voice would be part of an open discussion and the members would debate differing beliefs with great freedom.

A "livelie" church without a dominant pastor who wielded a busy pen gets little attention these days. The shortage of eye-catching qualities in Newport's First Baptist Church has let historians overlook the significance of the style of religious association there. Yet possibly it, more than doctrine or ceremony or special modes of prayer and devotion, constituted Clarke's most noteworthy contribution to "radical religion" in early New England. And surely in the years before the Great Awakening, his strand of resistance to a hardening New England orthodoxy had greater effect than the comparatively ephemeral radicalism of Gorton or William Pynchon.

Probably Clarke would have mixed feelings about being put into the category of radical religion. By his lights he was strictly conservative on how a church should operate, even when he was dazzled by hopes for an imminent Second Coming. Like Massachusetts Puritans, he wanted to go back to the kind of church organized by the Apostles. He condemned the Massachusetts men for forsaking the purer practices of an earlier Puritan time and for refusing to accept the better light on the subject of baptism. Dwight Bozeman has described how Massachusetts Puritans tried to return to a primitive Christianity, not merely in a legalistic sense of following the precedents of the early churches as described in the New Testament, but also in actions that would make them ritually at one with the sacred times of the early Christians.[1] As we shall see, Clarke wanted to practice an even more rigorous primitivism.[2]

Clarke's labors to get the Rhode Island charter also need a closer look. His part has been treated cursorily in most instances. In some accounts he becomes a hero of Rhode Island who overcame great obstacles to perform heroic feats, in others a malicious enemy of John Winthrop, Jr., who was getting the Connecticut charter. So far, the best historical studies have seen him as part of Winthrop's story.[3] I have looked at the episode the other way, with Winthrop as part of Clarke's story, and have been less impressed by Clarke's skills in negotiation than some admirers have been. Yet in the end he negotiated one of the more notable constitutional documents in early American history. Its provisions for religious freedom are well known, but it also contained a redesign of the colonial government which, although much elaborated on from time to time, lasted until Rhode Island adopted its first constitution in 1843.

In ways that went well beyond his intent, Clarke also made an afterlife for himself in his town, church, and colony by leaving a donation of land as the basis for a charitable trust. His trustees had to cope with most of the changes in the colony's fortunes between 1676 and 1718 and to decide how to use the profits. They did their best to manage the estate during a period of wars, governmental upheavals, and shattered public authority. Having weathered the storms, they settled into a habit of using the proceeds for their Baptist friends and relations until challenged by the town of Newport, which wanted to make the income a public fund. After a complex dispute, the trustees made the estate largely an endowment for Clarke's church. These events had a part in the development of governmental and ecclesiastical institutions in early eighteenth-century Rhode Island. In particular, when the trust became a benefit for First Baptist, the effect was to spur a move away from Clarke's standards for a church and toward a structure resembling the urban post-Puritan churches in Boston.

Even more notable, however, was the trust's impact on the relation of church and state. Clarke was one of the most ardent and effective stalwarts in the campaign to separate church and state in seventeenth-century New England. The colony and its towns (after a few months of other hopes in the earliest years) adamantly refused to treat government as having a divine source or to put secular power behind any religious purpose. They wanted their churches untouched by the corrupting hand of secular government. They created a government that did not violate true religion by mocking worship in such practices as oaths. It followed that they rejected the belief that government, to be effective, must be regarded by the governed as having a delegation of divine authority. This concept could be upheld as long as the churches had no desire to own property. In the early years the churches had none and believed that they should not want any, but Clarke's trust contributed to a change of attitudes toward and beyond the end of the century.

Because the terms of his will were loose enough to admit diverse readings of his intent, the town council, First Baptist Church, and the trustees became caught up in decades of strife over the proper use of the proceeds. Despite occasional conflicts, the town and the church cooperated much of the time. They tried to maintain the appearance of unsullied separation but in reality acted in an intimate fashion. Moreover, the colonial government was provoked by the Newport fracas to enact a law providing in general terms for the protection of charitable trusts. Thereafter, the now multiple churches of Rhode Island could and occasionally did avail themselves of this benefit. So, little by little, the church became dependent on secular power. Telling this story brings some clarity to the now characteristic relations of church and state in the United States by showing an example of how they began.

It shows an example, too, of the tangled and difficult evolution of legal affairs in a pioneer community pledged by its charter to honor a parent tradition of law that did not translate readily into a far-flung colonial environment. The struggles over Clarke's legacy provide a detailed example of how Rhode Islanders, including professional lawyers hired by the Newport town council and the Clarke trustees, had to maneuver to represent local interests without dangerous deviation from English legal principles or laws. How the Charitable Uses Act of 1601, for instance, was variously applied, adapted, and skirted in Rhode Island is an intriguing chapter both in the emergence of American colonial law and in the complete history of that important parliamentary statute.

1

John Clarke, from Suffolk Through the Antinomian Storm to Rhode Island, 1609 - 1649

Dr. John Clarke had a prominent place in the settlement of Newport, Rhode Island, and in the establishment of the colony. As he wrote his will just before his death in 1676, he could think back over an eventful life and a record of accomplishment, and he knew that what he had helped to build was a notable legacy. Yet far more than he foresaw, he was preparing a different legacy through the charitable donation or trust he founded in his will. For it helped to change what he had built, change it away from what he had favored. A dispute over the trust in 1718–22 brought a connection between the colonial government and the church Clarke had guided through its early years, a connection that he had opposed, and the income from the trust, which was used mostly to pay the minister of the church, fostered a pastoral eminence that he had avoided.

Clarke deserves a fuller appreciation than he has received. He was a many-sided man, and yet his modest fame rests on dim and somewhat inaccurate knowledge of only two of his accomplishments: founding the first Baptist church in Newport and winning the royal charter for Rhode Island in 1663. In both of these achievements his reputation has been put into competition with that of Roger Williams, without doing justice to either man. Beyond question, Williams had the better mind and pen. He also had a superior talent for dramatizing himself and cultivating the friendship of high-ranking contemporaries. All the same, Clarke built much more that lasted and set a course for the future.

The debate over primacy is sterile. Clarke's good name need not be magnified by shrinking another's. Surely Williams won the first charter for his colony in 1644 and was the first Baptist pastor in America, but his charter was a frail platform and he left his church after a very short time when he came to the conclusion that there could not be a true church of Christ on earth in his day. A few enthusiasts have insisted that Clarke should be considered the real Baptist founder in America because Williams left no lasting imprint on the denomination, whereas Clarke certainly did.[1] He took the lead in Newport, much the larger community, and remained constant in his Baptist affiliation.

He attained wider renown as Rhode Island's agent in procuring the famous royal charter of 1663, which remained the foundation of government for 179 years, with its oft-quoted provisions for religious freedom in the colony. Roger Williams had precedence as a champion of that cause. He upheld it from the start in Providence, with the support of his fellow townsfolk. By contrast, the Newport settlers initially wanted a single town church roughly in the Massachusetts fashion. They swung around to religious liberty only when they fell into disagreement on doctrine and how a church should be conducted. Clarke's part in this development is not known, but he probably was on the side of freedom all along. He did not invent the underlying ideas in the charter of 1663, but its most eloquent rhetoric was his, as was the tough and lonely campaign that won approval of the tiny colony's "lively experiment."

Throughout his life (to the distress of the biographer) Clarke practiced the Christian virtues of modesty and self-effacement. He left little on paper to advertise his actions and thoughts. In his church he was irenic rather than a stickler for doctrinal rigidity, though he spoke forthrightly for his own beliefs when he had to. At times he went so far as to publicize himself as the servant of a good cause. Though by disposition a peacemaker, he could be driven to anger. In the classifications used by historians today he became a religious radical on the fringes of the Puritan movement, but unlike so many other radicals he never became a flaming zealot.

By his own lights he was not a radical at all but rather an advocate for the pattern of the earliest Christian churches. In this respect he was hardly unique: all Protestants thought they were going back to the primitive ways. But for all their agreement on the goal, they disagreed on when they reached it. They kept "restoring" different things. Going back to the old turned into a design for the new.

Clarke knew that his beliefs about how to restore the old brought him to conclusions that others regarded as dangerous errors. He could maintain his poise in the face of hostility. He was sustained by his knowledge that he often clung to the ways of early Puritan conventicles when others were departing from them, whether in the direction taken by the Massachusetts churches or the Quakers. Not only did he believe he knew how to return to the Apostolic era, but he had confidence that he was faithful to the best of the recent past.

Clarke's principles reinforced his moral values. He seldom claimed a special leadership for himself and in crucial respects positively did not want one. In his church he opposed having a dominant pastor. In the government of his colony, he served willingly in a system that resolutely prevented any concentration of authority in a few hands. If we were to paint a diorama depicting Clarke's career, many scenes will have him somewhat inconspicuous among other figures, other scenes will have outlines partly lost in shadow.

He was born on 8 October 1609 (Old Style), on the manor of Westhorpe, Suffolk, eighty-eight miles from London. The bare genealogical data were entered by his father in a new copy of the Geneva Bible printed the year before.[2] According to this record, he was the fifth of seven children. His sister Margaret was the oldest, born more than eight years earlier. After her came Carewe, then Thomas, then Mary—and after John, William and Joseph. The family's social and economic standing is unknown. The most we can determine is that it was below the gentry and above the ordinary village tenant. Thomas Clarke's choice of a Geneva Bible suggests a Puritan leaning. That translation was preferred by Puritans.

More remarkable was John Clarke's education. Nothing survives to show beyond doubt where he studied and with what results. One theory has him a Cambridge scholar, another an Oxford man.[3] In his mature years he considered himself well versed in Hebrew, so he must have had a fairly extensive university education. He was a physician, but his medical training at Leyden is only a plausible guess.[4] Even if the specifics are unknown, the mere fact of his extensive education is striking. There is nothing to suggest that any of his brothers had comparable schooling, and John was the third of five sons.[5] Moreover, his father died when he was eighteen.

Why—and how—did the father gather the money to provide his third son with the education for a learned profession? If the funds were there for John, why not earlier for Carewe or Thomas? Were his parents so keen in their observation and so quick to act according to what they saw that they evaluated their sons and chose John for higher learning? Or did someone outside the immediate family sponsor him? Carewe and William went into commerce and did moderately well but scored no successes in life to make them memorable. The other two sons ended their lives as operators of medium-sized farms near Newport. Somehow, John stood out.

Just as obscure is his marriage in about 1634 to Elizabeth Harges, a daughter of the lord of the manor of Wreslingworth, Bedfordshire. For him this was a step up, but it turned out to be several steps down for her. They remained loyal to each other through some difficult times and disappointments. She followed him into the Baptist church, and he asked to be buried between her and his second wife. It is a fair guess that Elizabeth and her parents expected that she would be the wife of a prosperous English physician. Instead, she became the spouse of a man who went to Boston in New England, took the losing side in a theological dispute, helped found a new settlement in a struggling port town, embraced an unpopular religion, took many ill-paid public responsibilities, could not make a living from his profession, tried husbandry and commerce, and accumulated enough land to live comfortably as long as he had a few tenants or servants.

If it is correct to surmise that Clarke's father picked a Geneva Bible on account of Puritan leanings in 1609, then John was brought up in a Puritan household and probably was taken into a Puritan circle in the parish church. His later life shows that he had a background in a fairly radical kind of Puritanism. He became the leader of the family after his parents' death in 1627. When he decided to move to the Puritan colony in New England in 1637, his two younger brothers and his sister Mary went with him. Later his sister Margaret came, too. She married and remained in Cambridge or Watertown, Massachusetts, while the others went with John to Newport. He never gave a public explanation of why they all moved to Newport.

According to his own account, John Clarke arrived in Boston in November 1637. This was the month of Anne Hutchinson's trial before the magistrates, the trial that culminated in her banishment and the disarming of seventy-six of her followers. It was no time for a newcomer to plunge into the fray. If he had been timid, he could have stayed out of the controversy. If he had lacked a previous conviction that put him on Hutchinson's side, which was called Antinomian by her enemies, he could have waited to gain a fuller understanding of what was at stake. Rather, he took her side at once. His temperate narrative, written when he no longer felt the original excitement and championed a different cause, hints at his rush into this conflict, the most heated and vital of the disputes over belief in early New England. For him it turned out to be the first of two surges into confidence that human society could be ruled by God's laws.

Hutchinson, in the few years since her arrival in 1633, had stirred up a storm. Thinking she was faithful to the teachings of her minister, John Cotton, she began to hold meetings to discuss sermons, where she propagated her beliefs and soon began to denounce nearly all other ministers and the magistrates who backed them. She gained a large following, especially in Boston. Participants on both sides fervently believed that the stakes were of cosmic dimensions.

The two sides also agreed on the doctrine of predestination—that is, that every person was ticketed for heaven or hell by God's timeless decree. The predestined saints at some point in their lives would become aware that God had chosen them. They would be united to Christ. They would come to know "saving faith," which meant a spiritually exhilarating delight in God's dispensation as well as a belief in the truth of the Bible and the correctness of theology. The disagreement broke out over how the awareness of grace would begin, over the possibility of preparing the soul for it, over what inward experience the union with Christ would bring, and over the evidence that would give assurance of the presence of grace in a soul. Contestants in the Antinomian controversy believed that they must achieve the absolutely right understanding of these subjects. Hutchinson's opponents not only thought they had the correct understanding but also that she was undermining the authority of the government and the churches.

In his cool language penned fourteen years later, Clarke wrote that the issues in dispute were "touching the Covenants, and in point of evidencing a man[']s good estate." By "good estate" he meant predestination for heaven. On one side, he wrote, "some prest hard for the Covenant of works, and for sanctification to be the first and chief evidence."[6] (Sanctification meant an increase of good conduct, pleasure in religious duties, and love of God's law in all its ramifications, including prayer and formal worship.) Merely explaining it in those terms showed that Clarke disagreed. Nobody in New England professed a "Covenant of works," but Anne Hutchinson and her followers said their opponents did. These opponents were "legalists" because they stressed obedience to God's laws. Actually, everyone agreed that all humans were so corrupt that they could not obey God's commands completely, no matter how hard they tried.

When Clarke characterized the Antinomians as pressing "for the Covenant of grace ... and for the evidence of the Spirit," he showed his affiliation with them. This side, he said, "was established upon better promises" and "a more certain, constant, and satisfactory witness." That is, he found the doctrine better grounded in the Bible and better expounded, the evidence of the Spirit a firmer promise of salvation—and the outward evidence of behavior an unreliable sign of standing among the elect. He believed that only the Antinomians genuinely upheld the Protestant conviction that salvation is by faith alone and the Calvinist conviction that faith is the fruit of God's free award of grace.[7] He said later that he was not surprised to find disagreement "about matters of Heaven" because that was only to be expected "upon Earth," but was dismayed to find a fervor to make one side or the other victorious.[8] This comment expressed his moderate disposition but seriously understated the passions raging in Massachusetts during 1637 and 1638. He deliberately chose to define the issues in the Antinomian controversy on the ground Hutchinson first took. He left much unsaid.

The legalists, Hutchinson said, taught that godly living (as well as a mortal could do it) could prepare the soul to receive awareness of grace and thereby made good works the focus of a religious life, even if they claimed to believe in predestination. Thus they denied the fundamental Protestant belief in salvation by faith alone. Besides, they taught that union with Christ probably would seem uncertain and would not bring any divine guidance beyond the providential—that is, what God's stage management provided through the inward prompting of attention to helpful Biblical texts, the workings of natural law to bring portents and reproofs, and experience in public worship, above all hearing sermons. They made the bloom of faith in the soul much more the result of a preacher's words than a burst of divine radiation. The legalist ministers tightened the grip of reliance on works by telling their anxious hearers that the receipt of grace might be no more dramatic than an intermittent glimmer of hope but could be confirmed by a record of sanctification.

All of this was accurate enough up to a point. Hutchinson's opponents indignantly denied that they secretly rejected the doctrines of predestination or salvation by faith alone. For them, further, the emphasis should be different. They insisted on the public and social character of Christian living through the interaction between ministers and their hearers, the collective help to bring up children to virtue and keep adults from straying, and reliance on the visible evidence of sanctification to preserve mutual confidence. The standing of the elect would be there for all to see in their behavior.[9]

True doctrine, Hutchinson said, would not compromise or blur or secretly deny the central point: that the covenant between God and the predestined elect in the human race was fixed and unchanging throughout all eternity rather than contingent on the behavior of the chosen ones. The elect would come to know their standing through the witness of the Holy Spirit in their hearts, a purely inward experience, and could do nothing to bring it about. It would come as a blaze of light rather than a flickering candle flame. After that they would have a special intimacy with Christ's spirit.

The disagreement had extensive ramifications. For Hutchinson, but not for all of her followers, they were strictly in the spiritual life. For the legalists they ran much further. For them, upholding the value of preparing the soul and of documenting the presence of grace by sanctification explained why a person should strive to be godly even though a wholly moral life was impossible. To promote upright behavior also contributed to social well-being both in the church and the civil community. For them, Hutchinsonian beliefs were a poison that threatened to dissolve the social fabric by making godly living purely individualistic.

The bad results were likely to go further. To the legalists, it seemed logical that Hutchinson's insistence on the passive receipt of grace and God's sovereign choice of who should have it would lead to disregard for the moral law or even rejection of it as not binding on the elect. Worse, her confidence in intimacy with the Holy Spirit would open the door to belief in direct divine inspiration. Hutchinson resolutely maintained that God's promise of salvation required the saved to have only true faith, a tremendous obligation in itself that divine grace alone could enable the saved to perform. Nothing else mattered. This twist on predestination got the label "free grace" during the seventeenth century, though the term was later applied to any belief in predestination.[10]

Significantly, Clarke did not mention Hutchinson's belief, which she disclosed only at the trial leading to her banishment, that she actually received direct messages from the Holy Spirit. The magistrates had suspected as much and pounced on her admission as the last evidence needed for her sentence. Because Clarke wrote nothing on this point, he did not mention the fears that belief in direct inspiration aroused. When Hutchinson's enemies pinned the label "Antinomian" on her, they had in mind more than the disagreement over the covenant of grace. The term meant "against law" and in its simplest sense pointed to Hutchinson's objections to the legalists without implying anything more.

Yet the term had a second, more sinister meaning: a belief in such a complete union of the soul with Christ that the believer acted by divine direction. Persons so joined to Christ would no longer feel bound by traditional law, such as was given in the Ten Commandments, and might do anything whatsoever in confidence that it had God's approval. They might think whatever they did was controlled by God according to determinants that mere humans could not understand or might think God had promised forgiveness of sins in such absolute terms as to amount to a moral blank check. Sin would not be sin.

The two meanings—insistence on justification by faith alone and belief in exemption from the usual moral law—might be distinct, and Hutchinson could sincerely insist that she spoke only for the first. Her opponents, however, thought that the two were inseparably linked, the first a preliminary symptom of a spiritual disease that surely would progress toward the second and spawn countless other errors in the process. Accordingly, the legalist ministers compiled a long catalogue of erroneous beliefs that they attributed to Hutchinson, mostly as necessary corollaries of her beliefs. By that time John Cotton had abandoned her and joined the other ministers in extending the list of heresies.[11]

Hutchinson insisted through every trial and interrogation that she was "against law" only in refusing to taint the doctrine of predestination, and she vigorously denied believing that the moral law did not bind the elect and that the elect were under divine direction in all things. Nevertheless, the magistrates strongly suspected she was lying and believed that even if she was not, she would reach this terrible extreme sooner or later, as would her followers.[12]

The magistrates had quite specific fears. They saw in the Antinomians people who were likely to follow the horrible path of the Anabaptists in Münster, who overthrew the government in 1534. Under the leadership of a man commonly known as John of Leyden, who thought he was given absolute rule as a successor to King David and was guided by divine visions, they dreamed of world conquest but in the meantime disregarded property rights. They also took to polygamy and murder of their enemies—or in John's case, one of his four wives. Like all educated Englishmen, the Massachusetts magistrates knew this frightful example of what could go wrong. They justified disarming seventy-six of Hutchinson's followers by saying, "there is iust cause of suspition that they, as others in Germany, in former times, may vpon some revelation, make some suddaine irruption vpon those that differ from them in iudgment."[13]

Disarming was only a stopgap. The dissidents must be driven out in time. They faced defeat. Clarke's readers did not need to be told about the trials and banishment of Hutchinson, the banishments and excommunications of several others, the disfranchising of more of her backers, or the voluntary exile that still more of them chose—either in New Hampshire with her brother-in-law, John Wheelwright, who was the only minister who remained on her side to the end, or with her in Rhode Island. Nor did Clarke want to rekindle old fears about the tendencies lurking in the first stages of Antinomianism. He thought they were groundless and left this point implicit in his story.

Besides, nobody had accused him of such secret errors. In 1637 and 1638 he probably was not considered important enough to warrant prosecution in Massachusetts. The evidence is unclear. He may have been disarmed.[14] He chose to leave Massachusetts voluntarily. Anne Hutchinson was imprisoned at the house of Joseph Weld in Roxbury until the winter was over in 1638. While she awaited her departure, the other Antinomians planned where to go and what to do. In these conferences John Clarke rose to prominence.

In a narrative written at mid-century, Clarke reported that he advised them to move away—but not far—because America had ample room outside Massachusetts. It is unlikely that he was the only one to think of this policy, yet possibly he was the first to propose it aloud. In any case, it was agreeable to the rest. They asked him and some others to find a suitable place. Because of the extreme heat of the previous summer, Clarke first went north where he found an even more daunting cold winter, so he turned toward the south, thinking of a location on Long Island or Delaware Bay. On the way, he and his companions let their vessel go by sea around Cape Cod while they traveled over land to the head of Narragansett Bay. There they met Roger Williams, who advised them of two good places nearby: Sowams and the island of Aquidneck (or Rhode Island proper). Sowams was the territory at the head of Narragansett Bay east of Providence. When the prospectors asked whether these places were claimed by any existing colony, Williams accompanied them on a journey to ask the magistrates at Plymouth, who said Sowams was in their patent but Aquidneck was not. So the committee of Antinomians bought rights to the island from the Indian owners and launched the large-scale move from Massachusetts.[15]

In broad terms Clarke's version of events is correct, but in some respects it misleads. Most surviving documents on the move to Aquidneck portray William Coddington, who chose exile rather than face prosecution, as the principal organizer, with Clarke in a subsidiary position at most.[16] Certainly Coddington described himself as the leader and only vaguely referred to an informal committee, of which Clarke presumably was a member, to examine possible sites for the Antinomians.[17] Roger Williams insisted that he obtained the rights to the island by virtue of the affection the Narragansett sachems bore to him, an act no amount of money could have effected.[18] He slid over the fact that he gave the Narragansetts gifts supplied by the Antinomians, thereby obscuring the English understanding of a sale with the noncommercial attributes of the transaction. Clarke had strong reasons to present the story in a different light: he was seeking English revocation of a patent granting Coddington rights as governor for life in Aquidneck.

Neither Clarke nor anyone else wrote a good narrative of what happened after the arrival. The story must be pieced together from skimpy governmental records, a few comments in correspondence, and the journal of John Winthrop, who was anything but a dispassionate seeker of truth. He knew nothing except at second hand and was happy to believe the worst. That propensity gives a special importance to his only known dealings with Clarke.

Winthrop consulted Clarke a few months after the Antinomian exodus to Rhode Island. Anne Hutchinson had become pregnant just after her release from imprisonment, or so she thought. It was actually a pseudopregnancy that ended in August 1638 with a "monstrous birth." Alarmed even before the "birth," she sent for Dr. John Clarke for medical advice. He realized her condition was dangerous and suspected the growth was not a fetus. Clarke was unwilling to do more than recommend that she send to Boston for some medicines, and later he observed what was expelled from her womb. The event might have been forgotten if rumors had not reached Boston and had her husband, perhaps in hope of keeping the rumors from growing, not sent an account to John Cotton.[19]

Cotton, by then quick to take an occasion to show that he had turned against Hutchinson, announced in a weekday meeting for worship that the monstrous birth had been "twenty-seven several lumps of man's seed, without any alteration, or mixture of any thing from the woman, and thereupon gathered, that it might signify her errour in denying inherent righteousness, but that all was Christ in us, and nothing of ours in our faith, love, &c." Surprisingly, John Winthrop, shocked by this public announcement of Hutchinson's misery, took Cotton to task for making it and brought him to announce his repentance.[20]

This was surprising because Winthrop, too, was eager to see a moral meaning in the event. He thought God's providence made it a lesson for everyone and published the news in his narrative of the Antinomian controversy that came off the press in 1644. Among the many ugly parts of that controversy none were uglier than the spiteful interpretations of Hutchinson's monstrous birth and the birth of a pitifully defective child of her friend Mary Dyer the previous year. For the seventeenth-century Englishman, nature was to be studied not only to discover its earthly attributes and gain practical knowledge but also to discover the allegorical meanings instilled in it by God's providence. Winthrop wrote a phantasmagorical interpretation of Mary Dyer's childbirth, intensifying the drama by adding a supernatural shaking of the bed where she lay. The defective daughter symbolized the Antinomian errors not less in her deformities than in her death after about two hours.

Further, Anne Hutchinson had assisted the midwife on this occasion and decided to keep the unhappy event a secret. She consulted John Cotton, who backed her and offered consoling reasons. So she helped bury the dead infant and broke the law, which required making an official report of the birth. The news got out, however, Winthrop gleefully reported, on the very day when the church in Boston excommunicated Hutchinson and she walked out accompanied by Dyer. So Cotton was upbraided for being an accomplice to the concealment, and the corpse was dug up and examined.[21]

What a switch, then, for Winthrop to upbraid Cotton for telling about Hutchinson's monstrous birth! If the minister had to repent giving publicity to the event, the magistrate vindictively broadcast the news in print a few years afterwards. Soon after Cotton's announcement, Winthrop wrote to John Clarke asking for a more exact description than the one provided by William Hutchinson. Clarke sent back a strictly factual report with little technical medical language. He described what came from Hutchinson's womb and declared it was not a fetus but otherwise offered no explanation of the event.

There is an evasive tone in Clarke's report, at least in the part of it that survives. His only reason to write it at all was to prevent wild imaginings from being taken for truth. Winthrop was dissatisfied and questioned Clarke directly—this is the only clue that Clarke returned to Boston in the months following his move to Rhode Island—and commented on Clarke's reply in the manuscript of *The History of New England*, now often called his Journal.[22]

In his "Short Story of the Rise, reign, and ruine of the Antinomians, Familists & Libertines," published in 1644, he made use of what Clarke had told him. Hutchinson, he wrote, "*brought forth . . . 30 monstrous births or thereabouts, at once; some of them bigger, some lesser, some of one shape, some of another; few of any perfect shape, none at all of them . . . of humane shape.*" The symbolic meaning had to be hammered out: "*And see how the wisdome of God fitted this judgement to her sinne every way, for looke as she had vented mishapen opinions, so she must bring forth deformed monsters; and as about 30 Opinions in number, so many monsters; and as those were publike, and not in a corner mentioned, so this is now come to be knowne and famous over all these Churches, and a great part of the world.*"[23] Quite possibly, Clarke had been under the impression that he had been asked for a confidential description and was outraged when Winthrop broadcast the event in print as part of his condemnation of Hutchinson. Small wonder that Clarke never trusted anyone named John Winthrop again.

Hutchinson's agony may have been one of the most public events in the early history of Rhode Island, but it had no importance in the organization of towns. Roughly eighty families joined the initial exodus, along with uncounted servants. They settled at first near the northern tip of Aquidneck, where there are short water passages to the mainland in two directions, a sheltered salt pond, and low flat ground. They called their settlement Portsmouth. They divided suitable land into small lots in common fields for immediate use and set aside tracts for a meetinghouse and jail. Later a committee assigned much larger farms for the principal men.[24]

From John Winthrop and a few others we get tidings of the manifold conflicts that shook the settlement almost at once. The Antinomian exiles had been united in their opposition to the "legal" teachings of most of the Massachusetts ministers and the magistrates who forced the exodus. No longer in opposition, they lost their solidarity. A rash of new religious doctrines broke out, although probably not the catalogue of crackpot notions reported by Winthrop. He was all too eager to take any rumor as evidence that the worst excesses of Antinomianism were finally coming into view.[25] The clamor of new teachings was enough, however, to explode initial plans for a town church. The meetinghouse never was built.

The form of government aroused bitter opposition. It was an avowedly theocratic regime with tightly restricted voting rights, conducted by Coddington as "judge," an office modeled on the ancient Hebrew one although it also had attributes of an English magistrate and Coddington relied on English law much of the time. In the covenant signed before they left Boston, the Antinomians declared, "We . . . will submit our persons, lives and estates unto our Lord Jesus Christ, the King of Kings and Lord of Lords and to all those perfect and most absolute lawes of his given us in his holy word of truth, to be guided and judged thereby." John Clarke's name was second in the list of signatures.[26]

This government was a strange, if ephemeral, application of John Cotton's teachings. Cotton advocated a code of law drawn from the Bible, and in a famous letter to Lord Saye and Seal in 1636 he wrote that God approved either aristocracy or monarchy, "yet so as referreth the soveraigntie to himselfe, and setteth up Theocracy in both, as the best forme of government in the commonwealth, as well as the church."[27] Cotton had in mind a government in close partnership with the church. The two institutions would be separate in two senses: the officers of one might not be officers in the other, and they would have different functions. The church would teach true doctrine to all and would provide the sacraments and ecclesiastical discipline to the putative elect, who would be members in full standing. The state would preserve society, punish wrongdoing, and give justice in disputes between citizens. Both institutions would be governed by divine law—the church fully so and the state as far as biblical precepts and precedents, plus reasonable deductions from them, would supply guidance.[28]

Even with the help of three "elders," Judge Coddington could not subdue the disorderly behavior that broke out among some men of inferior rank, as well as among the voters. Some people who were poor or who had come as servants became resentful. They felt they were entitled to land—or at least more than the meager portions given to them—and a say in the government.[29] If Winthrop had been as interested in these matters as in heresies, he could have interpreted the discord as proof that Antinomianism wrecked the social fabric.

This turmoil shocked Coddington and Clarke profoundly and sent them in search of patterns of order for their societies. In important respects they recoiled from the ongoing ferment of radicalism. Although they took different paths fairly soon, at first they traveled together and, with several other prominent Antinomians who left Portsmouth in 1639, founded Newport at the opposite end of the island. There they organized their town government in the fashion they had used earlier in Portsmouth, but they changed the award of land. Instead of planning common fields, they assigned house lots near the spring that flowed into the splendid harbor and parceled out farms elsewhere, giving large allocations to the leaders and little or none to others.[30] Coddington, bred to commerce, surely saw the advantage of the fine harbor as well as the fertile acres. Like Clarke and most of the other leaders, he built his house near the harbor and put servants and tenants on his farm to do the work. The result was a cluster of houses near the water, loosely arranged around a crowsfoot of streets and less compact than in most other early New England towns. None of the dwellings was very large. Coddington's house, constructed in 1641 and still in good shape when it was demolished in 1835, was rather small by later standards but reputed to be the grandest. In all likelihood, Clarke's house was considerably smaller and less durable. Nobody bothered to record when it was torn down.[31]

The founders of Newport, at least during the earliest years, wanted a community where the lower ranks accepted their subordination and where religious discord had its limits. They kept the theocratic and oligarchical government for a year, then went over to a secular foundation and the use of English law. They declared "unanimously" that their government was a "DEMOCRACIE, or Popular Government." They explained that this meant that "It is in the Power of the Body of Freemen orderly assembled, or the major part of them, to make or constitute Just Lawes, . . . and to depute from among themselves such Ministers as shall see them faithfully executed."[32] (Cotton thought God disapproved of democracy.³³) Nevertheless, they still gave the vote only to a few.³⁴ The change in the theoretical foundation, however, signaled a sharp abandonment of hope for a society regulated by divine law.

Less plainly, a parallel change began in the town church. The government decided that church should be founded and so presumably considered it as the ecclesiastical face of the community. Possibly John Clarke served as a minister of sorts in it. The evidence is extremely thin.³⁵ The outburst of religious novelties dogged it for a short time but subsided to the point where disagreements could produce a schism but not chaos. Under the circumstances, the government prudently gave up hope of spiritual unity and adopted a policy of religious freedom. In March 1641 it decided "that none bee accounted a Delinquent for Doctrine: Provided, it be not directly repugnant to ye Government or Lawes established."³⁶

Putting aside earlier desires for a church and state in partnership implementing divine law, Newport—and Clarke—henceforth embraced the pattern that came to prevail throughout the colony. No longer was government conceived of as having a divine source; no longer would secular power be put behind any religious purpose. Only a church—and not a monopolistic church—must be operated according to divine rules. The schism in the church that occurred soon after, therefore, did not by itself make a political disturbance (see chapter 2), but it marked the beginning of a long and important opposition between John Clarke and William Coddington.

Clarke inevitably began to take a hand in civil government, too, although a lesser one than might be expected from the leader of the move to Aquidneck, as he had described himself. Judging from the list of land allotments, he stood fairly close to the top in the town's estimation of rank but far below Coddington and several others. His rank may show that he had come with more than ordinary financial resources, or it may show the value his companions placed on having a physician in town.

Clarke as an educated citizen had responsibilities. Rhode Island, unlike Massachusetts, never kept church leaders out of civil office. Among other tasks, he helped survey the Antinomians' island and lay out allocations to the Newport settlers.³⁷ He also served on a committee to write to England requesting a colonial charter to embrace the two communities of Antinomians.³⁸ Nothing came of this effort, although steadily thereafter he envisioned a charter as the only means to secure the autonomy of the Rhode Island settlements.

There is nothing to hint that Clarke had a significant voice in designing the early governments in Portsmouth or Newport or the early colonial governments that embraced these towns, but he evidently accepted them. He acquiesced in all the changes. There is no sign that he held strong opinions about secular organization. He accepted both the highly stratified social order implicit in the first land grants and the later softening of the gradations of allocations. He accepted both the original oligarchy of citizenship and the extension of political rights that made the Aquidneck towns a full-scale democracy by 1655.[39] If he did not expound his views on these topics, his actions outlined a shift away from accepting the traditional allocations of power to a ruling class in a united state and church. In fact, during the 1640s he became an ardent champion of separation of church and state and then or later a backer of equal political rights for male citizens.

Quite early, in fact in 1641, Coddington decided that his colony was going in the wrong direction.[40] Although he remained governor, he began secret negotiations with the magistrates in Massachusetts and Plymouth to find a way to combine Aquidneck with one of them on terms that would assure his supremacy. He was alarmed when the Aquidneck towns joined with the mainland towns of Providence and Warwick to send Roger Williams to England to ask for a charter, and he was quite bitter when Williams returned with a charter in 1644. For five years Coddington had detested Samuel Gorton, who he thought was a dangerous fanatic and who surely was the most outlandish religious radical in the region. Gorton had defied Coddington's judicial authority, had stirred up violent controversy in Portsmouth and Providence, and had finally withdrawn with his followers to found Warwick. Coddington, who was happy to have nothing to do with him, now found himself put into the same jurisdiction with this menace.[41]

Coddington, with some other Aquidneck men, kept the island government alive if feeble and staved off plans for a larger colonial jurisdiction until 1647. During these three uneasy years, he increased his dealings with Massachusetts and Plymouth, trying to form an association either with one of them or with the United Colonies of New England (a confederation of all except Rhode Island) in order to keep Aquidneck out of a jurisdiction that included Providence and Warwick.[42]

Coddington remained confident in his own ruling-class status and deplored the increasingly wide distribution of authority after he was reduced from judge to governor and given an advisory council. He thought that because so few of his neighbors approached his rank, there could not be a solid phalanx of gentlemen to control public life. So association with the gentlemen of Massachusetts or Plymouth looked attractive. Until late in his life he felt entitled to power because of who he was rather than what he could do. When he failed to negotiate a merger with a neighboring colony on satisfactory terms and the United Colonies would not admit an independent Aquidneck, he decided to pursue personal authority.[43] In 1649 he returned to England and procured an English patent making him governor of Aquidneck for life, required to share power only with a council that was chosen by the freemen subject to his veto.[44]

When Coddington was in England, Clarke served twice as the colony's treasurer—by far the highest office he had held so far, though one that actually must have put a light burden on him, because the colony had so little public money.[45] Clarke's sense of his place in the world was utterly different from Coddington's. He deliberately limited his leadership in the church, he did his share in the work of government without seeking power or titles. When he rose to high importance later, his service was diplomatic. He represented his colony in England both to get the annulment of Coddington's patent (issued in 1651), and later to get a charter that would allow the citizens to elect their own officials.

While fulfilling these church and state duties, Clarke had to provide for himself and Elizabeth. Unavoidably he departed from a traditional social pattern. Life in Newport in its first few years could not copy English patterns. The settlers had to make the place over to suit their purposes. They had to survey the territory, clear fields and pastures, lay out roads, put up fences, erect a few outbuildings, and build the small cluster of houses near the harbor and the scattering of dwellings on farms to the east and the southwest. For all their hopes, the would-be commercial center was little more than a hamlet. Moreover, given the small and rather healthy population, a physician's fees probably were sparse. Treating fevers and fluxes, coughs and rashes, could not command a sizable income, even when supplemented with fees for attending a few abnormal pregnancies or determining the causes of violent deaths. Probably Clarke went beyond the narrow bounds of an English physician's practice, which consisted mainly of consulting and prescribing and excluded everything in the realm of the surgeon or apothecary. In a raw new community a doctor might have to dress wounds or set bones, mix medicines and sell them as well as prescribe them, possibly even extract kidney stones and abscessed teeth. Nevertheless, in a show of respect for proper professional boundaries, the town of Newport in 1641 authorized a different man "to exercise the function of Chirurgerie."[46]

If he could not earn much as a proper physician, Clarke as a prominent founder could get awards of land. At the outset he got 148 acres.[47] He probably exchanged some and bought more, at least as early as 1650.[48] Although the size of his original allocation looked small next to Coddington's, which was almost five time larger, only a few other men received more than Clarke. In the early years people went to Newport and left again in fair numbers, so land changed hands often and mostly fell to a core who became permanent residents. When the sifting was over, Clarke had a farm of about 150 acres east of the harbor and beyond Easton's Pond and a 36-acre home lot just northeast of the harbor.

The island of Aquidneck was blessed with good soils and near freedom from predators, so the major landowners seized the opportunity to raise livestock. After some early diversity, they specialized in sheep.[49] The leaders of the town were mostly men with little experience in rural life, so they brought servants and tenants to do the work. Although Clarke had grown up in an agricultural village, he probably spent little time working his farm. Judging from later documents, he decided quite early that his land was large enough to support 180 sheep, but he wanted others to tend them. The big home lot was as much as he wanted to manage. Later he employed servants to do the work and turned his energies to retailing.

Because John and Elizabeth had no children, probably a source of sorrow for them, they did not have the usual incentives to build a family economic base. Instead, John had to contemplate the prospect of his heirs having a social standing similar to that of his father in England. John's brother Joseph and his sister Mary produced the next generation of the Clarke family in Rhode Island—and also several members of the church—so the doctor had a swarm of nieces and nephews who would carry on the family; and rather than build on his advancement into the learned professions to lever the family up, they were farming and learning crafts. With unknowable emotions he observed the beginnings of marital interconnections among his relatives and fellow churchgoers of even lower standing. The trajectory of his life was far from what it seemed to be during the years of his education.

After the excitement of the Antinomian controversy and the pioneering in Newport, Clarke seemed to be sinking into obscurity. Later he would be called to a prominent role, but for the time being he did his most creative work in guiding a church. His actions require a closer look because they set up an ideal that was so different from the insistence on a full catalogue of correctness that was usual in the early seventeenth century. His ideal has a great appeal to Americans in the twentieth century, but it was hard to foster in his day.

2

"A Teacher: I will not say an Elder": Guiding an Antinomian Baptist Church, 1641 - 1649

During his first decade in Newport, John Clarke moved from a secondary role in the Antinomian settlement of Rhode Island to leadership in a church that rejected infant baptism. Because it adopted this tenet, the church has been called Baptist. Looking back, we are justified in applying the label, although strictly speaking it was anachronistic during the church's first years. English people began to give clear meanings to such denominational tags only during the 1650s.[1] Clarke and his companions took what they regarded as the best of the Puritan past and went further. In short, they set up an Antinomian church that soon became Baptist. Remarkably, it was the only lasting church to grow out of the Antinomian upheaval.

Clarke's experiences in the two tumultuous years of controversy swirling around Anne Hutchinson left him open to new ideas about how to organize human society. Old assumptions had been debated angrily, and a new settlement had to be shaped. After arriving in Newport, he thought through the convictions that he believed would give the best guidance to the world until Christ Jesus returned to reign as king, convictions he held the rest of his life. Some of his conclusions were quite radical by the standards of the England he had known, but they were much less so in comparison to several novelties that burst onto the English scene after 1640. He neither rejected as many traditional elements nor favored such startling replacements as the flamboyant radicals of the English revolution.

He did less to guide secular government in its progression to democracy than he did to lead a church. He and his fellow Christians in Newport sought to establish a true church of Christ in the pattern of the Apostolic era. They shared this goal with Puritans in Massachusetts and, indeed, with Protestants of all sorts. Like the others, they scoured the Bible for instruction on how to proceed. Clarke came to his own conclusions on what characteristics a true church should have and led a group of his fellow townsmen in creating a fellowship that shared some traits with other groups but in a combination that was distinctive: they did not adopt a ready-made formula.

Although Clarke made the establishment of a true church his main purpose, the result had extensive implications beyond the narrowly religious. His church had a resolutely democratic flavor. He refused the traditional ministerial eminence. He served as pastor but was never ordained, and he welcomed other men as preachers and administers of baptism. He encouraged lively discussion in church meetings. In all these ways he rejected a vital component of the traditional hierarchy that put the clergy in a position of spiritual superiority. In both church and state he claimed no more prominence than his education and accomplishments justified. Tacitly, he rejected traditional beliefs in a system of rank largely determined by birth. Tacitly, he rejected even more, including the many versions of the belief that a web of relations must bind individuals and churches and society into a coherent whole. Out of this complex rejection he wrote only about his conviction that church and state must be separate, but that separation was enough to break the web.

The church in Newport surely had more behind it than its members' experience in Massachusetts. Presumably it drew something from the examples of dissenters in the mother country, but no clues survive to hint at what the founders had in mind. In fact, it is hard to know enough about the background of dissent from the Church of England. Information—or purported information—came from spies, recanters, faithful dissenters giving forced answers to slanted questions, or from the hostile interpretations that the orthodox clergymen made of secret publications that fell into their hands. Such of these fugitive publications as survive tell only a small part of what we would like to know. For most of the sixteenth century, the orthodox ignorantly or maliciously lumped together all manifestations of the religious underground as Anabaptists, regardless of their beliefs about baptism. Continuing this practice, Massachusetts ministers in the seventeenth century called any dissenters Anabaptists, even though the clergy there were accused of leaning toward Anabaptism.[2] When the church in Newport decided that infant baptism was wrong, it automatically was branded Anabaptist, but quite inaccurately.

The name "Anabaptist" suggests much more than it should about the Newport church. The word meant simply rebaptize. To opponents of Anabaptists, whether in England or Massachusetts, the word also carried two implications that occasionally were legitimate. The first implication was that Anabaptists were subversive of the fundamental pattern of authority in their world because they considered the official church too corrupt to be a true church of Christ. They thought they must depart from it and form a pure church. It followed, at least for some dissenters, that baptism administered by the official church was not valid. So people who joined a pure church must be baptized in it. In practice, this meant a second baptism. For most dissenters, the new baptism would be received in their adult years, and some, though not all, extended the practical likelihood into a tenet: baptism must be for adult believers, not infants. Further, some who decided that the only correct way to perform the rite was by total immersion then insisted on a second rebaptism. To the rulers in church and state, such fine distinctions were insignificant: a second baptism was an act of rebellion, no matter how it was justified. Anabaptists were enemies of all constituted authority and should be fought with force as well as words.

This conclusion was underscored by the second implicit meaning of Anabaptist: the English dissenters were offshoots of the Anabaptists of the Dutch Netherlands and nearby Germany, and so were likely to follow the dreadful lead of the Anabaptists of Münster. This, however, was not the case. Although some connections existed, the English dissenters usually avoided association with the continental sectaries. In the face of prevailing opprobrium, Clarke and his companions in Newport came out against infant baptism, although they did not proceed to rebaptism.

Clarke's congregation drew quite different practices from the radical past. In the record of persecuted English sects and Puritan conventicles, despite the incomplete or suspect evidence, we can see a profusion of precedents for what was done in Newport. During the sixteenth century and even earlier there had been coteries to study the Bible, to discuss doctrine and the ritual of worship, to give artisans and women liberty to preach or at least to repeat and discuss homilies, to resurrect (as they thought) the closeness of Christian love and the ceremonies that gave it expression. Especially under a strong leader, a few of these groups turned into tightly organized sects in spite of official hostility.[3] The best-known example was the Yorkshire Separatist church of John Robinson, some of whose members founded Plymouth.

By the early seventeenth century, some of the less tightly organized of these sects had become sufficiently alike to deserve the name "Baptist." In some ways, Clarke's church in Newport followed the same pattern. These English churches rejected infant baptism and did not ordain pastors or form church covenants. By 1640, if not earlier, they tended to an open style of fellowship, making few demands for adherence to a rigid creed, letting all sorts of people exhort, and welcoming discussion. The Newport church did not follow their example in all respects. It did not accept preaching said to be at the inspiration of the Holy Spirit or reject the doctrine of predestination. Unlike Clarke, the earliest English Baptists rejected the belief that a soul's destination, either to heaven or hell, had been decreed by God regardless of individual conduct. Instead, they believed that all souls might be saved but probably most would not; individual behavior would be the determinant. For this reason they eventually got the name of General Baptists or Arminian Baptists. When the predestinarian Baptists organized, these older ones often were called Old General Baptists.[4]

The practices of the dissenters gained greater currency when they were brought cautiously into the official church. By the end of the sixteenth century, Puritans often formed pious societies within parishes to study the Bible, repeat and discuss sermons, and encourage more exacting standards of conduct than the bishops required. Of course, these groups avoided preaching by the nonordained. When led by a Puritan-minded pastor, they enhanced the intimacy of religious fellowship beyond the scope of the official parish and sometimes included encouragement of radical views. When organized against a pastor who opposed Puritan reform, they were even more open to wide-ranging discussion of doctrinal matters and their implications for the devout life.[5] Most likely, Clarke had some experience in a Puritan conventicle of the kind that spawned a radical reform and an egalitarian approach to Christianity. Hutchinson's gatherings in Boston began as a conventicle to repeat and discuss Cotton's sermons. She departed from orthodoxy, and her followers went further after their exodus to Rhode Island.

Ultimately, the Newport church was classified with the English predestinarian Baptists, but it drew on their example in only a few ways and only after it had set its own course. Such churches appeared in England around 1639, growing out of the Puritan movement in somewhat the same way that the Newport church did, and within a few years they achieved a moderate degree of definition. They favored a clearer distinction between pastor and flock than the earlier Baptists had made, sometimes a distinction solemnized by ordination. They also insisted on a greater clarity in a creed, a fixed routine in worship, and sometimes organized a church with a covenant among the founding members. This last point, however, was especially controversial. A covenant, said the objectors, made membership in the church a product of agreeing to the covenant rather than the soul's dedication to Christ as commemorated in baptism. Moreover, some of the early churches of this stripe made acceptance or rejection of infant baptism optional. Such was the case with Henry Jessey's church in London. For it, other traits of the fellowship were crucial, but not a single standard for baptism. These predestinarian Baptists favored a more orderly—a more traditional—plan of worship than the earlier Baptists had used.

As will be seen, Clarke's church in Newport, though predestinarian at least in its leader's convictions and orderly in its worship ceremonies, resembled the General Baptists in its hospitality to a multiplicity of preachers and to free-wheeling discussion of doctrine in meetings distinct from formal worship, in its avoidance of a rigid creed, as well as in its choice not to ordain a pastor or adopt a covenant. Because the Newport church was formed at roughly the same time as those of the first English predestinarian Baptists, it could not and did not follow their lead, although Clarke saw in them his spiritual friends and associated with to them when he returned to England in 1651.

Although nothing is known about his earlier experience, Clarke's thoughts on the church as they had developed by 1651 are known. His spiritual progress to that point had taken a clear direction. In addition to steering his church to the basic Baptist practice, Clarke was shaping a distinctive style of religious fellowship. A few bits of information or purported information come from other sources, but the bulk of what we can know about this subject comes from his book, *Ill Newes from New England*, written both to tell his beliefs and to condemn the persecution he had suffered in Massachusetts during a missionary visit in 1651.[6] Because the book dwelt on matters where he thought the churches in Massachusetts were wrong, it is fairly safe to suppose that he often agreed with the beliefs and practices he did not mention.

Clarke and Coddington left Portsmouth for Newport in 1639 partly to make a stable and orderly church, but they soon disagreed on how to do that. Coddington wrote that the church was gathered—that is, formed by agreement among the prospective members—and planned to choose officers, above all a minister.[7] We know nothing about the characteristics of the church at its founding. By 1640 Robert Lenthall had arrived to serve either as the minister or as coteacher with Clarke. Lenthall had been called to be the minister of the town church in Weymouth, Massachusetts, but probably was not installed in that office. According to John Winthrop, whose reports of Antinomianism always must be suspect, Lenthall's views on grace were similar to those of Anne Hutchinson and he opposed infant baptism. When the magistrates got wind of his beliefs, they summoned him and told him to retract them, which he did in court and again at Weymouth. He thought better of this submission and left for Rhode Island, where he stayed for two years before returning to England.[8] His brief service at Newport marks the first time clearly Baptist convictions are known to have appeared there. In some measure the church resisted the burgeoning outburst of new teachings that followed the Antinomian exodus to Portsmouth and so fell victim to schism rather than shattering.

Dr. John Clarke pondered Lenthall's new doctrine for a while and then embraced it, surely by 1644 but probably by the time of the schism in summer 1641—in fact, probably touching off the schism. Coddington and others broke away from the church for reasons that are unknown but may be suspected. We must brush aside Winthrop's notion that they believed a Christian became so united with God as to be under divine direction in all things—the ultimate in Antinomianism that he and the Massachusetts ministers had expected all along. Although Coddington and some others later wandered restlessly for two decades until they found in Quakerism a tightly organized church based on direct divine inspiration, just before summer 1641 and twice shortly afterwards he said he was satisfied with the Massachusetts churches. Probably his assurances implied approval of the partnership between the churches and the government.[9]

If Coddington was seeking reconciliation with Massachusetts, so were other prominent Antinomians. William Aspinwall deserted Portsmouth about the same time to return to orthodoxy and public office in Boston[10]—until he returned to England and burst forth as a flaming millenarian. Among the men who left the Newport church in 1641 were William Brenton, John Coggeshall, and Nicholas Easton. Winthrop specifically said that Easton had reached advanced Antinomianism, and he may have been right for once. He may have been right about Coggeshall, too, but certainly not about Brenton. Brenton not only gave up Antinomian tendencies for good but returned to live in Boston for several years.

Rather than agreement on doctrines of the soul's union with God, these dissenters of 1641 were united by wealth. A quick glance at the land awarded to the first settlers in Newport shows Coddington, Easton, Brenton, and Coggeshall at the top of the list. By contrast, the members of the remaining flock, as listed for 1644, were far below the most favored. Clarke was well ahead of the rest but far down the ladder from the leading dissidents. The others who stayed with him had much smaller grants or none at all.[11] The roster of members for 1644 may have been incomplete, but it was right as far as it went. (It was made by a man who moved to Newport in 1648.[12]) Except for Clarke, the men were laborers and farmer-artisans, owners of forty or fifty acres at most, so the division in one dimension was social.

The split probably began because the economic leaders saw in antipedobaptism a socially disreputable or threatening tenet. Not only were opponents of infant baptism in England generally of low standing, but the continental Anabaptists who had given the tenet a bad name in the sixteenth century were lower-class rebels. Coddington may have sought peace with Massachusetts because he thought the legalists had been right to head off a reenactment of Münster in 1534.

If the prominent Newport men feared that opposition to infant baptism heralded a plunge into social depravity and a chaotic church fellowship, they were wrong. John Clarke was no John of Leyden. Throughout his life Clarke held firm to the customary moral law, never proposed to tamper with property rights, and preserved decorum in the church. The dissidents still needed a strictly ecclesiological objection to link their worries to their decision to withdraw from the fellowship. The likeliest objection, in view of Coddington's assurances that he accepted the Massachusetts churches, was the prospect of the Newport church's calling for rebaptism. When Williams and others at Providence rejected infant baptism in 1638 (reportedly urged on by Anne Hutchinson's sister), they baptized each other, an event immediately reported to Winthrop.[13] The implications were horrifying. Such actions implied a belief that previous baptism as infants was invalid and that all churches that baptized infants were dangerously false. This belief looked like the first step toward the outrages of Münster.

Clarke, we may be confident, did not start rebaptism at Newport. If he had done so, Winthrop would have heard and reported the news as further proof of the evils lurking in Antinomianism. Several years later Clarke participated in rebaptisms but never regarded them as essential. When writing on baptism he never mentioned the practice, though his reasoning could be used to defend it. In 1641 these developments lay well in the future, so if the dissidents expected them shortly they were wrong. Whatever they imagined, they thought they had grounds for leaving the church.

They left Clarke to shepherd a small flock of Baptists. The roster included himself, his wife, two of his brothers, and John Peckham, but not Peckham's wife, who was Clarke's sister Mary. As has been suggested, the list may have been longer, but not much. All subsequent lists for seventy years were fairly short—in the range of twelve to twenty-four names. It is impossible to escape the conclusion that the church restricted full communion to those who had felt the divine assurance of election to grace.

Clarke did not explain how they imposed this restriction. He opposed the legalists of Massachusetts, who required evidence of godly behavior as proof of grace. He may also have opposed their insistence on a recital of spiritual experience as a precondition for membership in a church. True to John Cotton and the original Antinomianism, Clarke believed that the witness of the spirit in the soul, rather than a pattern of behavior, was the reliable evidence of election. If his church accepted professions of faith and relied less on its own evaluation than was common in Massachusetts, the result was the same, at least to outward appearances. A small core of people who took communion sat among a larger number who attended worship. There may have been an inward difference of some consequence. The Massachusetts legalists made joining a church much more a reciprocal union than the Antinomians did because the outward evidence of sanctification was there for the other members to judge. Reliance on the inward witness of the spirit lacked this social quality.

dissent in "the carnall Israel . . . was but a type of this spirituall Israel of God" in the Christian era. Christian practice must be different from Hebrew. This was almost an aside. He rested his positive case on the precepts of the Apostles and the precedents of their churches.[39]

When Clarke made no use of typology in his discussion of baptism he silently denied the covenant formulations so relished in Massachusetts. If he had believed in something along that line, he would have been obliged to explain why believer baptism served as well as infant baptism to hold the web together. In fact, he hardly used the word "covenant" at all. His understanding of secular society, the church, the individual's relation to God, and the force of moral law put no reliance on such theology. A form of radicalism lay implicit in his silence, and we would be glad to know what it was, but its specific features have been lost.

His most adventuresome line of argument appeared in the series of propositions on baptism. Most of these used nothing but syllogistic reasoning on precepts and precedents found in the New Testament and introduced no figures of speech except scriptural ones—and even those sparingly. When making the case for baptism by dipping, however, Clarke cut loose from the ordinary. His assertions at the head of the section on baptism had special prominence. They avoided familiar ideas about cleansing sins or dedicating the baptized to God. Instead, he made dramatic use of metaphorical passages in selected scriptural texts that were typological themselves. He began by comparing baptism to death! Baptism by immersion was like drowning, or being cast into the ocean, or obscured by a cloud as the Israelites were when crossing the Red Sea, or overwhelmed by its waters as the pursuing Egyptians were. It was like death and burial.[40]

Then he cut the gloom by saying that these were figures of the death of the child of wrath and the new birth of the believing Christian. But they were more, he continued, as he expounded the Biblical metaphors. The burial was like a seed being planted. The baptized person "doth visibly put on Christ Iesus the Lord, and is hereby visibly planted into his death, holding forth therein a lively similitude, and likeness unto his death; whereby onely through faith he now professeth he hath escaped death, and is in hope to obtain life, and peace everlasting." Thereby the baptized person would "have fellowship with . . . [Christ] in his death, as to be dead with him, and thereupon to reckon himself to be dead indeed unto sin, Sathan, the law, and the curse." Clarke continued to define the experience of regeneration. "This appointment of Christ, [namely,] Baptism, is an ordinance whereby the person that submitteth thereto, doth visibly and cleerly resemble the buriall of Christ, and his being buried with him, so as in respect of the old man, the former lusts and conversation, . . . [are] taken out of the way, and seen no more."

Clarke went over the point again to show how the experience of baptism—the experience of a mature person rather than a baby who could not understand it—should have a deep psychological impact. "Baptism," he wrote, "is an ordinance whereby the person that submitteth thereto, doth visibly, and lively hold forth herein the resurrection of Christ." Baptism "declares him, whose life was taken from the earth, to be alive again, who although he died and was buried, yet was he not left in the grave to see corruption, but was raised again, and behold he liveth for evermore." And as hereby the baptized person "holds forth the resurrection of Christ, so doth he also his own, being planted into the likeness thereof, so as to reckon himself to be in his soul and spirit quickned, and risen with Christ, from henceforth to live unto God the fountain of life, and to Christ Iesus the Lord who died for him, and rose again." The new Christian would be ready "to walk in newness of life in this present evil world, being also begotten unto a lively hope, that in the world to come he shall be raised, and quickned both in soul, and body, to a life everlasting."[41]

Ritual identification with Christ's death and resurrection would be the earthly act to complete the making of a Christian.[42] (Clarke, even more than other Puritans, avoided the traditional Catholic emphasis on Christ's sufferings and crucifixion, as in the images of Christ on the cross or the procession through the stations of the cross.) After this conspicuous departure from his usual style of exegesis, Clarke went back to syllogisms using precepts and precedents to make the case for believer as against infant baptism.

Giving the ceremony of baptism such importance was fully in accord with his insistence that a church needed "a visible way of worship," that is, a framework of basic ritual and practice.[43] He proposed to maintain the pattern, however, without the usual reliance on a minister.

Characteristically, Clarke became open-minded on the subject of a pastor's qualifications. He never doubted the value of a university education for a minister, but he came to regard it as desirable rather than essential. He cherished his knowledge of the ancient tongues and perhaps as a compensation for the absence of others so qualified in

Clarke wrote nothing that showed a burning zeal to keep people out of church membership. His thinking tended the other way. Bring suitably inclined people to worship to learn what being Christian meant and bring those who felt God's election into membership in the church where they can encourage each other. The inner circle of the church should be for those who felt the assurance of God's grace, but anyone might be deceived and misled, or the advance toward ultimate understanding of God's truth might go in unexpected paths, so a church should reject only obdurate sinners and persons holding unmistakably antiscriptural beliefs. He relied on Christ's Spirit of promise to guide the elect into the church and opposed setting more than a few credal barriers. He did not write directly on this subject, however, so we may suppose he accepted the usual practice of the Massachusetts churches in expelling the unworthy.[14]

He firmly upheld a "liberty of prophesying" for those who attended worship. By "prophesying" he did not mean preaching at the direct inspiration of the Holy Spirit, but rather religious exhortation or simple exercises in Biblical exegesis. He wrote cautiously about direct inspiration and left his views ambiguous, although probably he leaned toward those of John Cotton and Anne Hutchinson. Cotton's teachings were reported most fully by Thomas Shepard, who copied the outline of a sermon on Revelation 4:1–2, delivered by Cotton in the months of the Antinomian exodus. In this discourse Cotton declared his belief in the possibility of direct revelation in his day, giving an almost ecstatic evocation of the heights of inspiration to which the Holy Spirit might lift a believer.

True, nobody should expect direct revelation to be common. Since completion of the Bible, "ordinarily tis not soe."[15] The faithful would find their guidance in the book nearly all the time. Cotton gave one example of recent direct revelation of exactly the sort Hutchinson claimed to have experienced. He mentioned God's direction of the believer's life and revelations of the sins of others. Dwelling on Biblical examples in expansive terms, he cautioned that nothing on the same scale remained possible "and yet there is a proportionable revelation in evill times to this day." By proportionable he meant in proportion to need. The Bible obviated most needs.[16]

Cotton's most striking passages were on the power of the Holy Spirit. Beginning with the revelations to John he quickly applied the words to believers in his own day. A man sometimes "is overcome or overpowered of the spirit" when reading the Bible. "It wholy captivates all a mans reason and judgement so as they stir not at all now but as instrumentall to him. . . . It overcomes all a mans naturall and sanctifyed reason so as no power here expresseth it selfe of nature reason or corrupt affection, but acted as moved by the holy ghost." Saint John's experience on Patmos could have its counterparts in Boston: "The spirit not only presents and increaseth spiritual gifts and graces but naturall gifts, so as he can see angells then and god then in a vision and a light and voyces then as John hears these voyces; so that a mans light and understanding is intended." Cotton compared the experience to drunkenness! John was "over come of the spirit as a man is sayd to be in drinke not only when full but overcome of drinke, which not only acts in him according to but beyond his reasonable faculty[;] so the spirit so overcomes the soule as that it is caryed above his reason not only naturall but above santified [sic] reason."[17] The extravagance of these ideas should be understood in part as a rhetorical device to make the ideas vivid to the hearers.

Clarke held similar beliefs but expressed them in a different imagery, imagery that came directly from the Bible and conveyed nothing about reason and the senses being overwhelmed. He never flatly contradicted orthodox beliefs that communication from God occurs only indirectly. Still, his words had distinctly Antinomian nuances. Although he used biblical texts, he chose the ones that most luminously told of what the believer would learn from the Holy Spirit. He carefully avoided a full-throated exposition. He went no further than orthodox divines when he spoke of his belief in the ability—indeed, duty—of a human being "to Hearken to ye Law [of God] written in ye heart."[18] He held an optimistic version of the orthodox belief that God's law had been written in the heart of Adam and survived in later generations in an imperfect state. There was something left, and opinions could differ over how much and how dependable it was.

Ordinarily, without explaining exactly what he meant, he used metaphors found in the Bible. He wrote of Christ's spirit as "a sparkling beam, from the Father of lights, and spirits," having dominion over man and extending "to all the inward and hidden motions and actings of the mind." He also wrote of the spirit "as a well-spring of living water flowing forth unto eternall life." Or as "the sword of the Spirit, which is his [God's] own word."[19] This figure implied that the Spirit was to be known from the Bible, just as Christ's teaching during the first incarnation, as reported in the Bible, "openeth the heart to understand the scriptures"—that is, the Old Testament.[20]

Clarke also wrote on the spirit in glowing words that could be interpreted either as Antinomian or orthodox. He mentioned "Christ . . . by his Spirit in man shedding abroad the love of God in his heart" and said the Spirit would teach all things, including the election of those chosen to receive grace. The spirit would lead believers "from truth to truth, untill they be brought to all truth."[21] These phrases suggest an expectation of direct transfer of divine knowledge to the soul of a believer. More tantalizing still, he wrote that when *"Christ Jesus . . . is come according to promise into the heart of a Christian, he [the spirit] shall not speak of himself, but as a messenger his office is to gloryfie Christ by taking of him, and his, and shewing it unto, yea writing it in the heart of a Christian."* The spirit also would nourish "a lively hope in the heart of a Christian concerning . . . [Christ's] glorious return."[22] The Holy Spirit would "sanctifie . . . [believers] throughout in soul, and spirit, and body."[23]

These statements might be interpreted as versions of orthodox doctrine in Massachusetts taken out of context; they fit better with Cotton's heterodoxy. In his writings Clarke never came out against the orthodox belief that communication between God and a believer's soul used only indirect means, mainly preaching by the ministers, participation in worship, and private devotions during which the mind would be steered to specific scriptural texts.[24] Still, he never wrote in support of it, either.

Clarke hedged his declaration. He was no enthusiast, no advocate of a spiritual stupor. True to Puritan orthodoxy, he wrote that the fallen condition of man left the soul "in a capacity by men and devils to be deceived, and so by perswasion to be mis-led" rather than to understand the promptings of the spirit correctly.[25] Then he made a surprising turn toward rationalism: he concluded that the spirit guides through persuasion of human agents using rational argument based on scripture. Such argument would convey the radiant truthfulness of the sacred text.

He was most explicit in saying that Christ's spirit by the law "written in the heart of a Christian" would tell how to conduct worship correctly. On this point he went beyond Massachusetts orthodoxy only in his emphasis on the work of the spirit to inform the heart over the legalistic construing of holy writ. The law was identical with the teachings in "the ministry of . . . [Christ's] Apostles, and servants"—that is, the precedents and precepts of the first Christians.[26] This statement embodied Clarke's central conviction that nothing received from the Holy Spirit would contradict the Revealed Word in the Bible.

If Clarke stayed with Cotton's teachings on the evidence of grace, he departed from it on other points, most obviously the doctrine of baptism. The paradox of radicalism flowing from a determination to return to the pattern of the first Christian churches was nowhere more obvious than in Clarke's turn against infant baptism. Although all Puritans, the pioneers of Massachusetts as much as any, shared his zeal for restoring primitive Christianity, few agreed with him on this point. On the contrary, they condemned his belief fiercely.[27] Clarke held that only those who had become genuine believers should be baptized. Faith must come first and then baptism would induct the Christian into the church. If Lenthall started Clarke thinking in this direction, the arrival of Mark Lucar some time between 1641 and 1644 kept him going.

Lucar, who had become a Baptist in England, moved to Newport, where he soon became an active member of the church. Before leaving London, he had come to believe that baptism must be by total immersion rather than affusion or some other symbolic substitute. He took this belief with him to Newport, where he persuaded Dr. John Clarke, if Clarke had not already come to it independently.[28] Because he had to uphold these views against centuries of doctrine and custom, Clarke in his public argumentation left many other doctrinal matters aside and concentrated on his reasons to believe that baptism was for adult believers only—"believer baptism," in short—and must be performed by dipping.

Since these tenets came in large part from a straightforward reading of the Bible, so we may well ask why so few other New England Puritans embraced them. In Massachusetts (setting aside the Maine district) only twenty-six people are known to have declared against infant baptism between 1639 and 1654, and some of them were talked back to orthodoxy or went on to reject all visible sacraments.[29] Even if the total were augmented by adding a small number of people in Connecticut, a somewhat larger number in the Plymouth jurisdiction, and an uncounted (and perhaps uncountable) number in New Hampshire and the Maine district, the sum will remain low. Certainly, the horrible example of the Anabaptists at Münster was often given as reason enough to oppose believer baptism. When old Antinomians adopted this tenet, they added new proof of its iniquity.

Keeping infant baptism was easy enough for those who respected centuries of tradition, as most people in Massachusetts did, and kept an ingrained feeling that the ceremony should be arranged by a conscientious parent because it was good for the baby.[30] Holding the line was much harder for Puritans determined to restore the primitive church by rooting out all human inventions, and especially for Puritans in New England. In the two decades beginning in 1635, they not only began to deny baptism to children who did not have a parent who was a member of a church but also began to baptize adults who qualified for church membership after having been denied baptism as infants, and some churches gave baptism by immersion when requested. They threw out the old customs of calling on godparents, which had given a substantial increase to the importance of baptism. These orthodox Puritans, who had gone so far toward the Baptist practice, furthermore, during the 1640s got into a long and bitter argument over the Half-Way Covenant—the plan to allow baptism to children of parents who had been baptized but had not qualified to take communion. With such perplexity over the use of infant baptism, an easy way out would have been to rule that baptism should be for adult believers only.[31]

The clergy hotly and quite successfully opposed this solution. They had to argue that baptism had an effect, difficult though the case was to make. Saying that it cleansed sins or attached the infant soul to Christ sounded like denying predestination, but those points were made.[32] Saying that it followed Christ's example was impossible. Saying that it followed the precedents of the Apostolic churches required a sophisticated reading of a few texts that relied on reasoning by analogy and proportion where a straightforward reading would not yield the desired conclusion. The ministers, when giving a full-scale theological defense, said that baptism symbolized the already existing attachment of the infant to a covenant with God. They could brandish texts about promises to converts and their seed. Besides, this view of baptism had the virtue of being exempt from verification. It had to be argued because it justified treating the infant as dedicated to Christ and as a fit subject for a church's spiritual nurture.[33]

The argument also used the typological variety of scriptural exegesis. Typology provided an argument for a form of continuity with ancient Israel, although the reasoning was hard to control. It led to the conclusion that a Christian practice was bound to be quite different from the Hebrew, but nevertheless connected to it by an imperfect analogy. (Analogies are hard enough to use without the requirement that they be perfect.) Precedents in the Old Testament were "types" and had discoverable though quite different counterparts—or "antitypes"—in the New. Typology could give fearful complications to theology, most obviously when New England Puritans wanted to combine it with other kinds of exegesis, especially with the simplest method, using the Bible to provide simple precepts and precedents. So they needed ways to distinguish when to use typology (or other sophisticated reasonings) and how to harmonize it with simple legal or historical argument.[34]

Typology looked very attractive as a means to argue that infant baptism was the Christian practice foreshadowed in Jewish circumcision—but much better. Baptism, too, signified participation in a covenant. When this argument collided with belief in predestination, the way out was to assert that although baptism symbolized an outward covenant, it did not signify an inward status among the elect.[35] By justifying a special spiritual nurture to baptized children that was not given to others, this defense of infant baptism indirectly defended the belief in preparation for salvation, which the Antinomians had denounced, and indeed it defended the whole system of covenant theory cherished by the leading New England Puritans, Cotton as much as any, by which they justified their distinctive partnership of church and state.[36]

The web of covenants formed an essential part of Massachusetts orthodoxy. The covenant with Abraham and his seed, like the monarchy of ancient Israel (as types) had to be seen as continuing, though in sharply modified Christian antitypical forms. The new version of God's covenant with the Jews defined the bonds of secular society in Massachusetts and its connection to the functions of the churches. This theory had to be maintained, or else anarchy would break out—or so it was said. Between fears of Anabaptism, traditional dedication to infant baptism, and pyrotechnical theology generated by the clergy, the bulk of the devout in New England outside Rhode Island was held back from going the Baptist route.

John Clarke was acquainted with typology and some other arcane methods of interpreting the Bible, but he rarely used them, and then only in a key passage to build an essential argument. For him, typology was an ornament. Kings of Israel were types of the kingship of Christ, he said almost as though inserting a commonplace thought that was considered obligatory when writing on this topic.[37] He made a similar comment to accompany remarks on Christ's priesthood—the priests of Israel were types.[38] Clarke also used typology to deny the legitimacy of using force against dissent. In an obvious riposte to Massachusetts divines who drew the opposite conclusion, he said using force against

Newport spent long hours improving his command of Hebrew. He and his church, like some early churches in Massachusetts, welcomed gifts for preaching among men without the traditional education for the clergy.[44] Lucar was the first to join him. Soon the Newport church had two more. Roughly a third of the men in the flock served as preachers, and one or two more had other parts in the ceremonies of worship. This fellowship took the opposite road from the one followed in Massachusetts, where "preaching brethren" were frozen out, leaving one pastor to speak during most of the three-hour services.[45]

Clarke went away from the Puritan concept of the ministry in other respects, too. There is no hint of an ordination for him, no hint that he considered himself a titled official of his church, no hint that he was paid. He may have assumed the role of teacher and surely had the role of pastor, whether officially or not. Even if not formally chosen by his flock he served by its approbation. A Puritan minister was, by contrast, a salaried full-time clergyman, formally chosen by the members of the church and ordained by them or at their request by ministers from nearby churches. Professional competence attained by study beyond a college education marked him off from others of equal devotion. He was a teacher and spiritual guide rather than a priest, but nevertheless a man of authority.

Moreover, as a further step into radicalism or a continuation of existing practice, Clarke insisted that all others in the congregation, at least men, should be encouraged to "prophesy" during a service for worship. He defined prophesying as "a plain, and brief declaration of the mind, and counsel of God, in words significantly and easie to be understood, confirmed by the words of the Apostles and Prophets of God, and brought forth for the edification, exhortation, and comfort of the whole."[46] He thought women should not raise questions during worship but wrote nothing against their prophesying.[47] He accepted women's voices in church meetings to debate doctrine as though women were normally participants.

In this openness to prophesying, he and his church carried on a development of early Puritan practice in England.[48] The freedom to prophesy was encouraged in some early Massachusetts churches (and most of the avowedly Separatist churches of Plymouth) until advancing clerical authority, codified in the Cambridge Platform of 1648, put an end to it.[49] Where prophesying was coupled with a multiple pastorate and acceptance of nonlearned preachers, it reduced ministerial predominance more than it did where it was a carryover from Puritan beginnings as a striving minority in the Church of England. More important, it kept alive one crucial attribute of the Antinomians, a spiritual excitement, an element that had been especially frightening to Anne Hutchinson's opponents.

When we look at the array of practices that were likely to disturb a fixed ritual—acceptance of several preaching brethren, prophesying, avoidance of an extensive creed—it is hard to see what Clarke cherished in the regularity of worship. Yet because he wrote nothing against the plan used in Massachusetts, we may suppose that he accepted it. There, morning worship began with an opening prayer, then a reading from the Bible and an exegesis of it, then psalm-singing, a sermon, a long prayer, more psalm-singing, then communion (once a month, usually), and a blessing. Afternoon worship followed the same pattern except that communion was not given but baptism might be, and any new members would be admitted.[50]

Clarke criticized only one ingredient in this formula; he objected to the "mixt confused way of singing which fills the ear rather with a loud sound of words, than the heart with any thing that is truly edifying."[51] He said this mode of psalmody had been introduced into Massachusetts, so presumably he preferred a mode that had existed previously. Evidently he was unaware that Baptists in England had rejected psalm-singing altogether on the grounds that it used "stinted imposed forms."[52]

Although much is known about the various translations of the Psalms and the tunes that were recommended for use when singing them, we can only guess at the actual sound. The novelty in Massachusetts during the 1640s came from introduction of the new translation known as the Bay Psalm Book. In order to help the congregations learn the new words, ministers developed the practice of "lining out." That is, the minister or someone else he chose would intone a line or two and then the congregation would sing it. Musicologists surmise that this resulted in such a great emphasis on learning the words that little effort was put into singing a tune. A less likely guess is that members of the flock were encouraged to embellish the tunes as they felt inclined in a mood of high piety, a practice that probably began later and certainly did produce a confused discord. There is evidence that the tempo of singing fell during the century and that some people made modest efforts to introduce a little harmony, which oftener than not gave another source of discord or even confusion over what tune was being used.[53]

The style of singing that Clarke preferred, like some other standards for the conduct of a church that he favored, came from pre-Massachusetts Puritan practice. Ministers of the Church of England who went into exile in Geneva during the reign of Queen Mary returned with livelier tunes than had been used in England before. John Calvin advocated using any well-known tune regardless of whatever secular, even scandalously secular, uses it had. French and other Continental melodies enlivened congregational singing by adding some catchy and rhythmic music. Psalm-singing had an immediate vogue and by the early seventeenth century had a fairly firm tradition—reliance on a few well-known tunes, sung unaccompanied except in cathedrals and usually without harmonization.[54] Clarke again looked to the immediate Puritan past while Massachusetts made innovations.

Clarke condemned two other changes underway in Massachusetts: required attendance at worship and taxation to support a church. He emphatically endorsed the earliest standards of voluntary attendance and voluntary contributions. His church surely had little of the goods of this world and stuck with the older view. Some Massachusetts towns, such as Boston and Dedham, proudly refused to levy taxes to support their churches. Laws to bring the power of government behind religious duty were an admission of failure, though not often described as such.[55] John Cotton, significantly, spoke on this point. In 1639 he declared that taxation for a minister's salary showed a decline of religion.[56]

The Newport Baptists probably never considered asking for such laws—and surely could not have obtained them. If Clarke thought he deserved a salary, his church could not afford to give him one, so of necessity he served it part time while making a living in other ways. During his lifetime, many Baptists came to the conclusion that pay for preaching was positively wrong.[57] Clarke wasted no time in lamentation. He preferred a church without an authoritarian pastor, but he had no objection to paying a minister, so long as the money came from voluntary contributions.

Moreover, Clarke opposed doctrinal rigidity. Maybe he had no choice in Newport's early years. The jungle-growth of opinions made uniformity impossible. Even after the withdrawal of William Coddington and others in 1641, the church still had plenty of diversity among its few members. And it continued to have diversity in spite of two more schisms, with Clarke on the side of holding everyone together when a rupture threatened. For him, an intense fellowship—not a highly defined organization—was vital. He favored a churning discussion of religion, not a procrustean creed.[58]

This point needs emphasis. At least since the eighteenth century and the writings of Isaac Backus, commentators on early Baptists have tried to sort them into categories with names, names derived from doctrinal tenets—above all, doctrines of salvation. Particular Baptists believed in predestination; General Baptists took an Arminian approach and thought anyone might be saved by dint of Christian living, although most people would probably fail.[59] These classifications were halfway adequate in England by the 1650s, but they were not appropriate in America until later,[60] and they did not fit the Newport church in Clarke's day. In some ways the Baptist church in Newport resembled the General Baptists more than it did the Particular Baptists, who organized at about the same time. Nevertheless, as a predestinarian himself, Backus regarded that tenet as decisive and, knowing Clarke believed in it also, placed the church on the same roster as the Particular Baptists. The result is a serious distortion. Clarke did not demand that the others believe in predestination,[61] and the evidence shows that many did not. Far from being the hallmark of their fellowship, the doctrine was not a subject of debate and was all but forgotten by the eighteenth century.

Exaggerating the distinction between Particular and General Baptists obscured important realities. When urban New England Baptists in the early eighteenth century began to go toward the style of religious fellowship of the orthodox post-Puritan congregations, ministers on both sides liked to brush aside the past and aver that good Baptists had never disagreed with Congregationalists in much more than rejecting infant baptism. Hardly anybody in New England wanted to admit that men like Clarke had created a distinctive kind of religious fellowship, and still less that they remained in harmony with most Puritans in England on certain points while those in Massachusetts concocted theoretical constructs to justify restricting baptism to the children of "visible saints," the presumed elect.

Supposing that Particular Baptists were a minor deviation from mainline Puritanism distorted the picture of John Clarke's world but rationalized the efforts by some Baptists and some Massachusetts Congregationalists to accept each other as brethren in Christ during the two decades before 1740. Actually, in those years, predestination had not been a salient point, while acceptance of a learned ministry was.[62] Especially when these high-toned Baptists professed the doctrine of indelible election, this pretense was highly convenient. Yet it cast into darkness the thoroughgoing contrast in the kind of church fellowship that had been crucial in the seventeenth century.

All in all, the church was shaping its own style of fellowship, which of course it said was drawn from the teachings of Christ and the precedents of the Apostolic era. It counted on interaction among the members and gave active roles to many men. They could not be markedly superior to the rest. It allowed women to vote and speak in church meetings. And they did. Although the church had begun in a disagreement over how to interpret the Bible and the doctrine of grace, it had made participation more of a face-to-face, voice-to-ear phenomenon than a quest for correct understanding of a text. By abandoning ordination, it carried forward a trait that had been in Puritanism from the beginning—the rejection of priestly superiority and reliance on mutual spiritual help among the adherents. But in Massachusetts ministerial dominance was growing. There, the bulk of public worship consisted of long sermons and prayers by the minister, who defined orthodoxy for a nearly passive congregation. Clarke's church did not draw up a covenant at a time when covenants were used throughout Massachusetts and were growing longer and specifying more and more tenets.

Clarke and his colleagues preached and prayed, but they accepted a variety of beliefs. They took firm stands only on what they considered the fundamentals of Christian association and refused to bend before a minority that demanded that all embrace its views. For Clarke, the goal was to keep the open interaction, the willingness to see new light, without casting off the scriptural anchor or the ordinances of worship.

3

"New Baptisme" and "the prophecies Concerning the rising of Christs Kingdome": Clarke as Evangelist and Visionary, 1649 - 1661

The events that took Dr. John Clarke back to England in 1651 and gave him a role in imperial politics and the tumultuous religious swirl of the Puritan Revolution began in an unlikely way. During 1649 he undertook a seemingly minor venture to encourage a cluster of religious dissidents at Seekonk (then in Rehoboth), which was in the Plymouth jurisdiction near the head of Narragansett Bay. Seekonk was ten miles east of Providence, where a Baptist church had existed for a decade. Clarke and Lucar learned that the Seekonk dissidents had rejected infant baptism and begun to worship apart from the town church. The two Newport men went to welcome them to the Baptist way and to baptize them by total immersion.[1]

Clarke and Lucar had every reason to expect that the journey would be seen as more than an inconspicuous expression of good will. For one thing, Seekonk was an acrimonious settlement. More important, the baptisms would arouse hostility in all directions, above all in Boston forty miles to the northeast. The dissidents, especially Obadiah Holmes, had quarreled with the town minister, Samuel Newman, in the past. Newman accused Holmes of swearing a false oath. Holmes sued him for slander and won—and went on to accuse him of high-handed manipulation of the church's disciplinary actions. Holmes was a pugnacious man, a hot-tempered fault-finder. His temperament was utterly different from Clarke's, and Clarke probably disliked him though he felt a duty to embrace him as a brother in Christ. Holmes had spent several years in Salem, which was such a reliable fountain of heresies as to raise the suspicion that there was something odd in the water. He had a forceful and nettlesome personality, yet he had a deep piety that ripened with the years, perhaps unnoticed by his neighbors. In Seekonk he was accused of sins ranging from drunkenness and abusive speech to adultery. After several quarrels had built up a fund of ill will, he renounced the church and took others with him. Defiantly he turned against infant baptism and embraced believer baptism in a rather aggressive and doctrinaire way.[2]

Staking the controversy on baptism lifted an ordinary village squabble to the level of a major public event. When Clarke and Lucar arrived and performed the baptisms, the news spread quickly. These were no ordinary baptisms; they were rebaptisms in the eyes of the orthodox. They implied a condemnation of earlier baptisms, an implication which extended to denying the validity of the churches and ministers who had given the infant baptisms. Horrified magistrates in Massachusetts wrote sternly to their counterparts in Plymouth, accusing them of conniving at the growth of error or at least doing nothing to stop it. The men in Massachusetts wanted action lest the heresy spread north across the border and hinted at cutting Plymouth out of the United Colonies of New England, a confederation of all except (and often against) Rhode Island.[3]

Roger Williams, who wrote John Winthrop, Jr., about the incident three weeks later, had a quite different view of it. He thought the baptisms at Seekonk were done in a manner "neerer the first practice of our great Founder Christ . . . then other practices doe" but regarded all sacraments as illegitimate. He believed no true churches had existed for centuries and so there could be no sacraments until Christ somehow refounded the church.[4]

Under pressure from Massachusetts, the town church at Seekonk excommunicated Obadiah Holmes, probably in 1650, the same year that the grand inquest of the colony presented him and two others for trial. (The colony's records do not contain the charges.) Holmes and his fellow dissidents met not only the glares of the magistrates but also four calls for action against them—one from thirty-five of their neighbors, one from the nearby church at Taunton, one from most of the ministers in Massachusetts, and one from the magistrates there.[5] The court ordered the three Baptists to desist from conducting a separate religious organization. But they disobeyed and thus brought down a new presentment from the grand inquest, this one including five more persons. Their sentence has not survived, but within a few years all but one or two of the accused moved to Newport.[6]

Knowing what an uproar he had touched off by the missionary excursion to Seekonk, Clarke surely could guess what might happen when he, Holmes, and John Crandall set out on a similar journey to Lynn, Massachusetts, in summer 1651. Their decision to go implied an intention to provoke a confrontation. The visit to Lynn was rather like the one at Seekonk. By means that are unreported, William Witter of Lynn had come to believe that infant baptism was wrong. Witter was described as old and blind, although he was less than seventy years old and had a peppery disposition and a youthful vigor. Five years earlier, he had been arrested for contempt of the holy ordinances of baptism as practiced by the church in Lynn. He had much more than contempt: he believed that the church was breaking the Third and Fourth Commandments. Witnesses quoted him as saying that to baptize an infant was to "take ye name of ye Father, Sonne, & Holy Gost in vayne, [and] broake ye Saboath." If that were not bad enough, he also said "yt they who stayed whiles a child is baptized doe wor[shi]pp ye divell."[7] Somehow he had got into communication with the church in Newport, which may have considered him a member, and either asked for a more direct acquaintance or let Clarke know that there were others in his neighborhood who would like an association with Baptists. However the exchange went, Clarke and his companions set out from Newport to visit Witter and the prospective Baptists in Salem.

Doing so almost inevitably would lead to a public controversy. The three missionaries expected to challenge the orthodox Puritans, most likely at a gathering for worship. Yet when they arrived at Lynn on a Saturday, as Clarke recounted, they felt no "freedom in . . . [their] Spirits for want of a clear Call from God to goe unto the Publike Assemblie [the next morning] to declare there what was the mind, and counsell of God concerning them." Instead, he and his companions held a religious meeting of their own with Witter and 4 or 5 Strangers, that came in unexpected" after Clarke had begun preaching. Suddenly, two constables burst in with a warrant from a local magistrate, Robert Bridges, to arrest the missionaries. Clarke looked at the warrant, told them that nothing in it forbade their staying to the end of the meeting and gaining firsthand evidence of what was said there, and advised them that if they thought it wrong to stay they might wait outside until the end, when the participants would, without resistance, submit to arrest.[8]

The constables, however, insisted on an immediate arrest, took the prisoners to an inn for dinner, and then wanted to take them to the town church's afternoon meeting for worship. "One of them said unto us, Gentlemen, if you be free I will carry you to the Meeting." Presumably, he meant free in conscience. Clarke replied, probably relishing the ambiguity of the word, free, "Friend, had we been free thereunto we had prevented all this; Neverthelesse, we are in thy hand, and if thou wilt carry us to the Meeting, thither will we goe." He went on to warn the constables that he and his companions would declare their Baptist convictions by deed and word. The constables said they had no instructions pertaining to that possibility, and so they took the Rhode Island men to the meetinghouse. Once there, Clarke "civilly saluted" the congregation by removing his hat, put it back on—whereas the congregation, as was customary, had taken theirs off during the worship—and pointedly read a book, presumably the Bible. Magistrate Bridges, who was in attendance, ordered a constable to remove Clarke's hat. Clarke made no resistance, but at the end of the service he rose and said he would speak on his beliefs. This was permissible by his rules—and the rules of the earliest Massachusetts churches—as a form of prophesying. Almost acknowledging the strength of this point, the minister, Thomas Cobbet, asked if he was a member of a church. Clarke did not report his answer.[9]

Bridges said Clarke might proceed if the congregation were willing, but that he must not speak against what the minister had propounded. Clarke agreed, but he began to explain his earlier behavior, which was a sign of dissent. First, he said with arguable correctness by the usual Massachusetts reckoning, the visitors were strangers to the congregation in Lynn and so lacked knowledge of the spiritual condition of the members, a knowledge that was considered essential to forming a church. Not belonging to the spiritual fellowship, the men from Rhode Island could not join in worship. A proper Massachusetts church rested on a mutual confidence among its members that they were all of the probable elect. But Clarke went on to say that he thought the people in Lynn were not gathered in the true faith, and thereupon Bridges and his companions ordered him to stop and be taken and held prisoner over night at a nearby inn.[10]

The next day, after they were arraigned and before they were taken to the jail at Boston, Clarke and his colleagues were sufficiently at liberty to go back to Witter's house, where Clarke held a religious meeting and gave communion to those who attended. Holmes baptized (or in the eyes of the authorities, rebaptized) three persons. When the three missionaries were brought to trial later in the week, they were convicted of holding unauthorized religious meetings, disrupting an authorized one, administering sacraments unlawfully, and maintaining that the churches in Massachusetts were not true churches and that baptism administered in them was false because it was performed on infants.[11]

The court handed down surprisingly differential sentences. It fined Crandall £5, Holmes £30, but Clarke only £20. If they did not pay they would be whipped.[12] Holmes's fine was the largest because he had been excommunicated at Rehoboth and had performed the baptisms at Lynn. Clarke was not an excommunicate but had given the communion sacrament. Crandall had done nothing ceremonial to offend the established church. The convicts maintained that they had done no wrong and refused to pay the fines.

Clarke protested that Massachusetts had no law that defined as a crime what the convicts had done. In return he got the sort of magistratical browbeating previously given to Anne Hutchinson and others. It reached the point where Governor John Endicott told Clarke he deserved death and seemingly challenged him to a debate with Massachusetts ministers. Clarke was eager for a public disputation and thought one was to be held. He wrote down four points that he would defend. After several equivocal statements, the magistrates left the disputation uncertain. Then friends paid Clarke's fine, and the court ordered him released, although he protested that he had not wanted anyone to supply the money. The possibility of a public debate vanished, leaving only the opportunity for a private one with some prominent ministers. Clarke did not want that, so after futile appeals for a public debate he returned to Newport.[13]

Crandall and Holmes fared worse. Crandall appealed, found a man to be his surety, posted bail for his return, and went home. Then he had a crisis of conscience that made him go back to Boston. The jailer refused to bother with formalities and assured him that he might go home again without putting his surety in jeopardy. But nobody informed Crandall when the next session of the court would be held to hear his appeal, so he failed to attend and the surety had to pay. Crandall went to Boston again to protest. The officials there made it plain that they wanted him out of the jurisdiction much more than they wanted to argue judicial procedure or the merits of his conviction, so he gave up.[14]

Holmes successfully avoided any payment of his fine and was whipped ruthlessly. He exulted in his martyrdom. As he reported it, "as the stroaks fell upon me, I had such a spirituall manifestation of Gods presence, as the like thereunto I never had, nor felt, nor can with fleshly tongue expresse, and the outward pain was so removed from me, that indeed I am not able to declare it to you." When the whipping was over, he continued, "having joyfulnesse in my heart, and chearfulnesse in my countenance, . . . I told the Magistrates, you have struck me as with Roses."[15] An old Baptist neighbor of his from Rehoboth came to comfort him at the end and was prosecuted, in spite of his protest that there was nothing unlawful in consoling a convicted man whose punishment had been completed. After the ordeal Holmes returned to Newport.[16]

Holmes's exaltation in the whipping was the response of a classic martyr. John Clarke was of a different sort. Although he led the mission, he suffered least. As he reported the story, he behaved with honor and intellectual consistency throughout. He was temperate and poised, whereas we may assume that Holmes was provocative and defiant. Clarke did his best to bring about a public disputation and give the Massachusetts authorities occasions to behave badly. He managed the technique of agitation very well. Three weeks in a Boston jail in the middle of summer were uncomfortable but well short of martyrdom. Unlike Crandall, Clarke had no agony of conscience when his fine was paid, and unlike Holmes, he escaped a whipping. Holmes probably had a far greater success in dramatizing the Baptist cause, at least to the populace in Massachusetts.

Despite the severity of his punishment, Holmes suffered less than several other dissenters. Religious persecution in Massachusetts ran a spectrum of penalties, beginning with being disarmed and proceeding through being fined, banished, whipped, whipped repeatedly, put to hard labor, mutilated, and, finally, being hanged. In 1651, the Baptists fell in the lower half of the range. The officials feared them less than advocates of total reliance on the Holy Spirit's guidance through the belief in direct divine inspiration and even fined them less heavily than the Anglican Samuel Maverick. The episode probably did not achieve what the magistrates intended: the public whipping called attention to the ideas it was meant to suppress.

Clarke broadcast the news to a wider and more important audience when he traveled to England in 1651. He went there to seek an annulment of Coddington's patent at the request of men in Portsmouth and Newport. They were continuing a colonial government under the charter of 1643/44—in hostility to Coddington's government—while the mainland towns of Providence and Warwick operated their own. The mainland towns chose to think that Coddington's patent had detached Portsmouth and Newport from the colonial union; the Aquidneck opponents of Coddington thought his government was a rather ineffectual attempt at usurpation. In this muddle, Clarke was to represent the island towns, which wanted Coddington's patent annulled in order to take the cloud off the charter of 1643/44. The mainland towns chose Roger Williams. They wanted a new charter for themselves in order to resolve doubt that Coddington's patent had in effect rescinded the earlier charter.[17] Thus the two agents had different missions, although both began with a campaign against Coddington.

The two men took ship in Boston in November 1651. Perhaps on the way, Clarke learned a lesson in publicity. When Williams had gone to England in 1643 to petition for a charter giving the four towns a colonial jurisdiction of their own, he had written *A Key into the Language of America* to advertise his value in converting Indians—and by implication, to point out Massachusetts's failure in this regard.[18] This was a marvelously indirect method but it worked. Clarke could not produce anything to compare with the brilliance of the *Key*. Rather, he followed the example of Samuel Gorton of Warwick, New England's most flamboyant believer in direct inspiration from the Holy Spirit, who had published a vividly colored narrative of his ordeal in Massachusetts under the title of *Simplicities Defence against Seven-Headed Policy*.[19]

Gorton had quite a story to tell. After antagonizing officials in Massachusetts, Plymouth, Aquidneck, and Providence, he and his growing flock of disciples settled on the west shore of Narragansett Bay at Shawomet. Still, a few of their neighbors across the Providence line thought they were intolerable, declared allegiance to Massachusetts, and in 1643 prevailed on that colony's magistrates to send a posse to capture Gorton and as many of his adult male followers as they could catch. The posse succeeded in getting Gorton and a number of others. All but seven were given minor punishments and released. The seven narrowly escaped the death sentence and were put in irons to be distributed among as many Massachusetts towns and set to hard labor. If they propagated their heterodox beliefs, they would be tried again and if convicted, put to death. Of course they did propagate their beliefs, but the officials prudently decided against another trial and ordered the prisoners released and banished—both from Massachusetts and Shawomet—on pain of death if they returned.[20]

Gorton and the rest went back to Shawomet anyway, then he and two companions went to England seeking a ruling that the place did fall within Rhode Island's boundaries. Gorton wrote *Simplicities Defence* as part of his campaign for the ruling and also to arouse widespread opposition to persecutions meted out by Massachusetts. (While he was away, Massachusetts authorized some Braintree men to settle a town at Shawomet![21])

Clarke had a less shocking tale to report and a less combative disposition, so his book lacked the sarcasm and dazzling twists of reasoning found in Gorton's work. Clarke's was dignified and less emotional. It was shorter, although like Gorton's it included judicial documents and correspondence between the magistrates and the prisoners. In fact, the narratives of persecution by Clarke and Holmes took up fewer than half the pages. Nearly all the rest expounded their beliefs about how to conduct a church of Christ and their reasons for thinking the Massachusetts churches were following the wrong course.

The relevance of Clarke's book to the campaign against Coddington was almost as roundabout as Williams's *Key* was to obtaining a colonial charter. Clarke believed that the magistrates in Massachusetts would tell its agent in London to spread adverse reports about the Baptist missionaries, which might stymie his protest against Coddington, so he wanted to present their side in as public a form as he could. In one way he succeeded beyond his hopes. His *Ill Newes* so alarmed the Massachusetts officials that they encouraged Thomas Cobbet, the minister at Lynn, to write a rebuttal. To Cobbet's credit, he tackled the central subject—government's function in supporting an orthodoxy—although he also gave space to attacks on the Baptist missionaries, especially Holmes.

Published in 1653 as *The Civil Magistrates Power in Matters of Religion Modestly Debated*, Cobbet's book gave a vigorous defense of the use of force to maintain the kind of church that he considered correct. Although he argued well, his work served less to defend Massachusetts than to confirm Clarke's attack. By the time it appeared, governmental enforcement of religious uniformity was in extremely bad odor in England, so a defense of it made apologists for Massachusetts quite unable to deny the colony's persecutions.

Clarke and Williams, with help from Sir Henry Vane, won something close to the annulment of Coddington's patent in 1652. The Council of State ordered the colonial government established under the charter of 1643/44 to continue until the controversy with Coddington was settled.[22] Williams sought a new charter for the mainland towns, with no success, and then returned to Providence, where he spent three years urging the others in Rhode Island to restore the single government specified in the charter of 1643/44. Clarke and his wife remained in England and may well have planned to stay there indefinitely. Clarke did a few more things as agent—notably getting a definitive ruling from Oliver Cromwell in 1655 reconfirming the charter of 1643/44 and procuring armaments for the colonial government—but otherwise his official business seemed to be finished.[23]

Like other Puritans who went to New England in the 1630s, he was excited by the revolution against Charles I and the opening it gave for further religious reform. Quite a number of New England settlers went back to England after 1640. Williams, who had traveled to England in 1643/44 for a charter, rushed into the debate over what the reform should be. Along with many other backers of the conflict against Charles I, he began to think that the series of events inaugurated by the revolution would lead to the Second Coming. Of course, he had his own twist on the prognostications; he was for religious freedom rather than a partnership between a purified church and state or a battle to determine the one true course of reform.[24] Even people who remained in Massachusetts began to think along similar lines, no one more than John Cotton, who expounded on the Revelation of Saint John in sermons preached in 1639 and 1640.[25] Before leaving Newport, Clarke caught the infectious millenarianism and voiced his hopes. Although no record of what he said or when survives, Williams knew enough about Clarke's views "Concerning the rising of Christ's Kingdome after the Desolations by Rome" to disagree with them.[26]

In *Ill Newes* Clarke made several allusions to the Second Advent, but without saying that he thought it was imminent. In one passage, echoed in a few others, he said the believers would nourish "a lively hope" for Christ's "glorious return" and must face "seducing spirits" in "these later daies." He had little to say on eschatology proper. He was not counting years to correlate the calendar to the beasts and vials mentioned in biblical prophecies, nor did he name an Antichrist. He merely concluded with a timeless exhortation to Christians to be ready for the Second Coming whenever it should occur.[27] Elsewhere he referred darkly to the Christian's hope for that glorious event as one to be awaited passively.[28]

In only a few passages did he hint at more specific expectations. Early in the book he wrote that "the lord is at hand." Twice he repeated this thought, noting that Christ "is alive, and will ere-long appear" to avenge attacks on his teachings. This could be construed as rhetorical technique if Clarke had not concluded by citing Revelation 22:20 and commenting on it: "Surely I come quickly, with the like closing therwith as there is exprest. Amen, even so come Lord Jesus."[29]

Clarke explained his understanding of Christ in *Ill Newes* in a section he said was written as his testimony of faith when he was a prisoner in Boston. In his usual straightforward style of exegesis, he showed that Christ had several roles, some of them distinct in chronology. Christ, he argued, was the Supreme Anointed One, anointed by God with "the oyl of gladnesse above all his fellowes," and so was above all others who had been anointed. He was the Anointed Priest, who made "a perfect attonement for all those that come to God through him," and so reconciled God and sinful humanity. He was the Anointed Prophet, the supreme teacher of divine truth.[30]

Christ also was the Lord, by which Clarke meant something different from king, or at least that was his meaning when he wrote around 1652. Christ as Lord governed his church. He appointed the mode of worship, gave rules for gathered congregations, knit the members together "by his Spirit," and ruled by "a spiritual law . . . written in the heart of a Christian by the Spirit of Christ" and not by "a carnall commandment seconded with carnall weapons."[31] By drawing the distinction between Lord and king, Clarke made the church an enduring institution apart from civil government.

Yet Christ was king as well, king with the power to heal the sick and raise the dead during his earthly career, and king as ruler of an earthly dominion at the end of history. Of the latter, Clarke said "that as certainly as he hath had a time for his Propheticall Office and for his Priestly, so shall he have a time for his Kingly; and as the dream of Nebuchadnezzer hath been found certain, and the interpretation of Daniel sure, concerning those four Monarchies or Kingdoms of men which should come to pass in the Earth, so certain and sure it is, that the day is approaching that the God of Heaven will set up his Kingdom by that despised yet Corner-stone that was cut out without hands. *Dan.* 44, 45." There would be a Fifth Monarchy. Christ would appear "in the form of a King, with his glorious Kingdom."[32]

Such was Clarke's doctrine in 1652. Shortly afterward his conviction that Christ's earthly rule would begin soon deepened, and in all probability he became a Fifth Monarchist.[33] His links to that movement have been questioned by scholars concerned with the reputation of the Baptist tradition and under the impression that only wild fanatics took up that cause. On the contrary, the movement attracted mostly urban folk, some of them of high standing and extensive education, who favored a strong moral code, intense piety, and a traditional social hierarchy.[34] At least by 1654 Clarke was caught up in the excitement of those who believed in the imminent return of Christ to rule as king on earth. Quite likely he was the John Clarke who signed a manifesto issued in that year by 150 men, many of whom were members of two Baptist churches in London with which he was associated.[35]

Three years later, in 1657, a John Clarke joined several known friends of John Clarke from Rhode Island in signing an address that begged Oliver Cromwell not to assume the title of king.[36] The next year our John Clarke probably was the man of that name arrested along with others who opposed Cromwell's rule. He was accused of saying that the present government existed by the permission but not the approbation of God and that God had called him to witness against it. He avowed that he held these ideas and had made his witness, but he denied that he had tried to alienate people from the government. He cited a 1649 law of Parliament against rule by one man. In this and other ways his defense resembled the one made by Dr. John Clarke in Massachusetts. In London he was acquitted on most counts but was fined and sent to jail for six months.[37]

Thereafter he gave up the political side of millenarianism. After Thomas Venner's pathetic uprising in January 1661, Clarke was arrested but released for lack of evidence of complicity. Within a few days he was probably the John Clarke who wrote a brief pamphlet denouncing the Fifth Monarchists who joined this rebellion against Charles II.[38] Clarke returned to advocating separation of church and state.

This skeletal narrative needs some flesh, and there is enough that fits the frame. Once Clarke no longer needed to hover around government offices, he set out as an itinerant preacher. Presumably, he was among the first "messengers" sent by groups of Baptist churches that were clearly of the Particular kind. The members contributed money to support these messengers, who were to oppose the messengers sent out by what we now call General Baptists. Clarke spoke against what he considered the General Baptists' errors of "freewill, and universal redemption, and spiritual baptism, and seeking."[39] That is, he upheld his old belief in free grace, predestination, limited atonement, and the need for a bodily baptism. He had already declared his opposition to the other side on these points and also on a cluster of errors that included Seekerism. In *Ill Newes* he had warned against the teachings of those who practiced "no visible way of worship, or order at all," no matter how they justified this neglect. Some, he knew, said "the outward court is given to the Gentiles, and the holy City is by them to be troden [sic] under foot." Others, like Roger Williams, held "that the Church of Christ is now in the wilderness, and the time of its recovery is not yet." Still others, like Gorton, claimed "God is a spirit, and so will in spirit be worshipped, and not in this place or that, in this way or that."[40]

When in London during the 1650s, Clarke associated with several Baptist pastors and congregations and eventually became a preacher in one.[41] The flavors of these associates again illustrate why the polarization into Particular and General Baptist should not be drawn rigidly. The first congregation he frequented, with Henry Jessey as pastor, had long welcomed members of different beliefs on various points, including infant baptism. Jessey himself held the doctrine of predestination, although probably some in his flock did not. Other congregations, such as the ones with William Kiffin and John Spilsbury as pastors, put more emphasis on agreement on free grace and so became Particular during the 1640s. Spilsbury was a cobbler and so not of the traditional standing of the clergy.[42] At times, Clarke cooperated with Hanserd Knollys, who also had been in New England, where he leaned toward reliance on direct inspiration from the Holy Spirit before returning to London and leaning toward universalism.[43]

More revealing was the array of men arrested with Clarke in 1658. They included an old Separatist and Baptists of different stripes, and they were rounded up at Thomas Venner's notoriously radical conventicle.[44] If Clarke had no significant connection with the Baptists now called General, he surely knew many and probably had his arguments with them. Like them, he strongly favored a congregation with openness to divergent teachings and full liberty of prophesying. Unlike them, he resisted letting the ignorant and women become preachers, and even more he opposed the proclivity for preaching thought to be at the prompting of the Holy Spirit. He sought reliance on Scripture and maintenance of an orderly pattern of worship. So again, the difference was more over style than creed, and it resulted in argument rather than separation.

Beyond this ecclesiastical variety, Clarke and his wife gained a valuable roster of friends. One was Robert Bennett, who had served in Parliament, on the Council of State, and on the Commission for the Approbation of Public Preachers. Possibly Bennett introduced Clarke to Captain Richard Deane, one of Cromwell's treasurers at war and later a London merchant. Of course, Clarke knew Anne Hutchinson's old champion, Sir Henry Vane. And he may have been related to John Carew, a prominent Fifth Monarchist from near Exeter (earlier a regicide, who was put to death for it in 1660) whose last name was the first name of Clarke's oldest brother.[45] And he became fairly widely known among Baptists.

Clarke also made some other friends who were particularly close. The most intriguing among them was Richard Baily. Almost totally obscure, Baily probably knew law. He had no wife or children so far as is known. He may well have given Clarke advice on petitions for the Rhode Island charter and some of the wording of the final document.[46] When Clarke returned to Newport, Baily went with him. He wrote Clarke's will and the subsidiary instructions that went with it; his hand penned them and his mind probably translated the dying man's wishes into sufficiently legal language. By the will he was to receive Clarke's books and the concordance to the Bible and the lexicon (probably Hebrew) Clarke had written. And he became the guiding member of the team of three executors.

Alice and Robert Osler of London also played a part in Clarke's affairs, although the context can only be guessed. There must have been a friendship extending back into the 1650s, judging from Alice's comments in a letter in 1671. When Clarke was angling for Rhode Island's royal charter, he sometimes had Robert Osler with him as an adviser. Because the government in Newport sent him far too little money, he ran up bills and began to borrow. He mortgaged his house and about 200 acres of land to Richard Deane for £130. He mortgaged other property to Hanserd Knollys, most of which he redeemed fairly soon. He also borrowed from Robert Osler and managed to pay him back in a short time.[47]

Well before the petition for the charter, Clarke and the Oslers talked of the imminent Second Coming. In her 1671 letter Alice wrote, "I would be glad to say sumthing to you of those affaires yt sumtimes wee haue conuersed about, but such is the intimation yt I haue from the scriptures of A uery darke and sad estate of things, before the worke of the lord be performed upon mount sion."[48] Alice Osler also did what she could to help John and Elizabeth Clarke in their financial concerns in England. She was in touch with Richard Deane, who waited for years and died without being repaid. He never claimed the property by foreclosure, although he might have tried to do so at any time after the end of 1663.[49] Deane was the kindliest—and therefore in the end, the most embarrassing—of creditors. (Probably he did not want a farm in Rhode Island, anyway.) Alice Osler had no need to cajole him for more time. Rather, she got his advice in trying to obtain Elizabeth Clarke's annuity.

Elizabeth's father, John Harges, had died and left her an annuity of £20, payable in two installments each year on the feast of Michael the Archangel and "ye Annuntiacon of ye blessed Virgin Mary." The heirs and executors had refused to pay it. Apart from avarice, their motives were perhaps shadowed in the terms of the testator. Michaelmas (29 September) and Lady Day (25 March) surely were traditional times for making many kinds of payments, but Puritans—Baptists at least as fervently as others—generally shunned such relics of the Catholic calendar. Mention of the old feasts suggests that Harges (or his lawyer) held firmly to traditional religion and used this language to show his disapproval of the new. He did not turn his face from his distant daughter who had joined a Baptist conventicle, but the rest of the family did.

In an effort to get payment of the annuity, John and Elizabeth signed a letter of attorney in 1656, empowering John Kinge to represent their interests. Either by John Harges's will or more likely, John Kinge's interpretation of the law, if the annuity was not paid, Elizabeth Clarke might enter the lands previously held by her father and distrain property to satisfy her claim.[50] Kinge got nowhere. Quite possibly the Clarkes chose not to attempt legal action but instead to rely on persuasion through intermediaries. After fifteen years nothing had been accomplished. Alice Osler and Richard Deane still were unsuccessful. Elizabeth's brothers sent Alice to their father's executors and the executors sent her back to the brothers.[51] As far as is known, Elizabeth never got a shilling.

Life was turning ever more bitter for her. In broad terms it is easy to sketch the circumstances that swept her along. The hostility of her brothers froze her out of her social standing among the gentry as well as the family solidarity she had every reason to count on. The engines of law did not turn for her. She was dependent on the husband whose promising career had gone so far off its projected course. He remained loyal and correct, probably devoted though not likely to let consideration for her deflect his plans, but her disappointments followed from his religious radicalism. And they had no children. The first journey to Newport had the excitement of serving a cause and building a future. When they went back in 1664, it must have seemed like exile to Elizabeth. Faithfulness to what were considered womanly virtues had brought her so little. At least Alice Osler, if unsuccessful, showed the cordiality and devotion that the Harges family denied. We cannot know how Elizabeth felt about these elements in her life. On the record nothing about her survives, not even in her husband's writings. Furthermore, she had died by the time Alice Osler's letter arrived.

But this is getting too far ahead of events. When John Clarke pulled back from assertive actions to bring on the rule of King Jesus, he had at least begun establishing a record of opposing Oliver Cromwell. After he denounced Venner's uprising in 1661 he had made arguable, if not plausible, his disagreement with the dangerous forms of Fifth Monarchism and his loyalty to Charles II. And a good thing, too, because almost immediately he was called upon for his greatest service as colonial agent, getting a royal charter for Rhode Island.

4

In Caesar's Court: The Royal Charter

John Clarke's best-known achievement was the royal charter for Rhode Island awarded in 1663. He served as the colony's agent and was directly responsible for several of the sections, including the best and the worst—the one on religious liberty and the one on jurisdiction over the territory west of Narragansett Bay. He had a hand, too, in framing the new design of government that the document prescribed and in persuading his superiors in Newport to accept it.

Originally, Rhode Island officials had in view no redesign of any kind, but when they learned of the king's restoration in 1660, they began to worry that the charter procured by Roger Williams in 1643/44 would be challenged because it had been granted by a commission of Parliament during the Civil War. At first they decided simply to petition for a royal reaffirmation. They drafted a letter to Clarke appointing him the agent for this purpose, but then they had second thoughts and did not send it. Instead, they considered sending one or two others for the task, chose committees for each town to solicit contributions to a total of £200 to pay for the mission, chose other committees in each town to consult the citizens on what instructions to send, and formed still more committees to collect the results and assemble supporting documents. After making all these plans, the colonial officials fell back on their first one, prompted by a message from Clarke, and sent him the year-old letter in August or September 1661. The only purpose they mentioned in the letter was to get the king's help in stopping the efforts by neighboring colonies to gain control of parts of the territory.[1]

There had been many attempts and more were underway. Massachusetts had tried to eradicate the Gortonian settlement and put another community in its place.[2] Also, Massachusetts, together with other colonies had sent military forces to intimidate the Narragansett Indians.[3] Plymouth at various times claimed land around the head of Narragansett Bay.[4] Massachusetts had claimed land on both sides of the Pawcatuck River as spoils of the Pequot War, but after years of dispute it had all but relinquished this claim to Connecticut, which was close to success in making it effective.[5]

By 1660, the Narragansett Indians no longer had the solidarity that had so impressed English newcomers in earlier years. Sachems were selling land rights to colonists in large tracts and small. Rhode Island men eagerly made purchases and took alarm when others did, too.[6] They began a town on the east bank of the Pawcatuck to counter Connecticut, but they feared more the combination of men based in Boston that was buying large tracts of land just west of Narragansett Bay, had plans for more, and emphatically wanted the whole territory to be under Connecticut rather than Rhode Island.[7] The competition for land gave urgency to Clarke's mission. Massachusetts, furthermore, had been limiting trade with Rhode Island.[8] That colony faced economic strangulation, if not submergence into the neighboring jurisdiction. Clarke, understandably, saw a threat to religious liberty, and maybe the officials in Newport did too.

He received his new commission by January 1661/62, well after his arrest the year before, and went to work. He labored under more handicaps than he realized. Although suspicion of his complicity in rebellion may have blown over, it could easily recur. He found some unfamiliar faces behind official desks and knew he had to establish a working relationship with them. He no longer had many useful friends in high ranks. While old antagonists in the ruling class were warily getting back together to support the monarchy, they could easily ignore a man like Clarke if they chose. Clarke did not understand how unskilled he was at negotiation or how much residence in England had affected his judgment. He saw the Restoration through the eyes of an

English Baptist Fifth Monarchist who had experienced the whole swirl of the Interregnum regimes, had mingled with their sectarian critics, and saw religious repression bearing down on him after 1660. His superiors in Newport wanted land; he feared loss of religious liberty. He compromised the one to secure the other, failing to see that his fears were all but unwarranted.

For him, lack of money was the biggest obstacle. He had to pay fees for legal advice and for filing petitions—and if successful, for issuing the charter. He also would have to use gifts to persuade some of the officials to aid his campaign. In Rhode Island the effort to raise the money by voluntary contribution had results that were slow and at best half-successful. After donations produced too little and a few other attempts failed, the colony's officials tried to impose taxation, though without much known effect.[9] All the entries in the public record tacitly disclose that the government got much less than needed for Clarke's expenses.[10]

Nor did it provide him with adequate instructions, and those it did send have not survived. There is no direct evidence on the occasions and reasons for most of the contents in the new Rhode Island charter—in short, for the radical change from the original purpose of Clarke's agency.

The charter of 1643/44 was vague and simple. It let the freemen of the colony govern themselves by any arrangements a majority chose, assured them ample judicial authority, let them pass any laws they liked so long as they were as harmonious with English laws as the circumstances of the place would allow, and sketched boundaries without any attempt at precision except for a clumsy one on the west. The territory would be bordered on the north and east by Massachusetts and Plymouth, on the south by the ocean, and on the west and northwest by the Narragansett Indians—and yet would extend well beyond them, "about Twenty-five English Miles unto the Pequot River and Country."[11] This demarcation was hardly precise; the Pequot River meant what now is called the Mystic in southern Connecticut and the Pequot country extended east beyond the Pawcatuck.

The charter obtained by Clarke designed a form of government, gave the colony a variety of specific protections from its neighbors, assured the settlers the rights of Englishmen, and added the extraordinary royal permission for freedom of religion. On boundaries, this document was less vague than the first but touched off eighty years of dispute over where they should be drawn on the ground. The parts can be explained with different degrees of confidence.

Steps toward the second charter began when Clarke wrote the first two petitions to the king, probably with little or no guidance from Newport. In the first appeal, presented in January 1661/62, he set aside the colony's original goal of guarding its territorial claims and made religious liberty the main theme. The settlers of Rhode Island, he said, had left England and then Massachusetts to gain it. They had allowed it to everyone who came to their colony—by implication, an adverse reflection on the other New England colonies—and they wanted the king to confirm their right to it.[12]

Clarke bolstered this plea with strong professions of loyalty to the crown, a topic on which he probably decided to say what he knew was necessary and trust the Rhode Island people to accept his judgment. Vigorously stretching the truth, he claimed they had always been the most loyal of subjects. He said they had appealed to Charles I for a charter in 1642, and then went on to say with some misty evasions that the result was the charter granted the next year by the commission of Parliament to regulate overseas plantations. The original decision to seek the charter had not specified a petition to the king—the people in Newport understood enough of the English Civil War to realize that they must address whomever was in power—but sought the help of Sir Henry Vane.[13] Besides, virtually everyone in New England sided with Parliament in opposition to Charles I.

Clarke could report truthfully that as soon as news of the Restoration reached Rhode Island, officials there decided to proclaim their fidelity to the king and ask for confirmation of their privileges.[14] He still was on safe ground when he declared that he saw the wonderful hand of God behind the return of the king, but he implied a delight in this turn of events which he surely did not feel. Nor was he entirely candid when he claimed that under the first charter the people of Rhode Island had "forthwith grownded their government thereupon." They had spent more than three years quarreling over whether to do so and how to do so, only to go on making changes in their form of government once they had started one. And there had been the disruption brought about by Coddington's patent. At least he was right in saying they had written a slate of laws based mainly on English laws.[15]

In a second appeal to Charles II, submitted a week later, Clarke summarized what he had said in the first and began to introduce the phrases that would appear in the charter. He said the people of Rhode

Island "have it much in their hearts ... to hold forth a lively experiment, that a flourishing civill State may stand, yea, and best be maintained, and that among English spirits, with a full liberty in religious concernments, and that true pyety rightly grounded upon gospell principles will give the best and greatest security to true soveraignty, and will lay in the hearts of men the strongest obligations to truer loyalty."[16] In this passage, "lively experiment," came from *Ill Newes*, which shows Clarke's hand in framing the address.[17] The document spoke in his voice, although surely he had advice and maybe a little guidance from a town and colony that had removed civil government from "religious concernments" more thoroughly than any part of the United States does today. He spoke for a unique society with no parish taxes, no specifications of parish boundaries, no grants of land to endow churches, no exemptions from taxation for church property, no laws to require attendance at public worship, no laws to call on the citizens to teach religion to their children or conduct family devotions, no legal authorization for clergymen to create marriages, no public support of education. Nor did the operations of government have the slightest flavor of religion. There were no invocations before the deliberations of courts or the legislature, no chaplains for the militia, no election sermons, no allusions to God in oaths of office or oaths to give testimony—in fact, no oaths whatsoever, but instead a solemn promise made in the awareness of the laws against perjury. With this background in mind, Clarke appealed boldly for a guarantee of religious freedom, adding the argument that this liberty would support rather than undermine both social prosperity and loyalty to the king. And the king took notice of it.[18]

In fact, he was sympathetic to it. In a cautious way Charles II favored legal permission for those who could not conscientiously accept the Church of England to form dissenting congregations. On his way back from refuge in the Spanish Netherlands, in the Declaration of Breda, he had offered to allow different persuasions, but in language that was deliberately ambiguous.[19] (Later, the Rhode Island charter contained phrases from this document.[20]) He was not on the throne yet, and so could do no more than express good will to people who were bound to be dissenters to whatever kind of national church might be reconstituted. He later tried to make toleration of dissent an accepted policy but had to yield to those who opposed him. Even his political captain, Edward Hyde, soon to be earl of Clarendon, resisted measures that would allow religious diversity.

After two years of uncertainty, the determined Anglicans gained the upper hand in England. At least, Clarke's first pleas were made when a liberal policy on religion still seemed possible. Of course, his requests were minor matters in English eyes. Hyde was willing to let American colonies have whatever religious arrangements they preferred, and the prelates of the Church of England were too engrossed in controversies over their form of Restoration to take much interest in matters across the sea.[21] Even as opposition to dissent grew strong, the king could condone religious liberty in a small and often forgotten colony at very little risk. Actually, the Restoration government never objected to religious liberty in Rhode Island. Rather, it objected to the lack of it in the rest of New England.

Without enough money, without detailed instructions, without enough legal advice or geographical knowledge, Clarke faced an emergency in spring 1662 and had to act as best he could. He cast caution aside and spent as much as he dared. By summer 1663 he had to borrow £130 from Richard Deane.[22] The emergency came when John Winthrop, Jr., got in ahead of him to obtain the award of the Connecticut charter of 1662. Winthrop's conduct has been debated ever since and the nuances remain hard to fit into a pattern. As a person, Winthrop was generous and ingratiating and kept the friendship of Rhode Islanders as diverse as Coddington, Gorton, and Williams. He even managed to radiate a sympathy for religious freedom, though he was the governor of the colony that outdid all others in suppressing religious dissent.

Winthrop brought instructions, of which he was one of the drafters. Part of the plan had to do with his colony's legal privileges and form of government. He was to procure a charter giving the same privileges as those previously given to Massachusetts.[23] Presumably, the privileges would include authorization to have a government like the one developed in the older colony.[24] The goal was a system where the freemen elected their governor and the other members of a council of "assistants," and the towns sent representatives to form the rest of the legislature. The governor and assistants would be an all-purpose board with legislative, administrative, military, and judicial responsibilities.

This part of Winthrop's aims posed no conflict with those of Rhode Island, but the boundaries he sought at first were little short of war. Partly at his behest, his colony wanted everything south of Massachusetts from the Plymouth line on the east to Delaware Bay on the west. His first petition for a charter followed this plan.[25] Plymouth had somewhat fluctuating estimates of its westward extent, but no matter:

if Winthrop got his way as first requested, Rhode Island would be wiped off the map. Winthrop could have justified this goal as best for all concerned, but in surviving documents he never did. Instead, he disclaimed it and said he had no desire to eliminate Rhode Island as a jurisdiction but thought its four towns had enough land in the islands in Narragansett Bay and around the central clusters of dwellings of Providence and Warwick.[26]

Winthrop and Connecticut publicly justified claims to a boundary at Narragansett Bay by the terms of a charter granted in 1632, which they never had seen. This document, which may well have been mythical, was issued by the earl of Warwick as president of the Council for New England and conveyed the territory between Narragansett Bay and the Pequot River, plus governmental powers over it, to a group of gentlemen, one of whom said twelve years later that he would sell it to Connecticut if he ever found himself in a position to do so. Winthrop inquired about the charter, found only what he said was a copy, probably grew skeptical about its validity, but went on with the assertion that by it Connecticut had acquired rights to the Narragansett country in existence well before the Rhode Island charter of 1643/44.[27]

Winthrop had a stronger motive than faith in an old grant. He had a share in the organization based in Boston that was trying to gain control of the entire Narragansett country and served its interests—as did Connecticut—tacitly.[28] Known as the Atherton Company or the Narragansett Proprietors, this group first bought two large tracts on the west shore of Narragansett Bay on either side of the large estate of Richard Smith at Cocumscussoc (just east of modern Wickford), who also was one of the partners. One tract extended north into what the leading men of the town of Warwick had bought a few years earlier on the south side of Greenwich Bay. The other, running down to Point Judith, the southeast corner of the Narragansett country, conflicted directly with the Pettaquamscut purchase made by a group of prominent Rhode Island men. So Smith and the Atherton Company between them claimed all the western shore of Narragansett Bay south of Warwick. More ominously still, the company had made a remarkable arrangement with the United Colonies of New England. The United Colonies punished the Indians for alleged misdeeds by imposing a fine they could not pay. The company then agreed to pay it for them in exchange for a mortgage on their entire territory, which they could not redeem.[29]

Rhode Island already had asserted a right to control private purchases by white men within this territory, had faced several who disregarded this assertion, had come to terms with a few, and had denounced the Narragansett Proprietors.[30] The colony opposed that group with special virulence partly on account of the huge extent of land involved and partly because the partners had begun large farms, which they operated by servants and tenants, and used them to raise livestock to export through Boston. Thus, if the Narragansett partners got what they wanted, Rhode Island would lose the economic advantages of the Narragansett region and would not gain much population. Winthrop knew perfectly well what he was doing, and Clarke regarded his conduct as treacherous.

Understandably, Winthrop took care to keep the Rhode Island officials in the dark when he set out for a charter. Instead of traveling by way of Boston, he first sailed west so as to cut down the chance that the purpose of his travels would become known in Newport, and arrived at New Amsterdam. There he asked and got the help of Governor Peter Stuyvesant in arranging passage across the Atlantic but surely never thought of mentioning his plans to pull the southern half of New Netherland into Connecticut. Of course, once he arrived at the English capital, he stayed away from John Clarke and found lodgings two miles distant.[31]

Winthrop went about his business skillfully. He renewed old friendships, found an ace influence-wielder and helpful men in high offices, gained the esteem of prominent scientists, and became a founding member of the Royal Society. And he arranged for the services of two lawyers of the Middle Temple, the more important being William Thirsby. Thus aided, he had a clear understanding of procedure—both formal and otherwise—and help in following the arcane protocol of requests to the throne. He was ready to approach the officials shortly after Clarke presented his first two petitions. Winthrop also had his own ready tongue and self-assurance among the mighty to make him effective when presenting his request. Personal qualities counted in this game. He succeeded in good time. His charter went through the elaborate procedures in about three months and was ready for release by May 1662.[32]

Clarke may have known fairly early in the process that Winthrop was seeking a charter for Connecticut. In March there was at least one meeting of the Privy Council to consider New England affairs.[33] Possibly at that occasion the Rhode Island agent became aware that the Connecticut agent had adverse territorial goals, but he neither grasped the full extent nor had the ability to mount a strong opposition. He was stumbling through the early steps of getting a petition acted upon. He needed more help with formalities than he got and needed more money than he had, so his business often stalled.

The order of events cannot be determined exactly. The surviving narrative by Clarke was incomplete, blurred chronology, obscured a few important features, and probably betrayed some serious misunderstandings. It was incomplete because he expected the officials in Newport to know what he had reported in earlier dispatches that no longer exist. Besides, he was not above telling a story so as to put himself in a more heroic role than the facts justified, as seen in a few parts of *Ill Newes*. For all its shortcomings, the narrative is a crucial document on his mission.

As he told it, he and Winthrop appeared before Lord Clarendon, who "exprest himselfe verie fauourably inclined to giue us [both] Charters." Clarke implied that this encounter took place well before May. According to him, he politely said to Winthrop, "now we being Neighbors there will be some difference I suppose between us touching or boundaries." So he suggested that they confer privately "so we may issue it . . . among or selues or call in friends to assist us." Clarke offered some reasons, but Winthrop "turned away and refused the motion & grew strainger & strainger." Clarke said he pushed for his own charter "wth double dilligence," though there is no hint of what he did, while keeping an eye on Winthrop as well as he could. But his rival "by the helpe of a silver key" hurried his campaign through the channels at court and got the award of a patent before Clarke was aware of it.[34]

When Clarke got an inkling of the contents he rushed to appeal to Clarendon and the king.[35] Suddenly the boundary was his foremost concern after all, not religious liberty. Clarendon said he would help and "called in" the Connecticut charter. The two official copies were at as many offices to be enrolled.[36] The earl certainly obtained a copy but may not have retrieved the official documents. He did, however, forbid their release for the time being.

Then Clarke angrily confronted Winthrop, who had his own story to tell, not least to subdue any annoyance that Clarendon felt at being hoodwinked into serving one colony at the expense of the other. Several times Winthrop wrote explanations of what happened, mixing the probable with the plausible to build a bypass around some ugly points. He said too much—that he only had sought a confirmation of the old grant of 1632 and so had no reason to think about Rhode Island, had not known that Clarke was Rhode Island's agent and had heard that somebody else would be sent or had been called upon, expected the colony to send someone with fresher knowledge of how things stood in New England, had known that Clarke had moved his family to England many years earlier, thought Clarke was acting in a private capacity and merely transmitted official mail from Newport to a certain Alderman Peake, who would serve as the real agent unless Samuel Maverick did; that he thought Rhode Island wanted to be in Connecticut; that the Connecticut charter would not take any territory from Rhode Island; that in any case Clarke could have got his charter if he had only tried before Winthrop even arrived. (Did he mean that it was fair to get a charter to somebody else's territory if the somebody else was slow at getting his own?) He sent a version of these protests to be told to important men in Rhode Island in order to prevent their believing Clarke. Winthrop had a good idea of what Clarke would say and later actually got his hands on at least one letter that Clarke sent back to the officials at Newport.[37]

Two items in Winthrop's catalogue of reasons need explanation. The fact of Clarke's moving his family to England several years earlier implied that he would not be an agent because the usual practice during the seventeenth century was for a colony to send an agent for a short time on a specific mission—ordinarily someone, such as Winthrop himself, who had taken part in planning the mission. Second, the allusion to Samuel Maverick. Maverick was an old settler in Boston, who was an Anglican and had been fined heavily by the Massachusetts government for signing a remonstrance against religious intolerance (and other evils). He had become a firm enemy to Puritan colonial governments and before his return to London began sending letters to the earl of Clarendon about changing the ways of Massachusetts and subjecting the colony to firm royal control.[38] But these are minor items.

Winthrop's exculpatory efforts would have been more convincing if they had aimed at the main point and referred less to secondary things. Still, what he said had some basis in fact. Quite likely he had learned before leaving America about the complex plans that beguiled the Rhode Island officials in winter 1660/61 to send agents and write their instructions. He had left before these plans were scrapped in favor of appointing Clarke as the agent after all. Clarke certainly had moved his family to England ten years earlier and maybe had entrusted papers to this Alderman Peake. Roger Williams at one point hinted that he would welcome an English plan to make Winthrop governor over all of New England.[39] Nevertheless, Clarke had not received his commission as agent until well after Winthrop reached England and so could not have procured a charter before that time, as Winthrop might have known if he had wished to ask. Besides, Winthrop had done his best to bring under Connecticut the Narragansett country that Rhode Island considered its choicest territory, had deliberately avoided telling Clarke what he was up to, even after learning that Clarke actually was the agent on the occasion when they both were pressing their business before Clarendon.

He had to let Clarke look at both the new Connecticut charter and what Winthrop said was the old one of 1632. Clarendon required this much. Clarke wanted to appeal to the earl again but refrained for fear of vexing him with still more trouble at a busy time (Catherine of Braganza was arriving from Portugal for her wedding with Charles II) and instead proposed arbitration to Winthrop, who seemed willing to accept this suggestion. They chose a panel, quite likely the three men introduced later in Clarke's narrative as chosen by Clarendon. Then Clarke was outraged by the discovery that Winthrop had persuaded Clarendon (by pestering and lies, Clarke said) to let him have the two official copies of the Connecticut charter either on the day the arbitrators met or the day before. So forthwith the Rhode Island agent went back to the earl after all to protest that Winthrop had got the documents "surreptuously and through verie great misinformacon & to ye verie greate prejudice of his Matie our selues & seuerall other Plantacons."[40]

As Clarke continued the story, Clarendon was amazed and indignant and said, "I thought you had bin agreed." Clarke accused Winthrop of deceit, and Clarendon replied, "well goe to him & tell him from me . . . that I take it not well at his hands he should serue me thus & bid him come to me." Clarke reported that he tracked down Winthrop the next day "and after I had dealt roundly wth him for this his base treacherous & under hand dealing" gave him the message, "wch did extreamely change his Countenance." Winthrop duly went to Clarendon, who summoned the two agents to appear for a hearing on 9 July.[41]

On the appointed day Clarke made his case, complaining that the new charter to Connecticut contained "many additions" to its territory, as it certainly did. Winthrop said he had seen the first Rhode Island charter and was willing to concede all the territory mentioned in it and more. Clarke quickly accepted the offer and said he would even be contented with somewhat less. Clarendon said they appeared close to an agreement and asked the crown's attorney general to examine the pertinent documents, but the attorney was reluctant, so the earl decided that Robert Boyle, Sir Thomas Temple, and Samuel Maverick should help the two agents.[42] Maverick has been introduced already. Boyle was an eminent scientist and friend of both agents, Temple a high-born royalist and Anglican who had spent time in New England developing control over Nova Scotia.

Clarke's report needs explanation. Winthrop interpreted the first Rhode Island charter as granting territory up to the Narragansett Indians, an interpretation emphatically urged by his partners in the Atherton Company,[43] which meant that it extended westward only to where the Indian lands lay. Clarke thought it granted everything to the Pequot River, including the Narragansett lands, so he greeted Winthrop's offer as one of more territory to the west rather than what it really was, a suggestion that a few islands or a little land west of Narragansett Bay might be consigned to Rhode Island. Either Clarke was unaware of what Winthrop meant or was happy to feign ignorance so that his adversary's words could be used against him once the soundness of the old Rhode Island charter was established. When Clarke offered to accept less than the territory as far west as the Pequot River he may well have had in mind Winthrop's acquisition of land on the east of the Quinebaug, a few miles west of the Pequot. Clarendon, probably with a sigh of relief, hoped for a quick end to the wrangle. And Clarke failed to realize that Boyle was less his friend than Winthrop's. At least Maverick was so adverse to Connecticut that he might take Rhode Island's side.

When Boyle, Temple, and Maverick learned of their assignment, they set a day for a hearing. In advance, Clarke and Winthrop each wrote a set of proposals for the panel to consider. Winthrop offered little, but he put it in the guise of magnanimity. First, he invited Rhode Island to join Connecticut and said, "provisions may be made for their inioyment of what so ever priviledges they now enioy as may be necessary." That was vague enough to be read as offering religious liberty by anyone eager to read it that way. In case Rhode Island declined the offer, he went on to propose boundaries that would limit the mainland towns of Rhode Island on the west either by a vaguely described line beginning at the Indian village at Cowesset (roughly, near Greenwich Bay where Warwick now meets East Greenwich) or a line running north from a point just east of Cocumscussoc, which would run just west of the original clusters of houses at Warwick and Providence. (Probably Winthrop wanted this proposal to be rejected because it would have surrendered part of what the Atherton Company had bought.) Or Clarke might get a charter stipulating a western border at Connecticut and a panel of arbitrators would determine where that was.[44]

Clarke showed much less caniness in his proposals. He offered too many and in some offered concessions that weakened his case for others. He revealed how far he would compromise much too soon. He wanted a western boundary at Pequot River and made that clear. He would reluctantly name a distance in miles between the east and west lines of his colony, preferring "about 35 miles unto ye Pequut River" but willing to accept "about 25 miles unto ye Pequut River &c That ye space which lies beyond ye 25 miles & between that & the Pequut River may be equally divided between us." (Referring to twenty-five miles had the slight merit of echoing the parallel passage in the first charter.) More unwisely, he suggested a boundary at the Pawcatuck River, which could be called the Narragansett River to get over the obstacle in the Connecticut charter, which set the eastern limit at "Narrogancett River, comonly called Norrogancett Bay, where the said River falleth into the Sea."[45]

Worse still, Clarke introduced the possibility of complex boundaries near the bay. If he could get a westward extension to Pequot River, the Atherton Company might have their purchases, provided they should "make a Plantation yr of" and sell parts to settlers rather than keep the land all for themselves as absentee owners—and the settlers could decide which colonial jurisdiction to join. Or if he could get territory only to the Pawcatuck, then the Atherton Company might keep only three or four thousand acres under the same conditions.[46]

On the day of the hearing, Winthrop came with his son Wait, his lawyer, and also John Scott, a brash young man from Long Island who had ingratiated himself with the Atherton Company and recently had come to England to serve their interests, or more accurately his own. Clarke was accompanied by his friend Robert Osler. The three arbitrators heard arguments and looked at documents. Scott and Winthrop's son perplexed them with what Clarke called "a fallce Map & fallce informacon," so they refused to make a firm declaration of who deserved what. They were the more reluctant because they learned—and Clarke learned, to his shock—that Winthrop had sent one official copy of his charter to Hartford. The arbitrators recommended that the agents settle matters among themselves and if they could not do that, to accept a western line for Rhode Island, proposed by Osler and Scott, to start at the ocean twelve miles west of Point Judith (the southeast tip of mainland west of Narragansett Bay) and run north parallel to the shore of the Bay, with compensation from Rhode Island to the Atherton syndicate for its claims to land on the east of that line.[47]

Clarke rejected this recommendation and consulted several friends and a lawyer who backed his judgment. He told Clarendon "yt all though I had exprest myselfe to be Content to take somewhat lesse then what is conteined in or Pattt yet I could not make it my Choise to accept of a therd part of what we could claim before upon as good a title if not better then they could theires & yt for seueral reasons but especially because it left out a verie Considerable purchase of Land & Plantation neuer Challenged by ym in wch neere an hundred Islanders were Ingadged." (He referred to the Misquamicut purchase that eventually became the new town of Westerly. He had a small investment in this project.) He would abide by Clarendon's determination, however.[48]

As to territory, the proposal was better than he thought. Although it meant the sacrifice of Rhode Island's tiny new settlement on the east bank of the Pawcatuck, that was a low price for the territory to the east of the line, which was the chief focus of rivalry. The payoff to the Atherton Company and its customers, however, soured the deal. If Rhode Island could not finance its agent, he could not commit it to pay an indeterminate sum to buy land rights that it had denounced as illegal.

Whether sincerely wishing for the conclusion or more likely taking advantage of Clarke's financial woes, Winthrop twice accepted the line beginning twelve miles west of Point Judith and urged Clarke to agree to it. On the second occasion, which was at a conference with Boyle and Clarendon, when Clarke refused, Winthrop said he was leaving on other business and his lawyer would hear anything further that Clarke had to say.[49] Clarke's lawyer recommended yet another protest to Clarendon—this time against Winthrop's dispatch of his charter—and a speedy request for a charter for Rhode Island. Clarke liked this advice and took it.[50]

Unaware that Clarendon himself had told Winthrop to send off his charter as soon as possible, Clarke misunderstood what happened next. He went to the Privy Council with a written protest and an appeal to Clarendon for his own charter "as neere the termes of the former" Rhode Island charter as Winthrop's was to the old Connecticut one of 1632. "Thereby," said Clarke, "we might be set again upon as euen ground as we weare before." He continued, saying, "so in case the Collonies cannot agree among ym selues toucheing theire Boundaries since ye Law is open as way of appeales they may take yt course to issue theire in."[51]

After some preliminaries, Clarendon said, "I haue perused yor Paper & as for ye desire to ye renewing yor Patt: according to ye former Boundaries in Gods name . . . doe it wth all my hart yt you may stand againe upon as euen a foote as he." All Clarendon asked was a statement from Boyle on what the three arbitrators had concluded. Clarke exited jubilantly, "blessing ye name of the Lord whoe had so wonderfully enclined his [Clarendon's] hart toward us."[52]

It is easy to see why Clarendon welcomed the prospect of consigning this troublesome squabble to arbitrators or the courts of law, but Clarke took his encouragement to mean that Rhode Island could have the boundaries it claimed. Much more likely, the earl had in mind what Winthrop believed the boundaries were,[53] but he was scrupulous enough to query Winthrop before dismissing the subject. Winthrop replied with another overabundant set of reasons why Clarke should not object to the dispatch of the charter to Hartford—and resolved to get the duplicate sent as soon as possible, which was done before long.[54] All the same, Winthrop could not take the document himself. He had to stay in England to keep an eye on Clarke, although his lawyer had already declared that Connecticut had a charter that could not be revoked.[55]

Clarke was distraught. His letter to the officials in Newport contained a wildly discordant combination of exuberance and anguish. Bitterly, he scolded the people back home. Their conduct was "stupid senceless [and] Baceless" in "not making use of those meanes . . . the lo:[rd] hath bin pleased to furnish you wth in plentifull measure so as to free yor selues from being a prey to ye teeth [of those] whoe could they come at you would teare you to [pieces]." He was chagrined when others, including "some at the sterne, . . . considered you a Coll: verie inconsiderable" and doubted that "[you should] be betrusted wth Gouernmt at such a time as this when you know what preparacon was made agst you by all your Neighbrs around about you." He went on, "you should . . . haue furnished me both wth Instructions & otherwise whereby I might haue bin able to haue borne up agt them. I cleerely see had you not bin backward & spareing Therein . . . I had procured you a Pattent before Wintrop had come" or could have been well ahead of him.[56] He denounced Connecticut and Winthrop in the most vituperative language in his vocabulary. He was angry at "the cruell deceitfull Barbarous Treacherous dealing of a professing People against theire Neigbrs whoe haue fled together wth Themselues to the extreame perill & hazard of their liues to enioie their spirituall liberties in those remote parts." Winthrop was deceitful, treacherous, underhanded.[57]

According to the surviving text of his letter of 8 August, which is a copy, Clarke went on to exult upon his prospective victory over the Atherton Company, saying in most uncharacteristic language that the reaffirmed Rhode Island charter would choke them with five provisions. By its terms all freeholders could vote in elections (not just members of governmentally approved churches), Rhode Island would extend to the Pequot River, the oath of allegiance to the king would replace the oath of fidelity to Massachusetts (a badly inaccurate prediction), all persons not of a scandalous life might be admitted to the sacraments, and any who wished might use the Book of Common Prayer. He resolved to rush energetically into the pursuit of the charter.[58]

Although the last two points were aspects of religious liberty that Clarke knew were forbidden in Massachusetts, the emphases were not his. Except for the second point, this whole list came from an even longer one compiled by Samuel Maverick, which was concerned with affairs in Massachusetts, not Connecticut.[59] Either Clarke was parroting Maverick, which seems unlikely, or the text of what purports to be Clarke's letter includes a concluding section by Maverick, whose approach to religious freedom was in the context of hostility to the restrictions imposed by Massachusetts. Clarke certainly had conferred with Maverick and was probably grateful for his help, but in Clarke's view, the goal of religious freedom was to allow religious advance and social peace rather than to punish anybody.

It is distressing to be without any documents to explain what took place between 8 August and 22 September 1662, because during this interval Clarke brought new elements into his dealings with the royal government. His petition to the king, which was officially accepted on 22 September, alluded to the conflict with Connecticut and asked for the most extensive territorial definition yet—not merely to the Pequot River on the west but also three miles east of Narragansett Bay, a proposition that found its way into the final charter and created additional discord. More interesting, Clarke went back to his constituents' desire for "liberty of Conscience" and asked for "such priviledges and immunities as haue been formerly graunted to the Mathathusetts Colony or of late by yor Royall selfe to Connecticutt Colony," which probably included a definition of the form of government along with a variety of other topics, such as encouragement for fishing and vineyards, ownership of land in the jurisdiction by the corporate government in something close to fee simple, and assurances of the rights of Englishmen for all the inhabitants.[60] The acceptance of the petition meant only that discussions might begin over how to word a charter.

Some passages were easy enough. At least Clarke had gained something from his recent woes and his talks with Maverick. He had learned to copy Connecticut in asking for privileges like those of Massachusetts, and in the end the basic plans for a colonial government contained in his charter were very like those for Connecticut. Conceivably he had new instructions from Newport, but if so, all trace of them is gone.

The new charter would have to contain clauses on boundaries, so it could not be drafted completely until an agreement had been reached. Winthrop would not budge. The dispute between Connecticut and Rhode Island, along with other sore subjects, led to an ominous development that made Clarke overeager to reach a compromise: the Privy Council, after approving Clarke's petition on 22 September, decided that a royal commission should be sent to New England to settle matters there.[61] Winthrop was much less alarmed and probably did not respond to most of the proposals Clarke made in the next month. As a result, Clarke gave up the high optimism of his report to Newport in August and began retreating from his hopes for a full-scale reaffirmation of the Rhode Island boundaries set forth in the charter of 1643/44.

He told Winthrop about a meeting planned for 9 October, at which they would both speak to the Council on Foreign Plantations, and said, "I could wish we might look each other in ye face ther as persons agreed" on the boundary "rather than to be found hotly contending each with other about yt wch in ye Issue may not Proue advantagious to either." On the outside of this note he wrote, "To his Beloued friend mr John Winthrop," but in the text he concluded, "I haue satisfaction in this that as I foresaw this euill [presumably, the projected royal commission] so I did my part to Prevent it, I shall not further trouble you but Remaine yors as I may."[62]

Of course, he troubled Winthrop again, probably because he got no response. The hearing was postponed until 16 October and then another time.[63] Clarke plied Winthrop with proposals much like the most conciliatory in his earlier document for the first three arbitrators. (After that unwise disclosure of what he might accept he had to offer variants on it but—a sign of his clumsiness in negotiation—kept repeating that if Winthrop did not accept one of these proposals, he would get the Pequot River boundary after all.) On one occasion he added a plea that religious liberty in his colony must be guarded.[64] As far as can be known, Winthrop did not reply and relied on the legal safety of his own charter. Clarke's hope that the Privy Council would settle the dispute evaporated on 13 December when the earl of Clarendon, who had been ailing earlier, became incapacitated by gout.[65]

Around that time the two agents decided to try a new panel of five arbitrators. This time it was composed of two friends of Winthrop, William Brereton and Benjamin Worsley, Clarke's friend Richard Deane, and two of unknown sympathies, Robert Thomson and John Brookhaven. On 19 December, three of them (Worsley, Brereton, and Thomson) produced a variant on what Clarke had proposed the previous summer. He should seek a new charter giving Rhode Island the same territorial definition as in its previous one, and Winthrop should declare his consent to the proposal, but the boundary later would be set at the Pawcatuck rather than the Pequot River. Further, the settlers both on the east side of the Pawcatuck and on the first Atherton Company purchases should have a year to decide if they would rather be under Connecticut, and after that time might choose individually if they had not reached a consensus, and any future disagreements should be settled by arbitrators chosen by the two colonial governments.[66] The three who offered this formula conspicuously did not include Clarke's friend, Richard Deane. The plan may have seemed Solomonic to the drafters but in retrospect looks calculated to make trouble.

Neither of the colonial agents embraced this scheme. So the winter dragged by without progress toward an agreement until Clarendon's health improved. Toward the end of February 1662/63 Clarke began to offer minor novelties to safeguard Winthrop's personal interests. If the boundary could be set at the Pawcatuck, then the owners of land—Winthrop or those to whom he sold his purchase straddling the Quinebaug—might choose to be in Connecticut if they were no more than six miles east of the river. This concession would be offset by three from Connecticut and the Atherton Company. These parties should agree to claim none of the territory claimed by the Rhode Island town of Warwick nor any included in the Pettaquamscut purchase. The syndicate should make "a Towneship . . . & so part with land to such as want it, upon reasonable termes" rather than "monopolize it . . . to ym selues."[67] Clarke's formula for the land near the Quinebaug betrayed an ignorance of geography that had grave consequences. He imagined that the Pawcatuck flowed closer to the Quinebaug than six miles. In fact, as Rhode Island's negotiators knew to their distress in many later parleys, the Pawcatuck rises a few miles west of Narragansett Bay, flows south, then swings west before turning south again to the sea at Block Island Sound.

Clarke already had thought out the subjects of disagreement and concluded that they came to three: boundaries, jurisdiction, and propriety (meaning respect for individual titles).[68] His distinctions seem illogical but actually got to the practical issues. He proposed the boundary at the Pawcatuck, the liberty of choice of jurisdiction for people on the Atherton Company purchases, and the agreement by the two colonies to honor all individual titles in territories under the jurisidiction. The illogic appears most clearly in separating boundaries and jurisdiction. And the limit on practicality came in the proposal to respect individual titles that came from different sources and often conflicted. Clarke's earnest effort to analyze the dispute so as to allow clear thinking on a solution came to naught, although the conclusions he drew from the analysis came close to the final agreement.

The two agents spent several tight-lipped weeks trying to get concessions from each other at the last hour, Clarke talking of the Pawcatuck as the boundary but mentioning the Pequot River occasionally, Winthrop saying he could not yield anything already granted in the Connecticut charter unless ordered to do so by the king.[69] Probably fear of the projected royal commission and the gathering strength of English opposition to any leniency to dissenters made Clarke increasingly alarmed, but he made no more concessions.[70] Nevertheless, it was better to get a charter than to leave his colony's fate to a royal commission. Winthrop had different worries. John Scott had returned to America and told the Atherton syndicate that Winthrop was too lenient to Rhode Island, so its officers instructed Winthrop to be firmer and sent Scott back across the Atlantic to serve as coagent. Still, they would not object if Rhode Island got a small part of the mainland that included only a thin slice along the bay in Warwick.[71] Also, by this time the leading men in the New Haven colony had learned that Winthrop's charter put their colony into Connecticut, much to their outrage.[72]

On 7 April, Winthrop finally gave in and he and Clarke accepted an award by a majority of the five arbitrators. By then, Clarendon had regained his health enough to resume official duties and could give his strong hand to the final approval. Winthrop confidently assumed that the arbitrators' conclusion would not undo the terms of his charter. He may have been pleased by another of Clarke's concessions to his personal interests—an explicit statement that Winthrop's Fishers Island should not be in Rhode Island. Alas, Clarke was unaware that all of this island lies west of the Pawcatuck.

The arbitrators' decision ruled that the Pawcatuck, as Clarke had proposed nine months previously, would be the boundary and that "for the future . . . [it would] be alsoe called alias . . . Narrogansett River," to make the name agree with the eastern border given in the Connecticut charter. Furthermore, anything within six miles east of the Quinebaug should be in Connecticut even if it was also east of the Pawcatuck. And the owners of land (resident and absentee) on the Atherton Company's purchases should have "free libertie to choose to which of those Coloneis they will belong." And finally, "That proprietie [i.e., individual title] shall not be altered nor destroyed, but carefully maintained through the said Collonies."[73]

All these provisions had been proposed by John Clarke. Winthrop had given up only Connecticut's claim to the territory between the Pawcatuck and the Atherton Company's purchases—and he believed he had not given up even that much. The boundary at the Pawcatuck produced trouble but nothing to match what flowed from the opportunity for Connecticut to have an enclave on the western shore of Narragansett Bay or the imprecise assurance of private land titles. Clarke was far better at speaking for religious liberty than his colony's economic or strategic interests.

Once this agreement was reached, Winthrop went home and Clarke steered the Rhode Island charter to final approval within three months. After all the wrangling over boundaries, the document set the western limit at the Pawcatuck (in much too specific terms), alluded to the agreement between the agents, but otherwise contained nothing from the arbitration award.[74] John Scott, back in England again, learned about this result and fought back doggedly, although with only one troublesome result.[75] He obtained an order from the Privy Council in the king's name calling on the other New England colonies to guard the Atherton Company and its purchasers against the molestations by Rhode Island.[76]

In the furor over boundaries, the other clauses in the Rhode Island charter aroused no debate that has been reported. Two central mysteries remain in Clarke's negotiations for the charter, and they probably never can be resolved. The first concerns the main legal terms. The charter made the original grantees—some named and the others designated only as freemen at the time of issue—and their successors in perpetuity a self-governing corporation. As a corporation, they should have a united personality in law capable of suing and being sued, carrying on other forms of legal action, acquiring land, and using a seal, just like any real or corporate person in England.[77]

The Connecticut and Massachusetts charters had nearly the same provisions,[78] so the concept was not unique to Rhode Island. But it was out of keeping with English imperial government otherwise. The charters to Virginia and Massachusetts had been for trading companies like the older trading companies. The Massachusetts Bay charter had been converted into a plan of government, but without English approval. Patents to proprietors, such as Lord Baltimore's grant of Maryland, had quasi-feudal characteristics. The royal bureaucracy opposed any more like it but could not prevent Charles II from passing out huge proprietary grants to reward his friends, new and old. Evidently the bureaucrats made no serious objection when the king and Clarendon decided to favor two minor New England colonies. At least the Connecticut charter served the bureaucrats' purposes by reducing the number of fragmentary jurisdictions in New England and preventing them from being gathered into Massachusetts. By contrast, the Rhode Island charter preserved the only small colony that actually survived.

The second striking feature of the charter of 1663 was its specification of a form of government. Connecticut plainly wanted a government organized like the one in Massachusetts,[79] but there is no evidence to show that Rhode Island did. On the contrary, the known instructions to Clarke called for nothing more than a reconfirmation of the charter of 1643/44, which left such matters to the freemen. Yet the new charter was accepted speedily and without a hint of objection. In the absence of evidence, I suspect that Clarke learned from Winthrop's negotiations that arrangements like those approved for Connecticut were as far as the royal officials would go in authorizing colonial self-government. Somehow, Clarke persuaded the officials back home to accept this view and let him seek a charter with clauses very like those in the new charter for Connecticut.

As issued, Rhode Island's charter certainly did resemble Connecticut's.[80] Both began with recitals of how certain prominent men asked for them, followed by a historical sketch of the beginnings of the colony. The text of the Rhode Island charter mentioned near the top evangelizing the Indians, a goal Connecticut introduced briefly later, and also the economic advantages the colony might offer to England, a topic not found in the Connecticut charter. Of course, Rhode Island uniquely included its famous clauses on religious liberty and briefly returned to the subject in allowing an engagement (now usually called an affirmation) instead of an oath of office. Connecticut's document, by contrast, was silent on religious laws (a tacit approval of a legally backed system of nonconformity with the Church of England) and dwelt on the procedure for taking oaths.

In the later portions of the documents the content was nearly the same on most points, although the subjects appeared in different order. Both gave further specification on how to choose officers. Both allowed the colonial government to create other official positions and decide on how to choose men to fill them; to erect courts; to make laws not repugnant to those of England; and to punish wrongdoing by fines, imprisonment, or other means used by corporations in England. These clauses gave a severely limited criminal jurisdiction, but clauses elsewhere in the charters somewhat vaguely implied an authorization for the colonial governments to define and punish crimes—such as murder, rape, and arson—that in England were tried before the king's courts.[81] The two documents contained nearly identical clauses on piracy, keeping it in the king's jurisdiction.

The two documents assured the colonists the rights of Englishmen, the rights to travel to and from England, to take unfree laborers to the colony, and to transport goods to and from it in commerce, so long as the king's customs duties were paid.[82] For Rhode Island, the right to travel within the king's dominions had special significance: it meant that the actions by Massachusetts in the past to banish Rhode Islanders on pain of death were rendered null. The king gave both colonies fishing privileges in the waters off New England and the associated privilege of using the nearby coastal land, so long as it was not privately improved, to salt, dry, and store fish.[83]

The charters diverged on a number of points. Both had provisos on military organization, but Rhode Island's were much more extensive. The same was true on the subject of fishing privileges. The Rhode Island charter forbade the several New England colonies to make war against Indians outside their boundaries without the permission of the governments with jurisdiction over the territory to be invaded. The document explicitly allowed Rhode Island's colonial government to set up cities and towns—a permission that was only implied in other New England charters.[84] Further, the Rhode Island charter had a few odd passages such as those on encouraging vineyards or reserving royal fish (sturgeon, whales, and so on) to the crown. Surely at Clarke's insistence it also contained a clause specifically authorizing the corporate government to appeal disputes with other colonies to the crown. If there was to be adjudication over the boundary, he wanted a clear channel to the king's courts.

The new document did not explicitly rule out many things done under the old charter, such as the various systems adopted from time to time allowing initiative, referendum, recall, and popular ratification of laws enacted by representatives, but it implied a rejection of such devices. The new charter gave the freemen wide powers to choose their officials but not to overrule them. The freemen should choose a governor, deputy governor, and ten assistants as the main governing council.[85] Because they served in one capacity as the high court, these elected officials soon became known as the magistrates. In addition to these officials chosen at large, each town should choose a specified number of deputies to sit with the magistrates to form a General Assembly. The Rhode Island charter was quite explicit on the number of deputies from each town, in contrast to the Connecticut charter, which said only that there should be no more than two,[86] and the absence of anything of the sort in the Massachusetts charter.

The General Assembly in Rhode Island could admit new freemen as well as choose other colonial officials, make laws and orders, set up courts, create local governments, and in most respects manage the public business of the corporation. To be sure, the laws (as in all colonial grants) were to be "not contrary and repugnant unto, butt, as neare as may bee, agreeable to the lawes of . . . England, considering the nature and constitutione of the place and people there."[87] The Rhode Island charter, like that of Connecticut, lacked a provision requiring that the laws be submitted to the crown for possible veto.

The new charter had provisions, almost completely absent in the old one, defining Rhode Island's place in the British Empire. The old charter specified only that the commission that had awarded it—the parliamentary commission on trade and overseas dominions—and its successors should have "Power and Authority for to dispose the general

Government of . . . [Rhode Island] as it stands in Relation to the rest of the Plantations in America as they shall conceive from Time to Time, most conducing to the general Good of the said Plantations, the Honour of his Majesty, and the Service of the State."[88] The new one contained nothing like that but had several provisions, mentioned above, about specific rights for the people in Rhode Island.

This mixture of corporate powers well beyond what English bureaucrats thought wise and guarantees of rights to fish and trade and travel within the English dominions were remarkable enough, but the most striking provisions, at least to the modern reader, were the clauses allowing religious freedom. The charter rehearsed the main ideas (and a few of the key words) found in Clarke's description of the history of the Rhode Island settlements in his first petition: the founders, with royal permission, had sought out a place of religious refuge at their own expense and hazard, had gone to Massachusetts and, encountering persecution there, had continued to Rhode Island.[89] The charter went on to use some of the phrases of Clarke's second petition: "it is much in their hearts (if they may be permitted), to hold forth a livelie experiment, that a most flourishing civill state may stand and best bee maintained, and that among our English subjects, with a full libertie in religious concernements; and true pietye rightly grounded upon gospell principles, will give the best and greatest security to sovereignetye, and will lay in the hearts of men the strongest obligations to true loyaltye."[90]

Then came the most astonishing clauses in the whole document. Charles II released them from the laws requiring conformity to the Church of England "because some [a polite reduction from all] of the people and inhabitants of . . . [Rhode Island] cannot, in theire private opinions, conforme to the publique exercise of religion, according to the litturgy, formes and ceremonyes of the Church of England, or take or subscribe the oaths and articles made and established in that behalfe." The document went on by using phrases from the Declaration of Breda: "our royal will and pleasure is, that noe person within the sayd colonye, at any tyme hereafter, shall bee any wise molested, punished, disquieted, or call [sic] in question, for any differences in opinione in matters of religion, and doe not actually disturb the civill peace of our sayd colony; but that all and everye person and persons may, from tyme to tyme, and at all tymes hereafter, freelye and fully have and enjoye his and theire owne judgments and consciences, in matters of religious concernments, . . . they behaving themselves peaceablie and quietlie, and not useinge this libertie to lycentiousnesse and profanenesse, nor to the civill injurye or outward disturbance of others."[91]

These lines in the charter have often been held up for admiration, while the clauses on the boundary with Connecticut have been deplored. Clarke produced both and, probably with advice from friends, borrowed the main architecture of the colonial government and many details in the rest of the document from the Connecticut charter. The authorization of religious freedom never came under attack, whereas the definitions of boundaries led to many years of contention. The design of government, much elaborated on from time to time, lasted until 1843, when Rhode Island adopted its first constitution. Ironically, what Clarke considered the prize dearly won was a prize nobody begrudged and what he fought over was the least successful.

5

Waning Years in Newport

John Clarke sent the charter on to Rhode Island as soon as possible, but he had to spend a few more months in London on other business. During this time he also signed up two servants, presumably to work on his land near the harbor in Newport. The contract with one of them survives. Richard Barnes would serve three years, after which he would receive thirty acres of land in Rhode Island. Young Barnes in due course went to the colony, served as bound, and ultimately became one of the founders of East Greenwich. (He never received the thirty acres, nor did Clarke pay the other servant what he promised. Both men accepted a small payment from his estate as satisfaction.[1]) In spring 1663/64, Clarke and his wife sailed back to New England on *The Sisters* of London, along with their belongings and a shipment of armaments.[2]

John Clarke had reason to think that he had done more than any other to shape a durable new religious fellowship and provide a firm foundation for his colony's jurisdiction, but his satisfaction was short-lived. During the rest of his life he endured painful controversies as his church changed in ways he disliked, he became a focus of political dispute, and his government rejected half of what he had done to settle the dispute over boundaries.

Well before Clarke's arrival in Newport, the new charter was received with rejoicing. Not waiting for orders from Whitehall on how to stage a public acceptance, the officers of the existing government gave instructions to change over to the new one.[3] As soon as possible, members of the new General Assembly met and began to elaborate the details left to their discretion and in doing so discovered ambiguities in the wording of the new document. They sent thanks to the king and their agent. Clarke must have considered the messages he received rather perfunctory as there was no money enclosed. The new government never paid all his expenses, and a bitter quarrel ensued when some of its citizens indignantly refused to pay a tax to raise the funds. Nor did Clarke's agreement with John Winthrop, Jr., resolve what he had hoped it would. Rhode Island's dispute with Connecticut alternately raged and festered for more than sixty years. His sour treatment by the new government was only the beginning of Clarke's disappointments.

When he first returned Clarke tried to go into commerce, but without great success. He had probably used servants or tenants on his large farm for a long time, and after living in England, he wanted even less to supervise his rural lands. Instead, he leased them to tenants and turned his energies to trade. His responsibilities as agent had included buying ammunition, and this may have introduced him to the London marketplace. Clarke tried acting on his own account while in England but depended on his brother Carewe to handle the business in detail, partly to convert what the colonial government offered on John's account into profitable goods. Carewe sold cloth, shoes, molasses, bedding, tobacco, and nails—some of these for other members of the family—and received for sale several items on the colony's account from a man named William Plumly.[4]

Thus introduced, John Clarke went further after his return. The consignment of firearms he brought with him was a small start—forty pistols, a carbine, powder horns, and accoutrements.[5] He sold some items to the colonial government or individual citizens but kept a pair of pistols and the carbine for himself.[6] Then Carewe, a widower since 1658, moved to Newport and sooner or later moved into John Clarke's house. (There is nothing explicit in the documents, but there is a faint overtone of Carewe becoming despondent or disabled in mind or body.) John transferred his business not to brother William, who may still have been alive and a small-scale merchant in London, but to a Mr. Johnson, who took various commodities in exchange for cotton cloth.[7]

These ventures were not very lucrative, and thereafter he lived on what little he could get from the practice of medicine, from managing livestock on his thirty-six acres near the Newport harbor, and from his rents—or more precisely, something like sharecropping. His tenants used his land and livestock, built fences and kept the existing improvements in repair, and turned over to him some of the increase in his flocks and some of the wool they sheared from his sheep.[8] The export of wool, coarse cloth, and meat were the mainstays of Newport in these years, so Clarke simply followed the known lines of profit.

If he hoped for a prominent part in the government under the new charter, he was disappointed. The town records of Newport for these years perished in seawater during the Revolution, so we cannot know what offices John Clarke held in local government. The colonial records, however, list his election as one of the six deputies from the town quite regularly from 1664 on.[9] After five years of this service, he was chosen deputy governor for a one-year term and again in 1671.[10] There is nothing listed in the colonial records after this, a fact that requires some explanation. Clarke's relatively minor position during the years immediately following his return resulted from a long controversy that prevented reimbursement of most of his expenses as agent. Inevitably, men who objected to paying the necessary taxes sometimes resorted to personal attacks.

The opposition sprang up in Warwick, the town with the smallest population. Most of the men there took offense with Governor Benedict Arnold in 1664, at first for reasons unknown but probably connected with his father's long hostility to the Gortonian settlers and their land claims. The Warwick men then focused on the tax levied to raise £600 to reimburse John Clarke, who of course wanted to redeem the mortgage on his house from Richard Deane. The Warwick men objected to this tax, giving the self-serving reason that they and their Providence neighbors had paid the expenses for their own agent, Roger Williams, and that Newport and Portsmouth, which had sent Clarke, should pay his expenses. The troubles with this argument came from two false premises. The divided agency lasted only from 1651 until 1654, when Williams went home to help put the colonial government back together. And when that was done, the government, without opposition from Warwick, asked Clarke to secure a royal charter.[11]

The men of Warwick conceded the weakness of these grounds and revised their argument to blame Clarke for not returning some town documents that Williams had transmitted to him, for charging too much, and for expecting to be reimbursed for living expenses in England when he had other sources of income, including payment for preaching.[12] In 1664 most people in Rhode Island regarded a "hireling ministry" as "none of Christ's," so what the people of Warwick disingenuously reported as a matter of the balance sheet was actually an accusation of grave sin.[13] It is hard to believe that anyone, even the authors in Warwick, took these reasons very seriously. The recalcitrant little town eagerly rushed into its genuine grievances—concerning far greater subjects, such as town boundaries and friction with resident Indians—enlisted support for the tax rebellion in Providence and maybe elsewhere, and carried on a long and intricate campaign that paralyzed the colonial treasury.[14]

The colonial government made things worse by appointing William Harris of Providence chairman of a commission appointed to collect the tax.[15] Harris was Warwick's chief enemy in the disputes over land and boundaries, and he showed special zeal—for the time being—in compelling Warwick to pay, which further inflamed the town.[16] He even lent Clarke a small sum. To avoid bending the knee to Harris or the General Assembly, the people of Warwick said they would collect their share of the latest tax and send the money directly to Richard Deane.[17] Things went on like that for several years until the political scene changed abruptly, at which time the town showed that it really had nothing against Clarke. It had little to say against plans in 1671 to send him to England again, firmly supported a tax for that purpose, and bitterly denounced the decision the next year to call off the plan.[18]

The tax controversy was more than a nasty political squabble. It withered Rhode Island's fiscal resources, prolonged quarrels over large private interests, and generally enfeebled the new government. The colony could not pay Clarke anything which he could send to Deane until 1666 and still in 1671 owed £61 14s. 3d. toward principal and interest.[19] The tax resistance fueled an existing controversy within Providence that several times led to rival town governments and also spread to Newport, where Governor William Brenton reported in 1669 that he had endured abusive language as well as repeated destruction of the fences that kept in his livestock. Brenton feared his house would be set afire, and he could get no assurance of protection from the town government. The distraught man resigned.[20] John Clarke escaped such manifestations of hostility, as far as we know, but the attacks on his integrity and morality surely were painful. Also, going without his reimbursement put him in financial embarrassment, and the controversy reduced his prestige in the colonial officialdom.

Despite his knowledge of the charter, Clarke had a surprisingly small part in the long and intricate boundary conflict between Rhode Island and Connecticut. Or perhaps he was regarded as knowing too much. It is not necessary to rehearse the story here in full, but some of the early events are germane because both colonies refused to accept the agreement signed by Clarke and Winthrop.

Connecticut, upon receiving its new charter, cheerfully accepted it and proceeded to assert its jurisdiction over the territory east of the Pequot River all the way to Narragansett Bay. First it claimed lands between the Pequot River and Weekapaug inlet, previously claimed by Massachusetts.[21] Then, in response to what it regarded as the unanimous desire of the people living on the Atherton Company's purchases and the land of Richard Smith in between, it appointed officers for this region and called it the town of Wickford.[22] The government of Connecticut had an additional justification for this action when it received a message from the king asking it and the other orthodox Puritan colonies to guard the Atherton Company and its settlers against molestations by Rhode Island.[23] After these steps had been taken, the Connecticut government for several years did little to back its officials in Wickford, who did little or nothing in an official capacity. This passivity was occasioned first by the arrival of the new Rhode Island charter and, soon thereafter, by the royal commission to settle controversies in New England.

Rhode Island continued to contest Connecticut and the Atherton Company. Before the new charter arrived, it relied on its interpretation of the old one that set the western limit at the Pequot River, but after 1663 Rhode Island accepted the Pawcatuck boundary—without honoring the clauses in the new charter about letting the owners of land in the first Atherton Company purchases choose which colony to be in. Rhode Island appointed officers for the Narragansett country, and these men exerted what little governmental authority was felt there.[24] No record survives of what John Clarke thought about these actions. When chosen to be one of his colony's representatives to confer with Connecticut's in 1664, Clarke did not go. For that matter, Connecticut sent nobody to the conference, so it was not held.[25]

The royal commission arrived a few months later and in still another way disregarded the arbitrators' decision on the boundary, as well as all the other charters that Connecticut and Rhode Island could brandish. The commissioners had been instructed to find out whether, as Samuel Gorton had written Clarendon, the Narragansett sachems had submitted to the sovereignty of Charles I in 1644, and if they had, to make their territory the King's Province.[26] The submission had been arranged by Gorton and some of his followers as part of their countermeasures against Massachusetts, and the Narragansett sachems cooperated because they had their own fears of Massachusetts. The submission had no effect at the time because Charles I was losing in the English Civil War.[27]

The commissioners found the document commemorating the submission, but they prudently staged a repetition by a team of sachems including one of the original ones, and then declared the entire territory of the Narragansetts as the King's Province. As described, it extended westward to a line running north from the Pawcatuck to Massachusetts, along the Massachusetts line to the Pawtucket River (now called the Blackstone), and on the east was bounded by that river and Narragansett Bay. Thus, as originally stated, the King's Province included Providence and Warwick.[28]

The boundaries, in fact, matched English grants to colonies rather than the extent of territory occupied by Narragansett Indians. The notion that there was a definable Narragansett country was much more English than Indian. In many ways, Indian reality was the village with its established hunting range, with affiliations among villages growing stronger and weaker over time and with functions of principal sachems—those with overarching authority—varying as the rank and file saw fit. The English newcomers liked the idea of Indians existing in solid tribal blocks with permanent names and sachems with authority like European monarchs. Actually, distinctions between Narragansett, Wampanoag, Niantic, and Mohegan Indians had been fluid, with alternations between hospitality and hostility, marriage and assassination, marking relations between the supposedly fixed tribal units.

Brushing aside these fundamental characteristics of Indian life as casually as the colonial charters, the commissioners carried out the plan hatched in London but had to spell out some implications in specific terms. The commissioners included Samuel Maverick, who went to Newport in the course of his duties to see old friends—surely John Clarke among them—and stayed as a guest with Governor William Brenton, who was a fervent enemy of the Atherton Company.[29] In any case, Clarke was one of three men who presented Rhode Island's views to the commissioners.[30] Perhaps as a result of effective presentations, the commissioners took a strongly pro–Rhode Island stance and all but apologized for ruling that what the colony had considered its mainland portion would be the King's Province. They softened the decision by making the Rhode Island magistrates justices of the peace for the King's Province and recommending that it be under the government of that colony until the king declared otherwise.[31] One commissioner advocated a new royal grant of the territory to Rhode Island.[32] Probably at his suggestion, the colonial government in Newport asked for this sequel in an appeal to the Earl of Clarendon and a petition to the king.[33] Nothing came of these requests, so the charter that Clarke had negotiated remained in force.

Rhode Island and Connecticut officially applauded the commissioners' decisions and then resumed their previous assertions, though far from consistently.[34] Connecticut continued to reject the result of Winthrop's agreement with Clarke, and Winthrop as governor concurred, although he did very little to carry out the implications of this policy. Without his participation,[35] his colony by 1668 had settled on an elaborate if not entirely coherent rationale: the charter of 1662 had given it the Narragansett country, the previous charter to Rhode Island was invalid because not approved by the king, the agreement between Winthrop and Clarke was nonbinding because Winthrop had ceased being an agent as soon as he had sent off the copies of the Connecticut charter, the Rhode Island charter could not take away what had been granted to Connecticut, the Rhode Island officials had violated the terms of the agreement anyway, the commissioners' ruling was invalid because Richard Nicolls had not been with the other three when they made it, the conflict between the colonies had resulted in Indians wasting and burning the territory, Rhode Island refused to join Connecticut to stop these evils, and Connecticut had done so by force on its own and so acquired a sort of right by conquest.[36]

This roster was not so much internally inconsistent as too long. If Connecticut's charter was solid bedrock, then Rhode Island's failure to observe its own charter or Connecticut's rights by something close to conquest were irrelevant. And yet Connecticut did not insist on the full territory specified in the charter but tacitly conceded Providence and Warwick without specifying how far west these towns extended. In the end, Connecticut wrote off almost everything the two towns claimed.

Rhode Island walked an even more crooked line. Never willing to honor the agreement that allowed the Atherton Company's purchasers to choose their colony, it nevertheless insisted on a very generous interpretation of the boundary at the Pawcatuck. And it accepted the commissioners' creation of the King's Province without allowing that Providence and Warwick might be in it. In 1666 Governor Brenton described himself and his colleagues as the Council of the King's Province (rather than Rhode Island) but disregarded the commissioners' narrow definition of their authority as justices of the peace.[37]

For a few years the two colonial governments avoided conflict. Governor Winthrop was especially artful at keeping Connecticut lackadaisical. Yet from time to time a confrontational incident made the officials say something or even do something. In 1666 some Rhode Island men began to overrun the west line of their colony. Also, a Connecticut man arrested an Indian east of the Pawcatuck and took him to a Connecticut court, which sentenced him to a fine or sale into servitude. The Rhode Island governor protested, and Governor Winthrop, after some delay, wrote a mollifying but evasive response.[38] The controversies over the property rights and the jurisdictional boundary in the Pawcatuck region continued.[39] Rhode Island declared that the settlers on the east were in the town of Westerly, while Connecticut maintained they were in Stonington.

At that point Clarke entered the controversy for the last time, but with no more effect than before. He had a surprising occasion to make peace with Winthrop in 1669, when Benjamin Worsley wrote to ask for his help. A friend of Worsley had been defrauded by his brother, who then absconded to Barbados and was reported to have moved on to Rhode Island. Worsley enclosed letters of attorney for Clarke and Roger Williams. Clarke could find nobody in his colony who might be the miscreant but learned from a neighbor who made inquiries in Boston that the suspect was in Springfield. (I suspect that Clarke took some satisfaction from this incident. After all the things said in Boston about criminals taking refuge in Rhode Island, it was bound to be pleasant to learn of one who had fled to Massachusetts.) So Clarke asked Winthrop to continue the search—and took the occasion to write that he was "desirous to forget those tedious & troublesome contests, which faithfullnes to our trust (as charity bids us beleeue) Put us upon beyond the seas."[40]

Winthrop did as asked, both in looking for the scoundrel and accepting Clarke's invitation to bury past antagonisms. Clarke took this reply as an opportunity to plead for a resolution of the conflict between their colonies. His argument resembled what he had said in London more than eight years earlier. The bickering made them appear vile in the eyes of the Indians and the king. They both knew what they had decided and both might be summoned to explain it all again to the king, which they would dislike, especially because neither had been suitably paid for their previous efforts. Then, in a way reminiscent of his braggadocio in 1662, Clarke hinted that Connecticut had better yield before Rhode Island received all it hoped for through an appeal to the king, which it had already begun. Connecticut, especially, should give thought to the commissioners' ruling. Then, again as in 1662/63, Clarke called for the colonies to agree among themselves or put the dispute to arbitration. If these methods failed, they should both appeal to the king. Clarke quoted the Rhode Island charter and the agreement of April 1663 but never mentioned the clauses about people on the Atherton Company purchases having a choice of jurisdiction.[41] He had gone back on the agreement just as Winthrop had.

For all his protestations of Christian love, Clarke's letters had an antagonistic tone still. He argued for the fullest extent of Rhode Island's claims and talked of getting the king's backing. Brotherly love was a religious duty, not a human emotion, for him in this case. No reply from Winthrop survives.

Negotiations between the officials gradually heated up as deliberate and accidental delays in arranging meetings provoked increasingly pugnacious messages. The two governments grew more willing to back their local officials who made arrests or intruded on property rights held by the opposing jurisdiction. Rhode Island not only planned to appeal the dispute to the king but proposed to send Clarke as agent.[42] The violence in Wickford and Westerly mounted until bloodshed seemed likely.[43]

The possibility of Clarke's further participation ended suddenly—along with his career in Rhode Island politics—when the officials elected in May 1672 abandoned plans to send him to London with an appeal to the king. Instead they decided on another round of negotiations.[44] This dramatic event has been described as the Quakers taking control. This explanation gained currency because Roger Williams used it repeatedly and gave it sinister overtones. True, concerted Quaker action in colonial politics began rather conspicuously in 1672, but hardly in an illegitimate way. Two things changed: the Quakers' desire to take an active role in public affairs and their willingness to do so as a bloc. The first converts generally had shunned public office. Several served at various times and a few were elected often, but only in 1672 did they seek election in large numbers. By then quite numerous—perhaps more than half of the church-affiliated population—the Quakers could swing votes if they could find candidates. If they could find suitable candidates, they easily could choose the six deputies from Newport and the four from Portsmouth, and often the officials elected at large from those towns.

But beyond that, the Quaker vote availed little. Few Quakers lived in Providence and Warwick, with four deputies each, or in the two newer towns, which could choose two apiece but seldom did. These towns with few Friends by a decision of the General Assembly provided men for five of the twelve positions elected at large.[45] So Quaker mobilization could—but never did—put Friends into a majority of seats in the General Assembly. At most they managed to send about a dozen and had a strong influence over the other choices of assistants.[46] In a General Assembly of thirty to thirty-four members, this ability was limited but included, in effect, a veto over the election of Dr. John Clarke.

Presenting this partisan rivalry as a clash over religion distorts the picture.[47] Religion had not been an issue before and now became one only in part. Previously, when most Quakers avoided public office, they saw government as extraneous to their faith. A few prominent citizens, such as William Brenton, Benedict Arnold (first of that name), John Cranston, John Sanford, William Coddington, and Nicholas Easton, filled the highest places. Brenton and Sanford, though old Antinomians, never rejected infant baptism and gravitated back toward Massachusetts orthodoxy although they had no church to join in Rhode Island. Arnold outwardly had similar leanings though he probably was the original nothingarian. Cranston may have kept a fondness for the faith of his childhood, Scottish Presbyterianism, but he went to Clarke's church in Newport. More concerned with this world than the next, these men prospered enough to make themselves appear worthy of high places in a world where wealth and power were considered natural partners. Before political contests polarized along religious lines, Arnold, Brenton, and similar men alternated in the upper circle with well-to-do Quakers like Coddington and Easton.

Just outside this small group of leading citizens, several Newport Baptists chronically served in office. In addition to John Clarke, there were Edward Smith, Richard Tew, Joseph Torrey, William Weeden, and the enigmatic Richard Baily. Hinting again at Baily's acquaintance with law, the General Assembly chose him as its secretary several times and on other occasions asked him to prepare official documents.[48] These men—Clarke foremost among them—clearly lined up behind William Brenton and Benedict Arnold when opposing sides formed. They favored waging the conflict with Connecticut with all means available.

When the Quakers entered the election of 1672 as a bloc vote, they had no narrowly religious program but rather sought peace with Connecticut in order to end the conflict over boundaries. The goal of peace had a pleasantly religious tone, but it had a price, which the Quaker politicians proposed to pay in two kinds of coin that were not religious at all. They proposed negotiation with Connecticut and, whether they knew it or not, a resort to John Clarke's analysis of the dispute into three categories: boundaries, jurisdiction, and individual property rights.

The Quaker politicians thought the boundary could be set at the Pawcatuck and the possibility of Connecticut's jurisdiction over the Atherton Company's first purchases could be eliminated if Rhode Island conceded the legality of those purchases. Then the Atherton Company's claims under the mortgage could be set aside. The chief obstacle to settlement on this basis had been the conflict with the Pettaquamscut purchase, in which William Brenton and Benedict Arnold were two of the seven shareholders—hence a vital nonreligious component of the political polarization. Legalizing the Atherton Company's purchases meant depriving the Pettaquamscut men of the territory they wanted most. (As it happened, some Quakers had bought parts of the Atherton tracts.) So Easton, Coddington, and their Quaker backers sought peace by giving up their political opponents' land in exchange for Connecticut's renunciation of jurisdictional claims. The scheme was not wholly unreasonable, however cheap it was for the advocates. If bloodshed could be avoided and the boundary dispute settled, the Pettaquamscut men would still have enormous numbers of acres free from the threat of Connecticut.

The Quakers who pushed this plan did not reckon on the stubbornness of Connecticut. The Rhode Island government legitimized the Atherton Company purchases at the expense of the Pettaquamscut men,[49] but negotiations over the boundary and jurisdiction failed again—and again and again and again. And claims under the mortgage lived on and on and on.

The political upheaval did not prevent John Clarke from marrying a Quaker soon after, an event that brought him some happiness in his last years. His domestic scene after his return to Newport in 1664 is hard to reconstruct. Brother Carewe probably moved in, along with young Richard Barnes and the other servant. Then Elizabeth's death reduced the household. In February 1670/71 John married a widow named Jane Fletcher, who died a little more than a year later after the birth of their daughter, who also died. Next he married Sarah Davis, recently widowed by Nicholas Davis.[50]

This almost mechanical sequence of remarriages was common in seventeenth-century New England. Generally speaking, the work to be done to keep a respectable household required the partnership of a man and woman: the usual division of tasks between men and women called for one of each. Practical considerations as well as the cultural norms that were absorbed as religious imperatives called for this pair to be husband and wife. Under these conditions, relations between husband and wife probably had a formularistic quality but worked fairly well as much because of it as in spite of it. For solid citizens like Dr. John Clarke, the course of life was easy to see. And many indications encourage us to think that they found more than practical benefits from being married.

In his case, the third wife gave him the most evident satisfaction. Clarke had probably been acquainted with Sarah Davis for several years. Her previous husband, Nicholas Davis, was one of the first settlers of Aquidneck in 1639,[51] but he did not stay in Newport. Rather, he became a merchant on the small scale then possible in southern New England. He moved to Hyannis but continued to do business in Newport and moved back in 1669.[52] An early convert to Quakerism, he had been haled before the authorities in Massachusetts in 1659 while on a combined commercial and religious mission and had been banished on pain of death.[53] If John Clarke opposed Davis's beliefs, he could share his opposition to the persecutions of the authorities in Massachusetts. Nicholas Davis was indeed a fervent Quaker and in his sloop carried the leading Friend, George Fox, from Long Island to Newport in 1672. Shortly thereafter Davis drowned.[54]

About a year and half later his widow married John Clarke. This link between a Quaker's widow and the leading American Baptist went beyond the ordinary. Even if Sarah had not shared Nicholas's devotion to the religion of the Inner Light, she probably accepted it as a dutiful wife as long as he lived. And marriage across religious lines was opposed by Friends and Baptists alike. Nor did Sarah have the glow of wealth. Quite the contrary: although she had a dower right to her husband's land, she doubted she could pay his debts.[55] So John and Sarah may well have found more than routine pleasure in each other's company. And he liked the children that she brought to the household; at last he had the completion of a proper domestic assembly.

While his political career came to a bitter end and his domestic scene brightened, the Baptist church had been moving away from the standards Clarke had set before 1651. This happened, ironically, when two of his policies undermined a third. Almost as soon as he sailed for England, the willingness to include Baptists with diverse opinions on other doctrines began to break down. His hospitality to new ideas and his avoidance of a single commanding pastor bore unexpected fruit. Two of the Seekonk brethren who moved to Newport—Obadiah Holmes and Joseph Torrey—joined Mark Lucar as preaching brethren, and along with John Crandall administered baptism.[56] These men kept the fellowship in operation quite well, but they were more intent on defining and enforcing an orthodoxy than Clarke was.

They got the occasion when some members of the church heard about a novel teaching brought from England to Providence, probably by Gregory Dexter. There, several men decided that Hebrews 6:2, in a passage listing six principles of Christ, called for the ceremony of laying on of hands to be performed on every believer, not just a pastor.[57] In this rite, a pastor put his hands on the head of the subject as a symbol of the power of the Holy Ghost being extended over this person. Putting every believer "under hands" emphasized spiritual equality within the church, played down still further a special role for a clergy, and often implied a reliance on the Spirit to provide preaching by direct inspiration. As long as they were taken in moderation—direct inspiration with great moderation—all of these attributes were compatible with Clarke's views.

Nevertheless, laying on of hands added a controversial third to the sequence of steps to bring a person into the church. Baptism and congregational approval of admission to communion had been enough before. The new idea spread to Newport quickly. Late in 1652, William Vaughan, one of the original members, went to Providence where William Wickenden and Gregory Dexter convinced him that all believers should be under hands. Vaughan received the ceremony and went home to advocate it. The Newport church promptly discussed it at a day of fasting and prayer. Several members, including Joseph Torrey and a recently arrived couple, Tacey Hubbard and her husband Samuel, favored it and received the rite.[58] These three and some others considered it good but optional. Within a few years, however, a group led by Vaughan became convinced it should be mandatory and after a controversy withdrew to form a second church, known either as Second Baptist or Six Principle Baptist. The desire to be inclusive was wearing thin.

The controversy and schism produced less estrangement between the two flocks than might seem likely. The division cut through a few families without breaking their solidarity. The shared opposition to infant baptism defined both churches as belonging to a beleaguered minority in New England. And several syndicates to buy large tracts of land from Narragansett Indians brought members of the two churches—and outsiders also—together, sometimes under the leadership of William Vaughan.

The original church narrowly survived the schism and slowly resumed its growth before Clarke's return in 1664, only to face a similar discord soon afterwards. This time the new teaching came directly from England, where Clarke had watched its rise, notably among some erstwhile Fifth Monarchists.[59] A few pious people poring over the Bible decided that the seventh day remained the sabbath even after the Christian dispensation. Other Christians, relying on a variety of texts but especially on Galatians and Hebrews, maintained that Christ had cut the cords of Jewish ceremonial law and fittingly replaced the seventh day sabbath, the commemoration of the Creation, with the first day as the symbol of the inauguration of a new era. Those who thought they should go back to the seventh day argued that it was laid down in the Ten Commandments and so was part of basic divine law rather than ceremonial law. (As many theologians pointed out, observance of the sabbath was the only item in the Commandments that could not be discovered in natural law by the human mind, so it had a uniquely strong obligation as the only one to rest exclusively on God's decree.)

Stephen Mumford, a regrettably obscure man who advocated the seventh day sabbath, arrived in Newport shortly after Clarke returned in 1664.[60] As with the introduction of laying on of hands, several Newport Baptists took up this novelty, including the Hubbards, once again with Tacey in the lead. The converts to the seventh day sabbath, subsequently dubbed Sabbatarians, initially decided to stay in the church. They would observe the seventh day, join the rest for worship on the first, take communion with them, and make no secret of their conduct. This course fit within Clarke's design for a Christian fellowship, if awkwardly.

The outward forms of tranquil fellowship might have remained if four of the original Sabbatarians had not reverted to the first day. The rest then withdrew from communion. Knowledge of what followed comes entirely from the Sabbatarian side, mainly from Samuel Hubbard, so disentangling the parts played by the leading actors can be difficult and the reports of the upholders of the first day may be biased.[61] The reports seem fair but may well do less than justice to what most of those on the other side said or thought. Even if slanted, what Hubbard wrote as a verbatim record of what was said in church meetings offers a striking display of how the fellowship worked. The church met several times for a vigorous argument. There was no hint of a firm pastoral control by Clarke or any of his colleagues in the leadership. Although the accepted preachers said more than others, and some in the group were silent completely, a surprising number joined the give and take, though women less often than men. Tacey Hubbard, of course, had emphatic words to say.

Once the four of the original Sabbatarians had given up observing the seventh day, they spoke and wrote against it and those who observed it. The Hubbards and the others who continued took offense not only at open opposition but at the church's refusal to reprimand the four backsliders. A Boston preacher persuaded the Sabbatarians to give up their objections to the church, but they stopped taking communion and lapsed into what was called a "halvish fellowship."[62] The public discussion heated up. Mumford and some others obtained defenses of the seventh day from English advocates and used them in the widening debate.[63] The central issue remained what the Christian dispensation had done to cut down the obligations given in the Old Testament, or as Hubbard characterized his opponents as believing "yt all the 10 commands are nailed to the cross & done away, but renewed again some of them." He commented, "I am sure that cant be, if nailed to the cross, no renewing again."[64]

Until 1670 the debate followed the known pattern of discussion within the church. Then the Sabbatarians again sought advice in England,[65] and Mark Lucar and John Clarke expounded their views by preaching on 2 Corinthians 3, especially verses 7–11 and 14, and the book of Galatians. In their sermons, the seventh day sabbath was condemned as part of the Jewish ceremonial law, swept away by Christ; the law to be observed was written in the human heart, for grace—rather than ritual—was sufficient.[66] Samuel Hubbard understood these opponents quite differently. As he interpreted them, "they are run out of ye gospel & Covt of grace & have espoused 'emselves to a new covt of works from wch can be no redemption."[67] John Clarke, as before, tried to avoid a showdown but spoke forthrightly when it came.

While the Sabbatarians protested that everything in the Ten Commandments amounted to moral rather than ceremonial law and accused him of deliberate provocation when he expounded Galatians, Clarke persisted. He said he preached on Galatians only because he was expounding the whole Bible and had come to it, but the Sabbatarians and some others who were distressed by the controversy asked for a respite. They got it. For them, the issues were great and agonizing. They wanted to preserve the existing church yet thought it failed to obey the law of God in a vital way. Could they continue joining in worship? Should they take communion? Could they remain when their distinctive belief was under heavy attack? Reluctantly, they considered withdrawing to form their own church.[68]

The disagreement might have been driven back to the earlier stage if Obadiah Holmes had not resumed preaching. Holmes, probably because of his harshness against the Sabbatarians, had been rebuked by Clarke in 1667 and had withdrawn as a preacher.[69] By an unknown series of events he decided to take up his active role again in 1671. Almost at once he delivered a strong attack on the Sabbatarians, saying they went back from Christ to Moses. William Hiscox, who had become the spokesman for the Sabbatarians, replied vigorously. He said the Ten Commandments—all of them—were a rule for Christians. This assertion drove at least some of his opponents to the untenable reply that the Commandments had never been a rule to the gentiles.[70]

The church then turned to a different subject, at least briefly. It called a meeting where the Sabbatarians were to justify their withdrawal from communion. The result was greater acrimony. Hiscox said they withdrew because of the four backsliders and since then had been further distressed by the preaching against the seventh day sabbath. Characteristically, John Clarke offered a mollifying comment—that Holmes had not spoken against anyone by name. Holmes, however, said he meant Hiscox and the rest. Hiscox then brought up an intemperate remark by Holmes to the effect that the Sabbatarians had no more conscience than dogs. The debate went down hill from there.[71]

At the next meeting, Joseph Torrey joined Holmes in the attack. He tried to prevent Hiscox from speaking. Samuel Hubbard refused to be a substitute and insisted that he deferred to Hiscox. Finally, Tacey Hubbard carried the defense for her side until several others chimed in. Samuel Hubbard burst forth with an elaborate confession of faith. Charges and countercharges were flung back and forth. As Hubbard put it, "They replied fircely: it was a tumult."[72] Torrey and Hiscox got into an argument. Clarke tried to calm things down. Torrey replied to Clarke: "good Brother Clark Speak plain and Say . . . [the Ten Commandments] are done away." But Clarke replied, "I may as well denie god to be god . . . at which mr Tory was grieved."[73] Clarke probably balanced his reply to Torrey with an accusation against Hiscox. Clarke said he had always held that the Commandments were moral law, not ceremonial, but Hiscox had borne false witness by saying Clarke denied this belief.[74] At the next session the discussion degenerated into vituperation until one of the four backsliders denied Torrey's view of the Commandments, and Hiscox with uncommon finesse said, "I shall leave you to debate ye matter among Your Selves."[75]

On a later occasion, debate started on a broader field—the basis for defining sin. The Sabbatarians, perhaps rashly, maintained that the Commandments were as essential as they had been under God's covenant with Abraham but that the Christian dispensation had brought new duties: to repent, to believe the gospel, and to convert all mankind. Torrey again insisted that the Commandments did not apply to the gentiles, that for Christians sin had a different foundation. He drew disagreement from more than the Sabbatarians. Hot words followed, which Clarke tried to stop by bringing in a diversion. He upbraided Hiscox for not getting adequate advice before adopting the seventh day sabbath. This tactic failed, and Holmes and Hiscox threw accusations of sabbath-breaking at each other—Hiscox piously defending himself by asserting that he had only worked on his sabbath when Clarke was sick. The acrimony mounted until the Sabbatarians left to form their own church in December 1671.[76]

Obadiah Holmes took the lead in bringing these events to a head, at least according to the Sabbatarians. Torrey was drawn in and at times spoke more stridently. Clarke stood by his beliefs and either could not or did not seek to forestall the schism. If he is to be thought of as the leader of the church, he was strangely backward. The controversy surely stretched his willingness to entertain disagreement in the fellowship in Christ, and it put this conviction into stark conflict with his belief that a church must have a basic ritual foundation.

When forced, Clarke opposed the Sabbatarians but with reluctance. He had baptized the Hubbards. His nephew Joseph had married their daughter Bethiah and had adopted the seventh day sabbath. So had John Crandall. John Clarke liked William Hiscox. The schism cut across strong emotional linkages. And it came to a head about the time when Elizabeth died and Clarke married Jane Fletcher.

Clarke endured one more disturbance in his church, one that led to several excommunications. Nearly all the surviving knowledge of this event comes from his report on the church's disciplinary actions on Giles Slocum and his family in 1673. More exactly, the action was against Giles's wife, Joan. She was accused "of Denying the man Christ Jesus to be yet in being and alive & therefore not to be Lord of all." It is not evident from Clarke's report whether she or he drew the conclusion, "therefore not to be Lord of all." She was excommunicated after she acknowledged her belief that Jesus was not alive.

Although Joan Slocum probably did not know it, this was a version of the ancient Arian heresy. In one form or another it had turned up for centuries. The root stock was the belief, in contradiction to the Athanasian creed, that the human nature of Christ had been a transitory phase, a mode of existence that partook of the imperfection of humanity and had come to an end with the Ascension. It followed that Christ was purely a divine spirit and so, some might infer, not to be Lord of a temporal kingdom on earth. Joan Slocum probably got the idea from George Fox, who during his time in Newport may have preached his version of the teaching of "the evil genius of Anabaptism," Melchior Hoffman, who held that Christ was the Word become flesh without the agency of Mary—"celestial flesh," as the concept has been called.[77]

Wherever she caught it, the heresy soon spread like measles to Slocum's husband, her children, and their spouses, and they were all excommunicated. Clarke's report sounds objective; it expresses a seemly sorrow.[78] In one respect—about some unsavory domestic details—it was decently reticent, in another it was misleading: Obadiah Holmes also believed that the human Jesus no longer existed.[79] The trouble came, or so Clarke's report said, in the corollary that Christ was "not to be Lord of all." In *Ill Newes*, Clarke had used the word "Lord" to mean spiritual lordship over the church, considered individually and collectively. If Joan Slocum had denied that, the family should not have been welcomed by the Quaker meeting. In fact, they became prominent members, which raises the suspicion that Clarke distorted the doctrines that led to their expulsion, or he may have given up his old distinction between Christ as King and Christ as Lord, meaning in 1673 by "Lord" what he had meant in 1649 by "King." Somewhere his report fell off target.

He may be forgiven. Against his wishes the church members had gone around to a kind of rigidity that he had opposed. Although they still shunned a formal creed, again and again they took sides on matters of ritual—first laying on of hands and then the seventh day sabbath. The Slocums probably spoke for more people than Clarke reported, but if not, they were the only case of discord over theology. And the church's leadership was growing old. Lucar, Torrey, and Clarke all died in 1676, and Holmes five years later. For the time being there was no new generation of preaching brethren. So in this respect, too, the original quality was withering away.

Clarke's death went almost unnoticed outside his church and family. Rhode Island was in the middle of a horrendous war. The Wampanoag Indians living east of Narragansett Bay had started it, but only after many years of small conflicts brought about by the expansion of the Plymouth and Massachusetts colonies. Those colonies and Connecticut carried the war also against the Narragansett Indians, who lived on the west of the bay, putting Rhode Island into the middle of the action for many months and threatening military conquest of the disputed mainland where the Narragansetts lived. The officials in Newport made a show of neutrality but in small ways helped their fellow English to wage war. The island of Aquidneck had an influx of refugees. The mainland settlements from Providence on south were nearly destroyed. Bands of armed men were stalking each other all over southern New England when Dr. John Clarke breathed his last in April 1676. His death was a minor event lost in the swirl of danger, but public neglect was, in fact, the norm. Unlike Massachusetts, Rhode Island ignored the deaths of all prominent figures in its early history.

While Providence smoldered, while Connecticut troops ravaged the Narragansetts and allied Indians killed their champion Canonchet, while other forces hunted the Indians across the hills and swamps of central Massachusetts, John Clarke thought over what to put in his will. Richard Baily stood by to give advice and frame the terms. It was time to think of what was dear and what family obligations should be met.

Clarke's brother Thomas had died two years earlier. Brother Carewe remained a widower, probably in John's household. Brother Joseph had a burgeoning family, including the staunch Sabbatarian, Joseph, Jr. Sister Mary Peckham had died years before, leaving four sons. Sister Margaret had died, too, in the rather remote location of Watertown, Massachusetts, but she had descendants, and John Clarke thought of them. He thought of a few friends. And there were also his church and his community—Newport, not the colony for which he had procured a charter. And above all, Sarah and her children.

Sorting out his feelings and obligations, John Clarke ran down the list of his property and decided how to distribute it. He had a surprising amount to give. In the heart of Newport he had a waterfront tract appraised at £10 as well as 36 acres and his house just back from the harbor, appraised at £300. To the east he had a farm of 150 acres and valuable marsh worth £500. He also had 10 acres by the sea, appraised at £30, at Applegate Neck on the way to Brenton Point. While he was in England his brother Thomas had bought this property for him and also interests in two new promotions, one at Jamestown and the other at Westerly.[80] The rights at Jamestown were good for 100 acres, worth £80, but the share at Westerly was problematical, at best worth £5. In addition, the town of Providence had awarded him a share right in the common land, also considered worth £5, as a mode of paying for his agency.[81] Clarke had an adequate supply of household goods and implements. He had abundant livestock, mostly sheep. He still had a big claim against the colonial treasury, although in the years following 1676 his estate stood little chance of getting it. The devastation of war made taxation unthinkable for the time being.

John Clarke also had to think about his debts. Maybe he could not remember them all, but his executors discovered them. He still owed money to Richard Deane. In 1666 the colonial government had promised grandly to assume that obligation but had done nothing to satisfy it.[82] Possibly, he owed the money to his brother Thomas for managing his affairs between 1651 and 1664—by then, a debt to Thomas's heirs, who were brother Joseph's children.[83] He owed more than £5 to William Harris,[84] and there were the unsatisfied promises to his servants.

In spite of his debts and the colony's inability to pay what it owed, John Clarke settled on a complex scheme in his will. Probably guided by Richard Baily, he mapped out a plan that relied as its central feature on a devise to uses. That is, he gave the bulk of his land, livestock, and tools, to three executors and the replacements, called assigns, that two of them would choose when one died or otherwise became unable to serve. They would be trustees responsible for using the property for the purposes he specified. To begin with, they would hold his farm, the Applegate Neck property, and the house and most of the land in central Newport for the support of Sarah during her life. Further, if she lived in the house, she should have the use of the property connected with it, about thirty acres. Regardless of where she lived, Clarke left her his biggest trunk and two beds of her choice, including all the furniture associated with them. The executors also would be trustees for a small tract at the southeast corner of his orchard. Subsidiary instructions told them that this was to be a burial ground for his church or any other use it might prefer.

Clarke had further plans for his property when Sarah died, but he also made a revealing set of specific donations. He instructed the executors to sell his lands or land rights outside Newport and distribute the proceeds to brother Joseph, a few of Joseph's children by his first wife, and certain descendants of sister Margaret. One nephew was treated specially: Joseph's son John, who was bequeathed six acres of the land in central Newport and the reversion of the other thirty acres and the house when Sarah died, preferably to be passed down to his male heirs. Here was a touch of traditional family pride: there should be an heir bearing the John Clarke name.

To Sarah's five children he gave more than to his own relatives (except John). Her son Simon was left the waterfront property. Her three daughters and her other son were to have money when they reached majority or were married, but in any case not before she died. Rather mysteriously, the amounts differed: Sarah Davis would get £40; Thomas, £20; Mercy, £20; but Hannah, only £10.

Further, brother Carewe was to be supported for as long as he lived. Quite likely he was sick in body or mind. If Clarke's widow Sarah continued to live in their house, Carewe was to go on living there, too, provided the two could get along with each other. If not, or if she moved, he would be supported by £16 worth of provisions each year from the farm, to be supplied by the executors and assigns. Likewise, they were to provide fifty shillings' worth of provisions for Mark Lucar for as long as he lived. Lucar had no wife and boarded with the widow Timberlake. Brother Joseph's entry in the family Bible hinted at the bleakness of this arrangement by laconically saying, 826: 10: mo: 1676:

mr Luker Departed Thies Life in the house of the wddow Tember Lake in nuport on rodiland."[85] Provisions for Lucar, therefore, amounted to very little.

Other items in the will were easier to settle: six ewes to Katharine Salmon and Clarke's books to Richard Baily. Mentioned in the will—a sign of what the testator prized—were the concordance to the Bible and the lexicon that John Clarke had written, his Hebrew Bibles, and a lexicon and concordance that he had used. Although nothing survives to show a motive, the six ewes for Katharine Salmon probably were a charitable gesture. She was one of the Baptist flock but was not known to have any special claim on John Clarke's generosity.

As important as what was in the will was what was not. Of the other preaching brethren, Obadiah Holmes and Joseph Torrey, not a word. Probably Lucar was poor and growing feeble, but Torrey was, too. Nothing about Clarke's other companion in 1651, John Crandall, who had gone off with the Sabbatarians. Nor were any of sister Mary Peckham's sons mentioned. The discrimination against brother Joseph's children by his second wife, who got only a shilling apiece, has no obvious explanation. Finally, the witnesses included Phillip Edes, a member of the original Baptist congregation, William Hiscox, and Thomas Ward. Hiscox, of course, was the leader of the Sabbatarians, and Ward then or later was a member. The inclusion of Hiscox showed Clarke's reluctance to let the schism break old bonds. Edes and Ward were younger men, and so made good witnesses in case of need for testimony in the future.

The plans for the trust after Sarah's death were put in vague and cautious words. In the will itself, Clarke stated that the income from his farm and the land at Applegate Neck should be spent "for the releife of the poore or bringing up of children, vnto Learning" in accord with subsidiary instructions. These instructions went on to say that the trustees should "haue a Speciall regard and care to Provide for those that feare the Lord." Literally, this clause put a very weak restriction on the trustees, but perhaps it was meant to favor members of Clarke's congregation. That is highly doubtful, considering his long preference for including people of diverse beliefs, his kindness to the Davis children, his reliance on Hiscox as a witness, and his continued regard for the nephew who had gone the Sabbatarian way. Rather than a strict congregational line, he drew a loose border of piety, which was quite in keeping with his lifelong convictions.

Inevitably, his wishes were hard to carry out.

6

Clarke's Estate, His Church, and His Colony, 1676 - 1717

After Clarke's death, his charitable legacy took on a life of its own. It became entangled in Newport family networks, engaged the town council for a time, helped pay for a new meetinghouse, and opened an important chapter in colonial legal history involving charitable trusts. On its way to becoming an endowment for First Baptist, it began to undermine Clarke's vision of a spiritual community aloof from worldly goods and gains. Thus at several telling points, the plan Clarke had sketched out in his will helped shape events in Rhode Island after 1676, yet it did so in ways that he had not foreseen and certainly had not desired.

Clarke's plan assigned the executors several tasks that appeared simple but proved hard to carry out, and it required them to manage property for the benefit of his widow as long as she lived. After that, their burdens would increase. To complicate matters, two of the executors died soon after Clarke, William Weeden within a few months and Richard Baily a short time later. Baily might have resigned anyway as, perhaps to his pleasure, he agreed to travel to England as one of Rhode Island's two agents in order to appeal to the crown against Connecticut's intrusion into the Narragansett country.¹ The agents were not dispatched before his death.² So within two years of Clarke's death, two of the executors were replaced by Thomas Olney and Thomas Ward—not as executors, but as assigns. The distinction was a nicety of law. For convenience it will be enough to refer to the executors and their assigns as the trustees.

The first changes in trustees had serious effects. Baily had the best understanding of the executors' responsibilities as well as of the legal procedures. Ward could replace only part of this knowledge and Olney virtually none because he lived in Providence, where he often served as town clerk and was pastor of the Baptist church that had decided against making the laying on of hands mandatory. He went to Newport occasionally to confer with Ward and Phillip Smith, the only surviving executor, but surely not often, and less and less until he stopped completely. As things turned out, Smith was the most active after 1678.

Baily had begun energetically. He and Smith filed the will with the town council, which served as a probate court, posted bond, and received letters of administration.³ He decided not to disclose the two documents containing subsidiary instructions, which the probate court did not see for several years. As Smith later explained, the object was to increase the executors' chances of getting the colony to pay its debt to Clarke. Baily told Smith, "if we sue for it to pay the testators debts, then [the colony] will soner pay it then if it should be published [as stipulated in the instructions] that the money when it is recouered is to goe to the widow." Baily may well have put this plan in a document outside the will precisely to keep it off public record as long as possible. Besides, he argued, the will contained an accurate expression of Clarke's intentions for the long run and "it was time innuf to place ... [the subsidiary instructions] to record when they wear called for."⁴ The instructions would need to go on record only when the widow died and the profits from the property would go for charitable uses—and then, only if the trustees' actions were challenged.

It is striking that nothing in Clarke's testamentary documents mentioned the money still owed to Deane, and that Baily chose to supply the widow in preference to paying the estate's debts. The executors knew that the colony had voted in 1666 to assume the obligation under the old mortgage. They also knew that the colony had not honored its promise. They wrote to Deane to inquire about what the estate owed. The letter took almost two years to reach him, and he waited over a year to reply, telling what he thought was due to him and saying he would cancel and return the mortgage as soon as he received the money.[5]

While waiting for this reply, Baily assembled information about the estate, told the widow she should pay the small debt to William Harris, and suggested that she do so in wool.[6] Then he and Smith went to the General Assembly in another futile effort to obtain payment of the colony's debt. As they pointed out, the accounts had been audited in 1672, at which time the Assembly had concluded that the colony should pay £200 worth of provisions (reckoned in New England currency[7]) to settle the arrears. As that had not been done, the executors now requested £100 sterling.[8] The Assembly chose a new committee to review the accounts and to inquire into where the executors stood in the business.[9] Two years later, after Baily's death, nothing had been done, and the Assembly chose yet another committee, which also did little.[10]

The colonial government's failure to act is understandable though disgraceful. In 1676 and for many years afterwards it had neither the ability nor the motive to meet a sizable demand on its funds. The devastation of the war with the Indians left the colonial treasury crippled. The quarrel with Connecticut over the Narragansett country grew fierce, with Connecticut having the upper hand. Then came a chaotic interlude during which the charter was abandoned and superseded by a vast viceregal jurisdiction, known as the Dominion of New England, covering English territories in North America from New Jersey north. It had no concern with old debts owed by the Rhode Island government. Its overthrow in 1689 was followed by an anarchic period until the crown reconfirmed the charter in 1693. Even after this news reached Rhode Island in 1694, the resuscitated charter government barely breathed for a few years and could not exert a tax power for even longer.[11] What John Clarke had labored to create nearly perished. When the government regained effectiveness, it found a working relationship with the imperial officials in London quite different from what had been anticipated in 1663. Throughout these troubled years, at least the town government of Newport went on as usual, although it gave the trustees no help. They had to turn elsewhere to pay the heirs of Richard Deane.

Some of their business was easy, if it actually took place, such as turning over the ewes to Katharine Salmon. Mark Lucar died so soon after Clarke as to need few provisions. The trustees quickly sold the land in Jamestown to Benedict Arnold,[12] and they began to distribute the proceeds, a business that remained unfinished until 1700/01, probably because the bequests could not be paid until the beneficiaries came of age.[13] The sale of rights in Westerly and Providence ran into complications and never resulted in payment to the beneficiaries.[14] Possibly the debt owed to brother Thomas had been paid to his heirs before John Clarke's death. If not, the executors and assigns may have satisfied that obligation. They "Cleared off the Demands of two men which Mr Clarke brought out of England with him."[15] Somehow brother Carewe was provided for. He did not live much longer. Sarah Clarke remarried and moved back to Hyannis, leaving her affairs in Rhode Island in the hands of her son-in-law, William Hedge.[16] She was back in 1691, possibly because her next husband died, too.[17] She went to the grave a few months later.[18]

Until then the trustees leased out the farm and the Applegate Neck property, took their stipends of £2 per year apiece, and paid the remainder to the widow. They took up their duties at a time when the farm was leased to George Brown, and they made a new agreement with him to run for seven years. He was to pay £34 each year for the use of the farm, house, and marsh, plus £10 for the use of the livestock, utensils, and the hay or straw he cut. He had to keep the house and fence in repair and promise not to remove timber or sell fodder or make any enclosures on the land without the lessors' permission. At the end of seven years he was to surrender the property and deliver twenty loads of English hay to the lessors.[19] The inventory of livestock and utensils showed 1 mare, 180 sheep, 10 pigs, 2 cows, and a heifer.[20] Nothing survives to tell how much rent came from the Neck land. The oldest extant lease for it shows a rent of £2 10s.[21]

If the rents were paid promptly, John Clarke's widow got a good income and could add to it by making her own arrangements or letting William Hedge make them to get profits from the land in central Newport. There is no sign that the trustees enforced the implications of Clarke's will that deprived her of the use of that property if she moved out of the house. Besides, title to it still was under a very dark cloud: the mortgage to Richard Deane remained unredeemed.

Clarke's trustees did what they could. In 1680 they at last heard from Deane. A brief flurry of action stirred up town governments to review what had been paid on the mortgage in the past, but no further payments came as a result.[22] Finally, in 1693 the trustees wrote Deane to say that they acknowledged the obligation, that the colony had agreed to pay it but never had done so, and to apologize for the disorder of the colonial government, ask again what was owed to him, and request documents on the debt.[23] If there was a reply, it does not exist. Deane died two years later. After more negotiations that do not survive, the trustees managed to satisfy the obligation, thanks to Jahleel Brenton, who had married Sarah Davis Clarke's daughter Hannah. She made an astoundingly good match. Jahleel was the son of William Brenton, who inherited much of his father's great wealth and also for a short time was the royal collector of customs for New England.[24] Jahleel Brenton bought the mortgage from Deane's heirs.[25] Then after Sarah's death, the trustees slowly saved up rent money to buy it from him in 1702 for £200.[26] After that, the property in central Newport may have been turned over at last to nephew John, though there is no record of this disposal. At least the farm finally was clear of the encumbrance and fully in the trustees' control.

Sarah died at a time when the colonial government of Rhode Island had reached its nadir. The long and slow recovery brought not only a new orientation to the British imperial authorities but also the entry into Newport of two new religions—Congregational and Anglican—that put John Clarke's old Baptist church into a radically different context. Instead of being the root stock from which all others deviated, the First Baptist Church had to occupy a middle position between traditional ones and radical offshoots. The Anglicans, especially, signified the connection of Rhode Island to the British Empire.

Both new faiths gave the colonial government occasions to reassert the separation of church and state that Clarke had so firmly favored. Although a Congregationalist missionary from Massachusetts was allowed to preach two sermons in the colony house in 1695, one to the General Assembly just after an election, objections from people of other faiths led the Assembly to vote that the "Collony House, in Newport, shall not be improved for any other use than judicial and military affairs; and not for any ecclesiastical use or uses of that nature."[27]

Later, when the Church of England established a congregation in Newport, the Assembly feared a campaign to get public support for it. The Anglican minister, along with his vestry, had been urging Queen Anne to appoint a bishop for New England and had called on the governor of Rhode Island for public money to support Anglican clergy in the colony's towns and to finance schools under their supervision.[28] These were calls for an end of religious liberty. Therefore, the legislators voted "that what maintenance or salary may be thought needful or necessary by any of the churches, congregations or societies of people now inhabiting, or that hereafter may inhabit within any part of this government, for the support of their, or either of their minister or ministers, may be raised by a free contribution, and no other ways."[29] Although this declaration lacked the panache of the charter's clauses, it made the point clear. In fact, it was the only rule ever laid down by the General Assembly to implement the charter's provisions.

Clarke's church went through a decline and reconstruction that nearly paralleled that of the charter government. Clarke died in the same year as two of his copreachers; only one survived—Obadiah Holmes. For all his heroism in the Baptist cause, Holmes was a minor prophet. He died in 1682.[30] After several dry years, the church ordained an obscure man named Richard Dingly or Dingle. He arrived in 1686 or 1687 and was ordained two years later. (This was the first reported ordination in the church.) By then, James Barker, one of the men who had made the inventory of John Clarke's estate, was "a ministering brother." Dingly continued as pastor until 1694, when he went to Charles Town, South Carolina.[31]

More arid years followed. Amazingly, the church turned to the leading seventh day Baptist, William Hiscox, to help in the pulpit. He had no other duties on Sundays and was improving himself by study. Regardless of his virtues, the church needed its own rather than a borrowed leader. The two sacraments could not be administered except when the preacher from the only similar Baptist church in the vicinity, Samuel Luther at Swansea, Massachusetts, came down to help.[32] At least the church in these years escaped extinction, a doom that befell a few other Baptist flocks in Rhode Island.

During this time, the trustees struggled with other adversities, including quarrels among the Clarkes. In spite of Dr. John Clarke's care to head off challenges by giving token bequests to his brother Joseph's children by his second wife, three of them tried to claim the farm intended for charitable uses, as soon as Clarke's widow died. Arrested on a charge of forcible entry, they escaped before they were interrogated.[33] Whatever happened next, their effort to get the property failed, and at last the trustees could manage the farm for charitable purposes, except for a brief controversy over the meadows that were part of it.[34]

At the same time, the town council in Newport became aware of the implication of the widow's death. In its capacity as probate court it called on the executor and assigns in 1693 to render accounts and tell what assets they had "that it may be ordered for ye vse of ye town for ye vses in ye will mentioned."[35] The executor and assigns had to reveal the subsidiary instructions and explain why they had not done so before. They delayed for almost a year.[36]

Before complying, they made a new lease of the farm for seven years, this time to Jeremiah Weeden, who already was using the property as the assign of the previous tenant, Edward Greenman. He got a lower rent—£26 10s. for the real estate, £8 10s. for the livestock. In addition, the rent would be reduced by £10 in exchange for his building a new lean-to on the house, replacing the old chimney, and putting up twelve poles of new stone wall each year.[37] This agreement began a descent into misuse of the estate. Jeremiah Weeden was a nephew of one of the original executors, William, and a brother of the trustee James Weeden. Although he married in succession two women bearing the last name of Clarke, they were of a different Clarke family.[38] Furthermore, he, like his wives, was of the church that had broken away from the first one that joined on the basis of insisting on the laying on of hands for all believers.[39] So financial benefits in the lease flowed from Weeden family self-help rather than financial prudence.

The town council wanted to direct the use of profits from the Clarke estate, but with weak justification, unless it was acquainted with how charitable donations had been taken over in England. The will said the money should be used for "the releife of the poore or bringing up of children vnto Learning." The tone implied a public scope, not one limited to Baptists—or to the town of Newport, for that matter. The will clearly called on the trustees, not the town council, to decide how to spend the money. The subsidiary instructions that aroused the council's curiosity limited the trustees' discretion only by telling them to "haue a Speciall regard and care to Provide for those that feare the Lord," make sure that they conduct the trust for "the good and benefitt" of the persons to be helped, and in the process glorify God. The will was fairly clear; the subsidiary instructions added some haze, but not to the clauses giving discretion to the trustees. If John Clarke had more specific limitations in mind than the instructions contained—such as confining benefits to his church and its adherents—he prudently kept them out of the documents. He may have known how English law was interpreted in England to frustrate charitable trusts for dissenters. More likely, Richard Baily had the important knowledge on this subject.

The difficulties lay on two sides. First, the courts refused to allow donations to religious uses outside the Church of England. Beginning during the Reformation in the sixteenth century, various measures were taken to prevent gifts, especially of land, to dissenting religious observances. The catchall term was "superstitious uses." Originally aimed at Catholics, the legal artillery was turned later against Protestant nonconformists. When an English court faced a donation to nonconformist religious purposes, it might transfer the gift to purposes that were deemed analogous but within the established church or were lawful public charities, often administered by arms of the church, such as parish vestries. There had been a few conspicuous cases before and after the Puritan Revolution and the Interregnum. Judges sometimes did likewise even after the Toleration Act of 1689 went on the books.[40]

Second, Clarke had to take account of the parliamentary Charitable Uses Act of 1601. Partly to skirt the religious battle lines—nobody knew what turn of royal policy might come next—the statute defined charitable uses in quite secular terms, though the courts had interpreted the words to allow a few religious purposes, notably repair of churches.[41] In 1676 no one could say definitively that the Charitable Uses Act applied to Rhode Island, but quite possibly it did. The colony was obliged to abide by the law of England "as neare as may be, . . . considering the nature and constitutione of the place and people there."[42] The charter also had guaranteed religious liberty, so the colony was at least exempt from observing English law in favor of the Anglican Church, but there was no easy rule to determine how far that exemption might modify application of the Charitable Uses Act.

Clarke wanted to serve purposes that English law and courts opposed. Certainly he did not want to finance any function of the Church of England and he did want to benefit his own church, but exactly how much is unclear. Equally unclear is the scope of philanthropy he intended beyond the church. If testimony from well after the fact can be trusted, he told the original executors that his "intent was to provide for religious as well as civil instruction," and expected them to pass this knowledge to their successors. By this reading, of course, he meant a Baptist pastor to provide religious instruction through preaching as well as other exercises of the ministry. He "did not insert the word ministry, lest the national [i.e., Anglican] clergy should lay claim" to the estate. This interpretation of his purposes came from Josias Lyndon, who became a trustee in 1730 and took part in decisions to spend most of the proceeds of the estate on a stipend for a Baptist minister.[43] Lyndon's statement is the only one that purports to clarify Clarke's will, so it must be evaluated carefully. Lyndon may have simplified or twisted the truth to justify his own policies, but he served in various public offices where legal knowledge was required, so he was not naïve on the complexities of the law. Lyndon's interpretation could be compatible with the will, but the record suggests that he exaggerated or distorted the importance of paying for religious instruction if he did not invent it outright.

Clarke's care to step around legal traps gave the trustees a free hand in choosing beneficiaries as long as they helped individual poor people and children. They might go beyond aid to individuals but would run some risk if they provided money for a Baptist church.

The town council both in 1693 and twenty-five years later tried to make the charitable trust serve as a public agency of Newport, leaving the trustees to manage the property while the council determined how to spend the profits. The justification for these attempts never was elaborated in a record that survives so must be figured out by indirect means.

In colonial Rhode Island, town councils were analogous to boards of selectmen in Massachusetts, but they had far greater authority. Among other things, they served as probate courts. A council was composed of six men specifically elected to membership each year by the town meeting plus any colonial magistrates who lived in the town—until a new law excluded the colonial magistrates in 1734. Newport was the home of many magistrates, from governor to justice of the peace, so it had an unwieldy council. The well-known provision in the charter of 1663 allowing religious liberty implicitly ruled out the jurisdiction of ecclesiastical authority exercised over inheritance in England.[44]

The councils without benefit of an adequate statutory authority had assumed what had been done by an episcopal court, the court of the "ordinary" in the parent country. That is, they supervised the transmission of movable property according to wills or rules of inheritance. From there the councils quietly expanded to supervise devises (grants of land in a will to persons who were not heirs by law and kinship) and inheritance of land, until they had full probate jurisdiction. They had for years supervised guardians of minors. In their capacity as the executive committee for their town, they took care to provide for the poor—or to keep paupers from moving in. Thus they had a duty to see that wills were carried out and a clear motive to preserve sources of funds other than taxes for support of the poor.

Supposing that the function of the town councils as probate courts might be an established colonial usage, it extended to charitable donations, at least when they were of personalty to be transferred like other bequests. If the Newport council was aware of the English Charitable Uses Act of 1601, however, and thought it applied to Rhode Island, the council might have taken greater responsibilities.

In England, the Charitable Uses Act provided a procedure to hold trustees to faithful performance, and that procedure had given way to another. Both were impossible to use in Rhode Island without great distortion. The first required that the chancellor appoint commissions—in practice they were for a county—to receive complaints about the misuse of trusts. Ordinarily these allegations would come from the parish officers, who were expected to be watchful over sources of funds to support their duties. When the commissioners received a complaint, they were to hear the interested parties and if wrongdoing seemed likely, to call upon the sheriff to impanel a jury to make inquiry. If the findings of the jury warranted action, the commissioners could give orders for a redress. The chancellor might modify these orders on his own initiative or he could do so after an interested party appealed to him.[45] This procedure, in keeping with the rather secular definition of charitable uses, held adjudication out of church courts. So far, so good: Rhode Island had no church courts. But neither did it have a chancellor or parish officials with powers like those in England. It did not even have counties at that time.

After the Interregnum, the use of commissioners had fallen into disuse and been replaced by another procedure. Upon the complaint of an aggrieved party, the attorney general would file an information against allegedly wayward trustees in the Court of Chancery. Then the chancellor would receive documents, testimony, and arguments by lawyers—sometimes a very long process—and issue a decree.[46]

But in Rhode Island, no court had that extent of chancery jurisdiction. The General Assembly ruled in equity on a few subjects, notably chancerizing bonds, but on none anything like supervision of trustees in control of estates. Besides, both of the procedures employed in England had been cumbersome and often either ineffective or unused for lack of somebody who would take the initiative to bring a complaint and spend the time and money to sustain the cause until it succeeded. Therefore, Rhode Island had no ideal model to adapt.

Conceivably, a substitute for the chancellor could be found in the town council, yet the council had no unquestionable authority over the Clarke donation before 1719. Actually, the council was more like a chancellor's commission than a chancellor. It also resembled English parish officials by virtue of having to aid the poor. If the council was to be put in the shoes of both a commission and the persons to complain of wrongdoing by trustees, then it would need a procedure to separate its roles as complainant and judge. At the very least, the Governor and Council—the tribunal that heard appeals on the councils' rulings on probate—should be the counterpart of the chancellor.

As a probate court, the Newport council could conclude that its duties ended once an estate had been transferred to trustees. As a panel of town fathers, it might disapprove of what the trustees did, but it had no clear authority to make them change their conduct. The Clarke trust was the first and for several years the only one of its kind. The council's obligations remained to be determined.

So in 1693 the town council apparently tried to put itself into the role of an English parish that obtained the right to control a charitable fund. Predictably, the trustees resisted. They held their own, and the town council relapsed into unconcern.

The trustees went on about their business but made some momentous changes. James Weeden became insane and in 1695 was replaced by his brother William, a choice with grave consequences.[47] The genealogical tangles get bewildering here. This William Weeden was another nephew of the original executor of the same name and was a brother of Jeremiah, who leased John Clarke's farm. The younger William had married Sarah Peckham, the youngest daughter of John Peckham by his second wife. (The first wife was Dr. John Clarke's sister Mary.) The Clarkes, Weedens, Peckhams, and Tews became so interrelated as to defy diagramming. Because Jeremiah Weeden had married a Mary Clarke of a different family, the intricacies can be confusing.[48] For the moment, the point is that the younger William Weeden was connected both to his brother Jeremiah, who adhered to the second Baptist church, and to the Peckham family, which stayed with the first.

When the trustees had repaid Brenton and began to have funds available for charitable purposes, someone again thought they should be watched more closely. They had not reported on their transactions for more than two years. The Newport town meeting asked the council to look into the Clarke trust.[49] The council remained apathetic, and the trustees stopped reporting.

Later, when the council insisted, it learned what the trustees had been doing between 1700 and 1718. To be sure, they pocketed their annual stipends to a total of £114. They took care of their assets. After paying the debt to Jahleel Brenton they claimed an allotment when the Newport proprietors divided most of the remaining common land. They paid taxes (c. £43), exchanged the Applegate Neck land and £80 in cash for a more lucrative tract at Spring Field, and made improvements on the farm—a cheese house, crib, cellar, barn, oven, and more than half a mile of stone wall. To make these improvements, the trustees usually paid Jeremiah Weeden or William Peckham, who was a grandson of Dr. John Clarke's sister. They spent over £162 on these projects. By contrast, their clearly charitable expenditures were on a small scale. They gave the town £20 toward building a schoolhouse and £4 for fencing the yard around it. They spent more than £29 to provide schooling for various children. About 64 percent of this amount went to young Clarkes, 15 percent to young Weedens. The other beneficiaries included some relatives. The trustees gave a slightly larger total (£31) to two widows, one of whom was a Peckham. The amounts given to individuals, even if legitimately to the deserving poor, came to little next to the £140 for building a Baptist meetinghouse. To finance these donations and other expenditures, the trustees used rents, mainly from Jeremiah Weeden. In 1702 his annual payment for use of the farm real estate went down to £24, and he was paid for making improvements rather than required to make them and deduct the bill from his rent.[50]

Defending this record as in harmony with Dr. John Clarke's intentions would require adroit argument. Support of a town school met every test except preference for the God-fearing. Benefits to Baptist widows and children were legitimate enough, although these were few and mostly to a concatenation of three families. The greatest difficulty lay in defending the improvements in the property, which mainly benefited members or cousins of the Weeden family, because the new trustee, William Weeden, gained practical control of the trust after Thomas Olney gave Weeden his proxy and stopped doing more than collecting his annual stipend of £2.

To an extent, the direction taken by Clarke's trustees was geared to the history of his church. In the doldrums after Dingly's departure and with few members, the church had only a small number of people who surely were God-fearing by Clarke's standard and also could be considered suitable recipients of the estate's bounty. If they were related, that was only the result of endogamous norms observed in a tiny population. True enough, Clarke's dislike of a doctrinaire approach to religion made preference for adherents of his old church questionable, but some beneficiaries—above all, Jeremiah Weeden—were Baptists of another kind. Under the circumstances, plowing back profits in the form of improvements made sense even if the first effect was to help the tenant at no expense to him.

The large expenditure for construction of a meetinghouse was another matter. Clarke's testamentary documents contained nothing to justify it, unless they be read as code language for endowing his church in all its aspects. In Clarke's lifetime none of the churches organized in Rhode Island cherished a meetinghouse. Quite the contrary, they usually prided themselves on following the Apostolic precedent of meeting in private houses or in groves of trees. Even when the First Baptist Church initially got a meetinghouse the event was not celebrated. Nobody can say when it was built,[51] what it looked like, who owned the land under it, or whether it was the only site for worship. By contrast, the church treated building a new one as a major event.

The old structure stood at Green End in the rural section of town, the new one in the heart of the commercial district. The move signified a change in the pattern of how the congregation was distributed in the town's territory and a growing taste for urban display. Green End was and is the place where the great ridge that slopes up from Newport harbor slopes down again on the east to meet Easton Pond—more specifically, the point at the north of the pond where it is fed by a stream. After the division of Newport in 1743 it fell into Middletown. At the outset it was approximately a central location, near Clarke's farm (which adjoined the farms of a few other members and lay near still more) and between Obadiah Holmes's land at Sachuest on the eastern end of town and the town center and the Brenton Point farms on the western end. With the growing concentration of inhabitants by the harbor, the practical center shifted. Even before the building at Green End was abandoned, the church may have gathered elsewhere at times.

It is also necessary to consider the significance of Green End. Delightful as the natural scene is there today, for seventeenth-century Baptists it had a decisive merit other than beauty: it was virtually the only place in Newport where they could perform baptisms in flowing water. Strictly observing biblical precedent on this point, they conducted the ceremony at the mill near the head of Easton Pond. Nor did they stop when they built a meetinghouse over the hill in 1708.

On this occasion the church took care to manage property transactions with full legal formalities. Eight brethren signed the deed selling the Green End property, two signed as witnesses, and then they took it before Governor Samuel Cranston to acknowledge their signatures and have the document enrolled on the public records. Trifling as these procedures might seem, they meant more entanglement with civil authority than would have been thinkable in earlier times. Property induced a subtle departure from old sensibilities. The new meetinghouse was erected on the small lot given by Dr. John Clarke, who had thought of using it as a burial ground but left the church free to decide. In some measure it was a burial ground all the same, for his body and some of his ideals. When the trustees contributed £140 for the new structure, Clarke's legacy was having effects different from what he had in mind. The church was learning to prize worldly possessions more than it had done during his lifetime. Its building gained importance at some cost to the old emphasis on the spiritual fellowship.

The new meetinghouse symbolized a new vitality for the church as well as the beginning of a shift of standards. More important than the building was the choice of a new pastor. In the past the church had not sought out one: it welcomed preaching brethren as they appeared, let others perform baptisms, and generally maintained a fluid and collective leadership. It set no limit on the number who might serve at once. If these men were ordained, nobody bothered to record the events—let alone the procedure—before Dingly, so if there were a ceremony, it hardly was a focus of pious attention.

But in 1708 the church adopted a new procedure. It considered two candidates and only in 1710 chose one of them: William Peckham. Moreover, it arranged an ordination the next year. This event planned as a major ceremony.[52] Thus the church gave its minister a new kind of elevation, and his position came to be rooted in his function to conduct worship in the new meetinghouse. The choice of William Peckham had an almost predetermined quality. He was a son of Dr. John Clarke's sister Mary; his first wife was a daughter of Dr. John Clarke's brother Joseph; and his second wife was Phebe Weeden, a niece of the William who was one of the first of the trustees and a sister of the second.[53]

Elder Peckham resembled Clarke's colleagues, such as Obadiah Holmes, in that he had no special erudition. Like Holmes, he was a weaver. Yet he would take the church in unprecedented directions. He took office when membership had sunk to seventeen (eighteen, if we count James Weeden who had recently gone mad) and set out to swell the ranks. This in itself was a project out of keeping with seventeenth-century norms. After eight years of labor Peckham asked for an associate in the pastorate. The church picked Daniel White.[54] This, too, was entirely out of the seventeenth-century pattern, and furthermore, White was not among the members of the flock. Dingly had been an outsider, but at the time there was no alternative. From the choice of White onwards, the church stopped looking for preaching brethren among its own and routinely searched beyond the membership.

The new directions taken by the church inevitably produced a conflict. It came into focus in a way that created an agonizing problem for Elder Peckham, split the church yet again, and resulted in a course of development that went still further from John Clarke's ideals. Ironically, his donation for charitable purposes—or rather, what his trustees did with it—set off the conflict.

7

The Dispute over the Clarke Trust

A crisis over the management of the trust was touched off by Edward Smith. Son of Phillip, one of the original executors, Edward was chosen by William Weeden and Thomas Olney in 1718 when Henry Tew died. Edward Smith had been a member of the town council several times before then but had not questioned the trust. Presumably, when he became a trustee he discovered what Weeden had been doing and objected, but found that he could do nothing because Weeden had Olney's vote. Still, the time was opportune: Jeremiah Weeden's lease was up for renewal. Quite possibly, Smith's decision to complain to the council was prompted or encouraged by the new associate pastor, Daniel White, who was outside the web of kinship that embraced Weeden, elder Peckham, and so many of the beneficiaries of the trust.[1] Although Smith was not closely tied into the web, his family had been in religious fellowship with many who were. Some others in the church later accused him of being devious when he went to the council.

Whatever aroused him to action, Smith began a complex wrangle that led to far more than he could have foreseen, both in the short run and the long. In the short run it drew the council into four years of legal battles with Weeden and threw the church into discord and ultimately schism. The council also tried to make the Clarke trust a source of support for the town's poor relief, only to fail completely after some initial success. In the long run the conflict determined the final shape of John Clarke's legacy and brought church and government into a new relationship that neither initially wanted.

In these eventful years, both church and state were transformed. For one thing, they began to form a loose and uneasy partnership, although each institution carefully refrained from admitting it in order to avoid the appearance of compromising their principles in favor of separation. For another, the town council had to assume new responsibilities and get a statutory foundation for its measures, which was something of a novelty for a governmental organ that had built its competence in several directions without much legislative guidance. So the General Assembly, too, had to enter a new field of law.

Further, the church, besides its unavowed new reliance on the state, had to rethink its style of religious fellowship. Although the church could not agree on a strong disciplinary procedure for William Weeden, it implicitly agreed that his conduct as trustee was a legitimate subject for church discipline. Previously, the church had condemned easily defined sins or had reached an impasse over points of religious practice. Weeden's misconduct was a new kind. Did it or did it not put him into the category of "tares" that Dr. John Clarke said should not be weeded out? There was no clear answer. Moreover, the church for the first time lowered its old standard of congregational autonomy by appealing to the sister church at Swansea, Massachusetts, to send brethren as advisers and arbitrators.

The unacknowledged partnership of church and state in this episode also revealed a remarkable effectiveness in the church's solidarity, even when it seemed flabby or fragile. The town council should have been able to act effectively by itself, because it could bring the force of law to bear on the wayward trustee. By contrast, the church shunned force and would use nothing stronger than suasion, admonition, and excommunication. These weapons seemingly had little power in a society where religious affiliation was strictly voluntary. The contrast was softened by the council's confusions over how to use legal compulsion and the church's disputes over when to apply its sanctions. With both partners in doubt as to how to act, the church's gentlest means, suasion, turned out to give the needed extra strength to the legal measures. Moreover, in the long run the church was able to gain control of the trust whereas the council could not. The struggle with William Weeden brought about changes that the contestants neither foresaw nor desired.

Records of the council's first moves have been lost, but they included a long-overdue demand that the trustees report their accounts. The trustees did so in December 1718, when they presented several pages detailing their transactions since 1700. These figures provided the council with evidence of mismanagement. The council never openly accused the trustees of wrongdoing in their choice of beneficiaries or their habit of making improvements to Clarke's farm instead of spending the rents on charity. Rather, the council officially questioned only the easy terms of Jeremiah Weeden's leases.[2]

After inspecting the accounts, the council instructed Nathaniel Coddington to write to Thomas Olney, the senior trustee, to ask what he could say for the conduct of the panel. Olney replied that the trustees had taken some prudent actions, that they had presented accounts to the town council regularly as long as Philip Smith had been alive, that since then William Weeden had taken care of everything and Olney had done nothing except collect his annual stipend.[3] William Weeden then went to the council and gave an unsatisfactory explanation of the accounts. The council thought Jeremiah had been charged too little rent for the farm and livestock, and it ordered the trustees to deliver all the livestock to administrators it chose. Weeden refused.[4] The next month the council ordered the trustees "to giue bond for the accott of theire proceedings" and chose a committee to consider how to stop mismanagement.[5]

Smith was willing to give bond but Weeden and Olney were not. Besides, they hurriedly leased out the land and stock for less than before. The council brashly declared that these "proceedings Appear very Contemptious & fraudelent & c." and went on to note that the leases were "Void in law[,] they not agreeing with the Will and Instructions which [missing] the Assignes" ought to follow.[6] This facile decision—that the leases were void—set the direction of the council's moves for the next two years.

If Weeden and Olney would not do as the council directed, at least they agreed to hold a meeting of all three trustees (the first for many years), which two members of the council attended. As a kindness to Olney, the meeting was held at Providence. Olney was willing to obey the council's order to surrender the livestock, but Weeden still held out against it. At that point both Olney and the town council went in search of lawyers.[7] Olney had the good fortune to find John Read, who was then moving from Connecticut to Massachusetts and an illustrious career.[8] The council engaged the services of the leading lawyer in Newport, Nathaniel Newdigate, an Englishmen who took great zeal in introducing the technicalities of English law into Rhode Island.

Newdigate remained a central figure in the imbroglio, and his troubles reveal how hard it was to adapt English law to a colonial setting. He was born in the same year as the Rhode Island charter and arrived in Massachusetts with a small capital at least thirty years later. He set up as a merchant and money lender in Bristol (then in Massachusetts) by 1703. There he married Sarah, a daughter of the prominent citizen Simon Lynde. The next year he was practicing law in Bristol and a few years later in Rhode Island, too, following in the footsteps of another Bristol settler, Nathaniel Blagrove.[9] Newdigate moved to Newport in 1714 and continued his business for another decade but turned more and more to law.[10] By 1717 he was appointed to a committee to prepare Rhode Island's laws for publication, but he was not admitted as a freeman of the colony until three years later.[11]

Newdigate was always at the council's elbow, and Read began to appear at meetings quite often, representing both Olney and Weeden. Perhaps because of his advice, the trustees—meaning Weeden—suddenly broadened their charity. Nothing more to Clarkes or Peckhams or Weedens. Instead, small amounts to a new and longer list of persons. In response to the council's desire to make the trust a source of money for the town's poor, the trustees made a big donation of grain for that purpose. They also nearly doubled Jeremiah Weeden's rent for the farm—from £24 10s. to £45—although he was to pay nothing for use of the livestock.[12]

As the council was being drawn into this contest, so, too, was the church. Soon it was embroiled in a tangle of arguments—over what—if anything—to do about Weeden, over some subsidiary grievances that came up, and over how to stop quarreling. The church was not explicitly a beneficiary of the Clarke trust, so it could have dodged the issue of Weeden's conduct and left it to the civil authority. Some members, however, insisted that the church must take disciplinary action against him. Others opposed this. The two sides lined up behind the new associate pastor, Daniel White, or the older man, William Peckham.

White became an unrelenting advocate of vigorous measures against Weeden, while Peckham resisted.

Peckham was William Weeden's brother-in-law and otherwise deep within the network of four families. He had rebuilt the church from a small and somnolent flock and probably regarded his labors with contentment. Understandably, he was reluctant to do anything that might disrupt the religious-familial fellowship he had nurtured. The two ministers probably also disagreed on whether to invoke the authority of the government. Peckham's opposition to harsh measures could not prevent discord. Antagonism mounted to the point where the two elders decided they must halt administering communion.[13]

By this time, the council had begun its investigation but paused for a few months to let the people in the church do what they could. Soon after the three trustees and two councilmen met in Providence, the church deviated a little from the traditional congregational autonomy, but no further than it thought justified by precedents from the early Christian churches. In April 1719 it called upon the only like-minded Baptist church in the vicinity, the one in Swansea, Massachusetts, to send a committee to hear "all our Aligations on both sides" and give advice.[14]

The arrival of the Swansea committee inadvertently made matters worse. White greeted its members with allegations, which he insisted were "to be first Answered or Else nothing Could be done." The full scope of his demands remained undisclosed for the time being. The offended committee went home and protested the action of "an Obstinate partie."[15] The Newport church began to break apart over the issue and for a year left formal action to the civil authorities.

Just after this futile expedition from Swansea, the town council sought the kind of aid that was then becoming common for local government in Rhode Island—an enlargement of its powers through a law enacted by the General Assembly. Usually such laws authorized what seemed practical in a way used in Massachusetts, which in turn had decided on something in a fashion resembling English laws. Yet since Rhode Island faced unusually delicate matters in legislating on charitable trusts, the Massachusetts model was inadequate.[16] Rhode Island could not innovate freely without violating its charter and could not import English laws unchanged. Rhode Island lacked the necessary court, and the composition of the populace—a great majority being outside the Church of England—made completely unacceptable those elements in English law and judicial precedents against endowments for non-Anglicans. So the legislature had to write its own laws in terms that could be explained as harmonious with English law. Ironically, its first attempt was closer to English law in one respect than the statute that went on the books. The episode illustrates the perplexities that faced colonials who tried to abide by English law and the uncertainties of the result.

The Assembly heard a presentation by Weeden's lawyer, John Read, but then in June 1719 it put on the books a law presumably drafted by Newdigate. This was "An Act for Ennabling and Impowering the Town Counclls within this Colony to Redress and Punish all Frauds Breaches of Trust and Mismanagements of Persons Entrusted with Estates Given to Charitable Uses." The preamble explained the occasion for the law, that the assigns of the executors of John Clarke had not carried out their trust properly and their "Breaches of Trust and Mismanagmt . . . [were not] Discoverable and relievable by Actions or other Process at Common Law." (That was a great understatement: the common law had done nothing whatsoever to regulate trusts, except in the tangential function of enforcing the chancellor's decrees.) So the statute specified that any trustees, "by any . . . means whatsoever Entrusted" with property to be managed "for the Reliefe of the Poor[,] Building of Hospitals or Schools of Learning[,] bringing up Children to School or other such like Charitable uses"—carefully omitting specific mention of the support of religious institutions, probably to stay on the safe side of English law—were accountable to the town council where they lived or where they managed property.[17]

The statute tried to end any doubt that the town council might enforce faithfulness on trustees. It made a council a "Court to Enquire into all Frauds Breaches of Trust & Mismanagements" committed in its jurisdiction. This authorization covered both donations of personalty, which may well have been under the council's purview already in its function as the ordinary, and realty as well. Thus the council got more than the jurisdiction of the ordinary by the addition of something properly in the region of chancery. Or in a sense, the council was to gain the functions of a chancellor's commission under the Charitable Uses Act.

To carry out this function the council was given extensive authority. It was empowered "to send for any Persons Writings or Records and to Examine and Enquiry make into the same by all Lawfull ways and means as shall by them be thought Proper," to fine and imprison anybody refusing to submit to this authority, "to pass such Judgmts and such orders to make for the Discovering and Redressing of Wrongs Done by such Breaches of Trust and Mismanagemts as to such Town Councill shall appear Just and Reasonable and to Enforce the Partys Guilty of such Willfll Breach of Trust or Mismanagement to make Good the Damages Sustain'd thereby out of their own Estates to the Partys Injur'd."[18]

The council's power to use "all Lawfull ways and means" may have allowed it to ask the sheriff to impanel a jury to hear allegations of wrongdoing, as the English act of 1601 had done, but if this was so, the possibility was not exploited. When a council decided that trustees had done wrong, it could "Issue out Executions Either against the Persons or Estates of the Delinquents for Satisfying the Judgmts given in such Cases ... as in Courts of Common Law is Usually Done." The statute gave the Newport council special authorization to replace trustees of John Clarke's estate if it saw cause. Unfortunately, determination of who were "the Partys Injur'd" was just as hard under this law as it was in connection with a charitable trust in England.[19]

Nearly all these provisions were like those of the parliamentary Charitable Uses Act and made the councils rather like the chancellor's commissions. The colonial law even had phrases like the English. One conspicuous exception was the council's power to punish contempt. In England, only the chancellor could do that; his commissioners could only recommend.[20]

Probably the clause in the Rhode Island statute about using the methods of common law courts also muddied the parallel, because the English procedures were in equity rather than common law, although the colonial law's lack of an explicit requirement that the council use a jury proved to be far more serious. Even more important was the English law's lack of clauses authorizing commissioners to displace and replace trustees. The act said that the commissioners could order only what was "not ... contrarie or repugnante to the Orders Statutes or Decrees of the Donors or Founders." This clause was solemn, if perhaps obligatory, nonsense: English officials had concocted a doctrine of general charitable intent to justify setting aside a donor's explicit stipulations and substituting others that the commissioners or the chancellor considered harmonious with national policy. As Newdigate read in one of his law books, which contained nothing on the procedures involved, commissioners had displaced trustees and chosen others in their stead.[21] In context, the clause in the Rhode Island act empowering the council "to Issue out Executions" as English common law courts had done probably referred to the methods for carrying into effect the decrees of the Court of Chancery or Equity.[22]

Those aggrieved by any action taken by a town council under this act were entitled to appeal to the Governor and Council, who heard appeals on probate matters. The Governor and Council were authorized "to Alter Mitigate reverse or confirm" the actions complained of "And to give A New and final Judgement and Determination in said Cause." In this function, the Governor and Council were to take the role of the chancellor as defined in English law.[23]

Armed with the new statute, the Newport town council in July 1719 ordered the trustees to appear and produce their records. It also summoned Jeremiah Weeden and another lessee, Philip Peckham, whose name will turn up later, to display their leases.[24] Olney did not appear; the council's records contain nothing legible about Edward Smith and the two lessees; William Weeden appeared with his lawyer.[25] The records are faulty at this point. The council ruled that Weeden (with Olney's help) had rented the lands at too low a rate and had refused to give bond or deliver the estate's livestock to the administrators chosen by the council. Then the council gave a judgment, which does not survive, and offered Weeden leave to appeal to the Governor and Council, "which he positively Refused." After that, the council prepared "to grant forth Execution" of its judgment.[26] The execution may have been deferred.

The council was relying on advice from Newdigate, but he evidently began to have qualms about the soundness of the proceedings. He sent away for more law books.[27] The delay in their arrival may have encouraged the council to go slowly for the next several months. It marked time for the rest of fall 1719 except when it was prompted by Edward Smith, who insisted that there had been a mistake in the council's casting of the accounts by omitting one year's rent on a piece of property, "Wherein the Judgment Given in said Case was part Wrong." So the council once more summoned Weeden and Olney to present their accounts.[28] Olney stayed away again, but the council declined to act against him on account of his advanced age and his passivity in the trust.[29] Weeden appeared with his lawyer but "positively Refused to Deliver the said Accots," so the council ordered him jailed until he decided to comply with its order.[30] Then the council suspended action while the church tried to overcome its difficulties.[31]

During this interval, Weeden, probably at Read's advice, gave Jeremiah Weeden a new lease at almost double the previous rent—£45 as against £24 10s.³² This was intended to show a change of policy on William Weeden's part, although it amounted to an admission that he had mismanaged the property before. The rent still was too low to satisfy the council.

Although shaken by the antagonism aroused during the first visit by the Swansea brethren, the First Baptist Church tried once more. The church remained divided over what to do, but the majority voted to ask the Swansea church again to send impartial men to hear the case. The delegation arrived in August 1720 and concluded after a hearing that the trustees should "Endevour to let out" the Clarke land "for its Just value"—that is, at a higher rent than Jeremiah Weeden had been charged—and devote the income every year for the purposes Clarke had stipulated rather than for improving the house and outbuildings for the tenants. William Weeden should confess his wrongdoing and start managing the trustees' assets properly. He expressed contrition and, presumably, was let out of jail.³³ His release was one of the most obvious signs of the unavowed cooperation between the church and the council.

The arbiters also made recommendations about restoring unity in the Newport church. Elder Peckham should acknowledge a minor affront to White, and White, amazing to say, should be excommunicated! He had been a member of the Swansea church before he moved to Newport. The delegation in 1720 revealed, apparently as news to most people, that White had left for Newport in the nick of time before the Swansea church could expel him for irregularities in conduct. Consequently, the Swansea church had refused to recommend him to the Newport church. When messengers were sent to Swansea to ask why, they were told the reasons but had presented a false report back home. The Swansea committee now shared their opinion with the people of Newport: White was "not a Legal Rightfull Member of Your Church" and should not "exercise ye authority of an Officer by Dispencing publick admonitions & Excommunications as he has done." Nor should he have use of the meetinghouse, which should be reserved to Elder Peckham and his side.³⁴ Arbitration obviously failed to produce all the desired effects.

The Newport church lacked an institutional system—that is, the members could not agree on a form of majority rule—to bring a binding conclusion, and so the council resumed its campaign. It found that Weeden had only pretended to change his ways. Although he had arranged a new lease at a substantially higher rent, he had continued to favor his relative with low payments for the use of the trustees' livestock in spite of the council's order. Besides, the council came to believe that William Weeden was profiting from his control over the Clarke estate.[35]

The council, surely advised by Newdigate, resolved to wield the ultimate weapon authorized by the 1719 statute. On 3 October 1720, the council voted to "Remove and suspend" William Weeden and Thomas Olney as trustees and replace them with John Wanton and John Rogers.[36] Rogers was the town treasurer, one of the overseers of the poor, and a member of the First Baptist Church who firmly opposed Weeden.[37] Wanton was not a Baptist, but he was a very prominent citizen, a member of the Governor's Council, and as such a member of the town council. In the Governor's Council he may have voted on the new law. As a member of the town council he had already taken a part in determining its actions and reactions to Weeden. In short, neither was an impartial outsider, and Wanton even more than Rogers was to give voice to the town's desire to use profits from the Clarke estate for civic purposes.

Once again the council summoned William Weeden and reviewed his accounts to compel him to settle with the new trustees. The council and he differed widely on the reckoning. Weeden said the estate owed him £59 14s. 5d.; the council maintained that he owed the estate £183 8s. 5d. in the colonial currency (roughly half the value of sterling). When he refused to pay this amount to the new trustees, the council ordered that a writ be issued to the sheriff to seize his goods of that value, or if so much could not be found, to put him in jail again.[38]

The council's next move was against Jeremiah Weeden. It ruled that he must deliver the movable property of the Clarke estate that he had in his possession to the new trustees and must pay them rent. Unfortunately, the council's records of the procedure and the decree have been lost. Jeremiah Weeden refused to comply, and John Read probably peppered the council with arguments to show that it had acted illegally. In the face of the resistance, the council waited until the following spring, when it became uneasy enough to delay until it could get from the General Assembly an "Opinion Whether the law of the Collony" made in 1719 was "Sufficient to [allow the council to] Grant forth Execution on Jeremiah Weeden And If they should not think it Sufficient that they Would Advise and Enable them by Such farther Measure as may lawfully Effect ye Same."[39] No response from the Assembly appears on the records.

In the meantime, Edward Smith resigned as a trustee. He refused to act either with Weeden and Olney or with the council's appointees. Weeden and Olney promptly selected a new Henry Tew as the third trustee, as though their power had not been affected by the council's action. Wanton and Rogers took Philip Peckham as the third man with the council's approval. Like Tew, Peckham was from the Baptist flock. He had leased the smaller tract held by the trustees but ceased doing so by 1719, when William Peckham became the tenant.[40] When William Weeden and Thomas Olney took Tew as the third trustee, the council decided that these men were guilty of contempt.[41] So Weeden went back to jail.

The next complication came to light soon. The town council learned that Weeden and Olney were "sending home to England by way of Complaint against the Counll Proceeding ... and against the Collony Law for the Management of Estates given for Charitable Use." The response was symptomatic of the colony's fairly new determination to keep its law harmonious with English law and the fear haunting the officials that the imperial government was eager to accuse them of failure and use the accusation as a pretext for action against the colony's charter. Governor Samuel Cranston and the town clerk, William Coddington, planned to report the whole story to the colony's agent in London to prepare him to defend them against the complaints.[42] Complying with English law was devilishly hard when the colony lacked the means and the parent country lacked the model.

The official alarm was undue. Presumably, Weeden and Olney had in mind a complaint to the crown asking for protection against highhanded treatment rather than a judicial appeal. Because William Weeden had refused to appeal the council's first judgment against him to the Governor and Council, he could not suddenly change his mind and go over their heads. Nor could Weeden and Olney appeal the incarceration of Weeden or the appointment of new trustees to the crown without going first to the Governor and Council. Even an informal appeal to the Board of Trade against the law of 1719 was a dubious step, because Rhode Island statutes were not subject to royal review.

Still, the officials in the colony took news of the complaint seriously. They became cautious, though the council put up a bold front for a few more weeks. Newdigate felt confident enough to bring an action in the colony's General Court of Trials (where the bench was the Governor and Council—so John Wanton, who held the office of assistant, presumably declined to take his seat). Newdigate left out allusions to the town council's earlier efforts and presented his case simply as an action brought by the new trustees against Jeremiah Weeden. The form of action was called trespass and ejectment, a poorly understood phenomenon of New England jurisprudence. Probably invented in Massachusetts, as were most innovations in early New England law, it was not a fictional action like ejectment in England but accomplished the same purpose of bringing competing claims to title into adjudication quite easily. It had the additional advantage of getting around a shortcoming of English ejectment, which did not allow a plaintiff to get an award of damages. To do that, a further action of trespass was necessary. (In England there was a "mixed action," also called trespass and ejectment, that had the same virtue but with a fictional component of ejectment.[43])

By putting trespass together with a nonfictional version of ejectment, New England practice created a simple and effective device. The name for it changed from time to time, but it was called trespass and ejectment in the early eighteenth century.[44] Earlier and later, it bore the name of plea of land; later, plea of land or ejectment of disseisin.[45] In the ordinary case, a plaintiff declared that the defendant had wrongfully withheld a tract of land, described by metes and bounds, to the plaintiff's damage of a certain amount. The defendant might make one or more of several replies but usually pleaded the general issues—that is, denied any wrongdoing—and then the two parties presented their competing claims to title along with any necessary legal reasoning to show why one was superior to the other. The court seldom awarded damages to a successful plaintiff.[46]

When Newdigate launched his action, he had a difficult time adapting the usual form to the task at hand. Evidently he could not think of a more suitable type of action. Instead of the usual grounds for a suit on a writ of trespass and ejectment, the derivation of an adverse title, he presented a recital of the origins of the Clarke trust, the mismanagement, the statute of 1719, and the council's actions to replace the trustees. He concluded that the new trustees had a lawful right of entry to gain possession of the land leased to Jeremiah Weeden and to use it for the purposes of the trust.[47] (By an understandable slip of the pen, attorney Newdigate wrote William Weeden in place of Jeremiah at one place.)

The declaration and complaint (to use the Rhode Island name) only revealed a little of what was to come. It named the game that

Newdigate would play, his opening gambit, and his opponent. There would be a much more elaborate presentation at court. There, in addition to presenting evidence on how and why the new trustees got their position and the derivation of the title of lands they held, he would have to make an argument to show why they could remove Jeremiah Weeden as tenant. For this purpose he had the council's ruling—which he probably had designed—that the lease to Jeremiah Weeden was fraudulent and therefore void.

To defend this assertion, he had various doctrines and precedents. Crucial to his case was the legality of the council's decree removing Weeden and Olney and substituting Wanton and Rogers. Unfortunately, he had his weakest legal material on this point. He could use allusions in his book on cases in Chancery to show that trustees had been displaced, but the allusions did not explain the grounds or the procedure and, worse, referred to examples of taking donations for dissenting purposes, such as ones to endow Puritan lectureships, and putting them to use for the Church of England.[48] He recently had learned from one of his new books that five trustees had been replaced by governmental authority, pursuant to an "ordinance of the Protector Cromwel," a replacement subsequently confirmed by the Court of Exchequer in 1657.[49] Cromwell was still in power when the Exchequer gave its ruling, which clouded its usefulness after the Restoration. Newdigate could recite the General Assembly's act of 1719, but could a colonial statute be observed if it contravened established rights of property? Could it be observed if it incorporated not only the parliamentary statute of Charitable Uses but also the workings of the Court of Chancery that had been built upon the statute?

If the appointment of new trustees could be sustained, it followed that they had the "seisin" of the Clarke estate. "Seisin" meant ownership and not necessarily actual possession, but it carried a right of entry. If Newdigate could get the court to agree with the council's decree declaring that the lease to Jeremiah Weeden was void, then the court would give the new trustees immediate possession. Even if the court accepted the lease as valid, the new trustees would get "constructive seisin," to use a modern phrase, until the lease expired, when they could enter and enjoy actual seisin or possession. At least Newdigate did not have to confront the common law's fervent protection of interests in real property. If the lease was considered valid, it ran for a term of years and so did not constitute an interest in real property. In the legal thinking of the day it was more like a chattel and so was designated by the oxymoron "chattel real."[50] (By contrast, a life interest, a right of reversion, and many other tenures without specific duration constituted real interests.)

Newdigate was equipped with citations on a variety of points that might be brought into argument by the defendant. He could show that a charitable donation was protected even when the terms of the donation were defective in the language used or the description of the property.[51] He had citations on leases that were voidable.[52] He had several citations that bore on the authority of the council.[53] He could show that an action of trespass would lie where a plaintiff had a right of entry but not actual possession.[54] And he had citations on possession and seisin.[55] As it turned out, he did not have enough.

In his plea and answer (again, to use the Rhode Island term) for Jeremiah Weeden, Read made a series of four arguments cast in the form of one plea in abatement and three in bar—all pleas to the bench to dismiss the action. The focus of the plea in abatement was that Philip Peckham could not be a trustee and so could not join as a plaintiff in the suit. The plaintiff's writ and declaration failed to set forth how the trusteeship was to be continued from Clarke's executors, and so it did not explain how any of the plaintiffs might be a trustee. Even if the town council was empowered by the law of 1719 to replace delinquent trustees, the law did not authorize the replacements to select successors to vacancies that might occur in their roster. Moreover, the selection of any replacements by the council was impermissible because it violated Clarke's will, which specified a system of cooptation to the position of trustee and no other method.

If the court did not choose to quash the writ on these grounds, Read said (in his first plea in bar) that it should rule for Weeden because the town council had not proceeded as required by the law of 1719. The power to replace a trustee had been granted only in case the council by legal trial convicted one of breach of trust, but the council had acted on mere insinuations that William Weeden had leased land at unduly low rent and that he and Olney had pocketed income from the Clarke estate. Therefore the replacements were not legally effective. The implication of this argument was that the council had not separated its roles as accuser and judge. It had not called on a jury to examine the allegations against Weeden.

If this argument, too, were rejected, Read offered a third—that accepting the council's appointed trustees would run counter to English law. There were English laws, he said, sustaining the trust and providing remedies for mismanagement. (This was a bold statement, indeed, considering that the remedies were unavailable.) Clarke's will observed the provisions of these laws. The Rhode Island Assembly "was led into" the act of 1719, which could not be valid because it contradicted parliamentary statutes. Here again, Read alluded to the council's failure to rely on a jury, but he went on to say that if the council could replace trustees it was "breaking in upon ye Manifest Will of the testator And Disinheriting . . . ye heir to whom ye forfeiture by Law is given which seemeth to be against Common right in ye greatest degree and is a thing Wholly unpresidented in ye English Laws." That is, if the trust were taken out of the management stipulated by the donor, then the land in the assets had to go to the donor's legal heirs.[56] The General Assembly could not invent a different outcome.

Maybe this was all bluff. Or maybe Read looked at the words of the Charitable Uses Act and did not know how they had been used to authorize the replacement of trustees. Finally, Read offered the simplest, and perhaps the most effective, argument against the suit: William Weeden and Thomas Olney had leased the land to Jeremiah Weeden before any attempt was made to replace them as trustees. In other words, the council had been in error when it declared the lease void because it set the rent too low. So Jeremiah had a valid right of possession for the remainder of the ten-year term and should not be molested.[57]

Unfortunately, nothing remains to tell how Read argued the case after presenting this plea or even whether the court heard further arguments by the two lawyers. Still, Read's initial presentation was effective, though not quite in the intended way. He found the two weak points in Newdigate's argument: the justification for discharging trustees and putting in new ones, and the procedural flimsiness of the council's ruling that Jeremiah Weeden's lease was void. And he deepened the doubt that the statute of 1719 could be harmonious with English law. Read unnerved the Newport men. The plaintiffs quickly backed down, asked for and were given a continuation, and then settled out of court. On 9 September 1721, the town council learned that the trustees acting under its authority had "agreed with Capt William Weeden and Company" in a document that no longer survives. One key provision was that the three new trustees would surrender their claims to hold the trust. The council approved the agreement, received the resignations, and ordered that Weeden be released from jail.[58]

The agreement was not so clear, however, as to settle anything for long. By the next month the council called on the two sides to pick arbitrators to resolve a quarrel between them over money allegedly owed by William Weeden to the trust. The council chose its arbitrator—Judge Nathaniel Byfield of Bristol (then in Massachusetts)—but Weeden would not name one, although he gave no reason for his refusal until later. He continued to insist that the trust owed him money.[59]

The town council then shifted its tactics. After the case had been dropped against Jeremiah Weeden and William Weeden had been freed, the Assembly repealed the law of 1719.[60] The legislators wrote a new law to replace it in 1721. This act cautiously adapted English law to the colonial circumstances. It continued to give the councils authority to enforce faithful conduct by trustees, but it abandoned the device of authorizing the Newport council to appoint substitute trustees for the Clarke donation and instead directly answered Read's implied objection against the council's failure to use a jury.

Under the new law a town council could use all "good & lawfull ways & means," as before, to investigate mismanagement of charitable trusts. It must call upon all parties to present their views. But the crucial feature came in the requirement that the council impanel a jury of inquiry composed of twelve or more men of the town. The jury would hear the interested parties and then, presumably (the law was silent on this point), either arrive at a verdict on the alleged mismanagement or declare its conclusions on the facts in controversy. Whatever the precise function of the jury, after it had been performed the council might "set down such orders Judgements [and] Decrees" as it thought likely to effect the purposes of the trust and have them executed by the sheriff. The statute gave it authority to hold trustees personally liable for their mismanagement. There was no longer a reference to procedures under common law.[61]

In these ways and a few others, the new act followed the English Charitable Uses Act of 1601 even more closely than the previous one. When the legislators responded to Read's criticism of the old one they borrowed a phrase from the English statute verbatim by declaring that the orders issued by town councils might not be "contrary or repugnant to ye orders, Statutes, & Decrees of ye Donors, or Founders."[62] Also after the English model, if an aggrieved party appealed a council's rulings to the Governor and Council, the council's ruling would be suspended pending the outcome. The Governor and Council, like the Court of Chancery in England, might reverse, sustain, or modify a town council's order, or even write an entirely different one as a substitute, provided it was "agreeable to Equity & Good Conscience according to the true intent & meaning of the Donors, or Founders." This provision allowed the Governor and Council more discretion than Read had thought proper, but it clearly reflected English law.[63] Still, Read's defense of Jeremiah Weeden had guided the General Assembly to revise the remedies for mismanagement by trustees.

For the time being, however, the new act seemed unnecessary. Edward Smith thought the prospects bright enough in December 1721 to resume acting as a trustee. He planned to do so after the council's appointees had withdrawn, and the council approved his return to the roster.[64] On the first day of January, however, William Weeden reverted to his old ways yet again. He asked the council to enter on its records that Henry Tew had been chosen a trustee in Smith's place. When the council "passed a vote that the sd Tew was not a proper Assigne [illegible] According to sd Clarkes will," Weeden "Refused any farther to Act According to Agreement made with the Trustees" the previous autumn. (The trustees referred to in the council's entry were Wanton, Rogers, and Philip Peckham.) He persisted in February and demanded that the old controversy over his expenses be submitted to arbitration. The council laconically set down a minute that Nathaniel Byfield should continue to serve as its representative in the arbitration.[65]

Three days later the council decided to use the new law. It ordered the colony's sheriff to summon a jury and cite the three trustees it recognized—William Weeden, Thomas Olney, and Edward Smith—"to appear at a Court of Town Counll" on 20 February "to answer to all such Mismanagement or breaches of Trust wch have been Committed by them."[66] At the appointed time Olney failed to appear and Weeden asked the council for more time to prepare his defense. It gave him twenty-four hours.[67]

The hearing took place the next day. The jury found "that Capt William Weeden by the Concurrance or Conniveance of said Olney (Mr Smith being Unactive) hath very Much abused the trust" he held and decided that Weeden owed the Clarke estate £183 8s. 10d. (two pence more than the council had previously claimed) for transactions up to 25 March 1720. The jury gave as its "Judgments and Verdict" that the farm leased to Jeremiah Weeden should have brought £65 annual rent (rather than the £26 more or less from year to year charged in the past), another tract should have brought £15, "and that whatever the sd Olney and Weeden have agreed to lett it for Under the sd Rent

Dispute over the Clarke Trust

is soe much Yearly prejudice to the poor; and therefore we Adjudg the said Weeden & Olney or the most Active of them [i.e., Weeden] shall pay & make good to the town Councell . . . out of his or their proper Estate the Yearly Rents of Eighty pounds from the time of the last Adjustments of Capt Weedens Accott by the town Councell." They also decided that Weeden and Olney should pay costs of the hearing.[68]

The council accepted the verdict and adjourned to the next day. On that occasion it gave Weeden ten days to pay £183 8s. 10d. to Edward Smith, gave Weeden and Olney the same time to turn over to Smith £80 they should have collected in rents for 1720, assessed court costs of £11 4s. 9d. against Olney and Weeden, and required that the trustees use the money turned over to Smith for the purposes of the trust. If the delinquent trustees did not obey the orders, the council directed its clerk to grant a writ of execution for the collection of the various amounts by seizure of their property or, failing that, their bodies.[69] Quietly, Weeden had given up his objections to accepting Smith rather than Tew as the third trustee.

Once again the council stayed its hand when it seemed about to wield the full power of government. During the spring it settled a few accounts of its expenses in the trial but did not order seizure of Weeden's property when he refused to comply with the judgment.[70] As on the previous occasions, the council marked time while the Baptist church invited Swansea emissaries in an effort to subdue Weeden's stubbornness by brotherly suasion. The outsiders also had the task of making recommendations to heal the widening split in the First Baptist Church.

To complicate the problem, in spite of advice by the Swansea brethren, the Newport church had let William Weeden remain in the fellowship, although he had not repented. This time the committee of visitors declared it could not see how any members of the Newport flock could continue taking communion with him "Untill such time as he submits ye Rents and Profits of the [Clarke] Estate . . . to be disposed of according to the Instruction, Together with a Manifestation of his Repentance for his Irregular Proceedings therein and Promise of Reformation for the future," a goal toward which the brethren should strive by beseeching Weeden to be reconciled to them. The Newport Baptists accepted this advice but did not act upon it straightforwardly. They urged Weeden to reform, but he yielded nothing.[71]

Probably this decision to take milder measures than the visitors recommended was by a majority vote. And it brought to a head the antagonism between Elder Peckham and Elder White and their followers. Ten of the twenty-nine members in full communion broke off with White as a separate church. Weeden, of course, was not among them, but John Rogers and Philip Peckham were. In fact, they comprised half the male membership in the seceding group.[72] They managed to build a meetinghouse but began to drift apart when some of the members accused White of violating the rules he had promised to observe. He stopped preaching. The meetinghouse was sold to a Congregationalist flock. Then White left for Philadelphia.[73]

For all that, the arbitration may have promoted a resolution of the conflict over the Clarke estate. After the departure of the schismatics, the remaining members of the First Baptist Church reembodied themselves—that is, agreed anew to form a church, apparently with Weeden still as a member. Even he may have been shaken by the disturbance he had occasioned. When Olney died in June 1722, Weeden and the other trustee (Smith rather than Tew) replaced him with the man who had led opposition to stern measures against Weeden, Elder William Peckham.[74] This decision was the first sign of softening in Weeden's stiff-necked attitude, though under the circumstances it probably was an easy one. It turned out to have great consequences because it gave the controlling voice to Peckham. John Clarke probably had not wished to put the pastor in charge of the endowment.

In August the town council got around to citing the trustees to appear and report what they had done to carry out the judgment given six months earlier.[75] The trustees had done nothing, so in September the council ordered writs of execution against Weeden for amounts he had been adjudged to owe, and in October another writ (scire facias) against the executors and administrators of the estate of Thomas Olney, requiring them to appear and show why the estate should not pay the amounts adjudged due from him.[76] Some representation duly appeared and, with the concurrence of Weeden, declared that Olney had had no assets of the Clarke estate.[77] Weeden remained obstinate, but the writ evidently was not executed against him at that time. In December and again later he was admonished by his church for withholding rents from the Clarke estate, "by which Evil ye holy Name of god and ye profession of his truths were reproached.[78]

The writ was finally executed in time to present the council with £183 8s. 10d. at its meeting on 5 February 1722/23. The council ordered that £160 be paid to Edward Smith while the remainder (taking a page from Weeden's book) was to be kept by the council "for ye Defraying the Sundry Charges Expended by the Counll in ye Action agt Wm

Dispute over the Clarke Trust

Weeden in behalf of the poor." The disposition of this amount indicated that the council paid the bill of costs previously assessed against Weeden, as well as fees to two attorneys and the sheriff.[79] The council gave no explanation for its surrender on the court costs or the sheriff's fee that ordinarily would have been extracted from Weeden. Perhaps he finally gave in and the council softened his defeat by relieving him of these burdens.

Whatever the agreement reached with William Weeden on this occasion, it was durable, and he stopped taking an active role as trustee of the Clarke donation. After 1722, Edward Smith and William Peckham acted together and so controlled the assets of the trust. For a time they adhered closely to the spirit of the council's rulings. They presented accounts to the council every year, gathered in assets in private hands, and devoted funds to charitable purposes.[80] In keeping with what John Clarke probably had intended, they gave benefits to all the poor, not just Baptists. In 1724 they donated £100 to the town of Newport "for the helping Errect a Charity house in the Town." Shortly thereafter, they gave the town additional money to pay expenses of the poor.[81] After that, however, the trustees began to give money to pay part of a stipend for an elder in the First Baptist Church. Gradually the contributions increased until the trust became virtually an endowment for the pulpit.

The struggle against William Weeden represented more than a triumph over corruption. In the long run, the means of winning were as important as the victory itself. What occurred within the church was somewhat deceptive. The church neither had a firm disciplinary technique at the outset nor developed one to use against the unscrupulous trustee. It was reluctant to initiate action, put it off for years, and for a time succeeded only in provoking a schism over how much firmness should be used against Weeden. Significantly, the side that was less legalistic and harsh, more inclined to moral pressure than formal action, remained predominant throughout. It scored only one conspicuous success, a vital one surely, when it prevailed upon Weeden to accept Elder Peckham as a trustee. This little victory was achieved by purely informal means, which worked because William Weeden chose to stay in the church and the others could not bring themselves to throw him out. Elder Peckham's policy was effective—or so it seemed.

Actually, this policy succeeded because it was a kindly approach amid calls for stern action. Within the church, White led the disciplinarians. The new device of formal investigation and nonbinding arbitration by emissaries from a sister church added calls to rigor, even against White. And the church surely knew that the council was looking for means to compel Weeden. The church probably welcomed the council's campaign—after all, Edward Smith had started it—though maybe with qualms.

The council entered the fray as reluctantly as the church. It, too, lacked an unquestioned jurisdiction or an established procedure, and it avoided action for eighteen years. At last, faced with the trustees' maladministration, the town fathers had to act. Possibly they tried informal private persuasion—in a small town such an effort was all but inevitable—but they had to proceed to formal and public legal procedures. As it did so, the council kept hitting limits on what it could accomplish. It could summon the trustees, but they might not obey and it did not dare to compel them. It could get them to present accounts but could not make them manage the trust differently. Its frustrations were reminiscent of those that plagued the colonial government at the end of the previous century. The council could not fall back on methods the church used. It could not tolerate a defiance of its orders. It was brittle where the church was supple. It needed a mechanism that could overpower any opposition rather than an elastic emotional net. Government had to be monopolistic; its authority would stand or fall on its ability to impose its decisions.

The council, moreover, could not prevail by its own prestige or by proving the goodness of its purposes or by relying on the social bonds that united the townsfolk. It realized that it must act as a local agency of central authority under terms close to those in English law. If the colonial government at first provided an inadequate delegation of power, the council was embarrassed and sought a revised delegation. Finally, it backed Weeden into a corner; the church gave him the face-saving exit of transferring control over the trust to Elder Peckham.

In this imbroglio the church and the state entered an unacknowledged alliance for limited purposes in a way that has become quite common in the United States. The result did not overturn John Clarke's convictions so much as cut away half. Religious liberty, he had asserted, would make loyal and law-abiding subjects of the king. And a church would be free only if it never touched civil authority, never relied on it in any fashion. But by 1718 the First Baptist Church had begun to rely on government to protect its property in lands and buildings. Now it sought government aid to keep benefits flowing to it from the Clarke trust. It would not say so, and throughout the controversy the church treated Weeden's conduct as a subject for disciplinary action. The first difficult task was to find a device by which governmental action would help the church without confining religious liberty. In the end, the church and the government managed to adjust their relations so as to avoid making either one dominate the other. They marked out a narrow zone where they would meet for mutual advantage: government would protect a trust that would benefit a church but would not give this protection to one church more than another. Ironically, nobody used the rationale that would be commonplace sixty or seventy years later, that churches taught the citizens to behave themselves in ways that were good for society and reduced the government's burden of punishing crime, which is ironic, because this idea was so close to Clarke's thinking. Instead, the basis for the alliance went unformulated.

The legal statement of the government's duties had to be put in general terms. One serious defect of Rhode Island's first statute on charitable trusts was its undisguised purpose to provide means to reform the Clarke trust. It virtually judged and condemned William Weeden. The act of 1721, however, was written in impassively general language. The wording camouflaged the actual purpose, but at the cost of extending governmental protection over all denominations, all sorts of secular endowments, and unforeseeable other things. This use of general terms, with its potential for unpredictable effects, has been characteristic of the devices by which American state governments have favored churches in recent centuries.

The denouement changed both state and church. The colony had a new law, a proven procedure to supervise charitable trusts. It also had gone through an instructive exercise in adapting English law in a difficult field. To be sure, the specific development in law had no immediate effect beyond the dispute that occasioned it. It did not inspire a host of donations like the Clarke trust, yet eventually, security for ecclesiastical or eleemosynary endowments would transform a society that had been confined to what little could be done for public projects by minuscule taxes and day-to-day contributions.[82]

The First Baptist Church changed in more subtle but more far-reaching ways. In the seventeenth century it had been a prime example of an institution focused on the present through the living fervor of devotion. It had done without everything that could tie it down to mundane calculations on preserving assets for the future. As a Baptist church it resolutely rejected the symbolic ceremony of taking infants under its ritual care and insisted that baptism should ritualize the new birth of a believing Christian. It had insisted on congregational autonomy. It had raised up men as pastors who lacked higher education and in other ways had reaffirmed its commitment to the spontaneity of the now. Except when forced to a showdown on a doctrinal point, it had preserved a latitude of convictions within the fold.

Unwittingly, its founder encouraged a radical alteration. He set up a trust that could give the church property, both directly and in the prospect of income, which drew its attention to maintaining and improving real estate, to proper ritual use of land or a meetinghouse, and to the possibility of what could be done with a flow of funds. By putting these worldly benefits before his old flock, Clarke entrammeled them in debates over church procedure and how to position themselves in relation to a sister church. Although nothing decisive or codified came of these advances into institutional regularity, merely considering how rules might be framed and how intercongregational assistance might be managed brought a new element into the church. More would follow. The church fell to the temptation to grasp the material benefits in the trust for its institutional ends, rather than for the welfare of the needy, and to frame its institutional plans to elevate the pastor. Although the church did not record a shift in principles, it was sidling around to a trained and salaried ministry, and the Clarke donation smoothed the way by providing a fund for a successor to Elder Peckham.

Ironically, then, John Clarke's legacy was a subversion of what he had created. Granted, one modest donation could not weave a magic spell on a whole colony, yet the donation and the controversy it created played a part in some basic changes. During his life Clarke had been the champion of separation of church and state in the charter of 1663, the founder of a church that rejected the trained professional ministry and concern with worldly goods and procedural rules, yet his benevolence at death left property in trust and led toward a fundamental transformation.

Epilogue

In the aftermath of the campaign against William Weeden, the First Baptist Church changed more obviously than the government. The church continued to move away from its origins and toward the pattern of a dignified, even elegant, urban Protestant organization with an erudite minister set well above the congregation, paid, and supported by a small staff of deacons. The government also cultivated procedural formality and a well-defined hierarchy of functions among its organs. It, too, departed from its beginnings and arrived at a redefinition of its part in the workings of society.

On the surface, the government seemed to subside into passivity rather than attempt new ventures. Certainly, it stopped being assertive as far as the Clarke trust and the First Baptist Church were concerned. It saw no need to write more laws or bring wayward trustees back to their responsibilities. The Newport town council gave up the attempt to put a non-Baptist into the ranks of the trustees. Presumably it had wanted its own man on the panel to get public benefits from the money in their hands. It got some, then made no objection when the trustees stopped making donations to the town.

The trustees, in turn, complied with the minimal requirements of the law. They presented their accounts annually or nearly so, gathered in assets in private hands, and spent money on charitable purposes.[1] Surviving documents do not tell what they did about the lease to Jeremiah Weeden, but before long the rents increased dramatically. The council was contented with a few donations from the trustees while Edward Smith was still alive. In 1724 the trustees donated £100 to the town "for the helping Errect a Charity house" and soon afterwards gave additional money to pay expenses of the poor.[2] These awards carried out what Smith, probably correctly, believed John Clarke had intended. When Smith died in 1730, however, Weeden and Peckham replaced him with Josias Lyndon, who thought Clarke had meant to endow his church. The council did not object, and the town stopped hoping to get funds from the Clarke trust.

The Newport council could easily forget about the subject after the division of the town in 1743. Clarke's farm fell on the Middletown side of the line, so the council there received the annual reports and for many years was satisfied with what it learned. When an attempt was made in the early nineteenth century to compel the trustees to resume payments for public charity, they won vindication from the General Council—that is, governor, deputy governor, and assistants, sitting as the court of appeals from the town council in probate cases. The General Council decided that the trustees used their income "according to the true meaning and intention of the ... will of the said John Clarke deceased."[3] Most likely, the mere accumulation of precedent—almost a century of use as an endowment for the First Baptist Church—rather than any interpretation of documents justified allowing the trustees to continue along the course they had established.

The contest with Weeden, in hindsight, might well seem like an aberration, although it left scars in the church that were painful for at least sixty years.[4] Before 1718 the Newport council had done nothing to watch over the Clarke trust; by 1730 it was again doing next to nothing. Yet the passivity after 1722 was not the same as the apathy before 1718. In the early eighteenth century the Newport council had dodged its duties, probably glad to stay away from a thorn bush and willing to believe that it had no well-grounded legal part to play. When it entered the fray, sure enough, it had doubts about its legal foundations and petitioned the General Assembly twice. But at that time, the town council wanted to lay a rather firm supervisory hand on the Clarke trust to coordinate it with other forms of civic development.

For a few years after 1722 the town of Newport received the kind of benefits from the Clarke trust that the council considered its due, but it had never openly accused Weeden of choosing improper beneficiaries and never openly criticized the choices made after his fall. Just as the General Assembly had changed from the language of the act of 1719—plainly an ad hoc measure against William Weeden—to the general phrases of the act of 1721, so the council changed from seeking to gain a voice in the management of the trust to leaving the trustees to do as they wished so long as they submitted annual reports and stayed clear of corruption. In Rhode Island after 1730, the government less and less tried to make its own determinations about what its people should do and more and more concerned itself with what they should not. In short, it set rules for everyone to observe and stood ready to cajole observance or punish violation.

This change, from deciding on goals and searching for the means to attain them to providing procedural rules for the citizens to observe as they pursued their own ends, could have several explanations. One would be that the citizens had reached a consensus on what kinds of social action were useful and proper, so the government no longer needed to prescribe them. Another, that they disagreed so much among themselves on what to do that they could agree only on procedures and the judicial mechanisms to enforce them. A third, that the growing diversity, complexity, and sheer size of nongovernmental operations reached a point where the political institutions could not steer their development.

What happened after Weeden had been subdued suggested that there was some truth in all three explanations. The transformation of the First Baptist Church in these years took it to a style of ecclesiastical behavior that had widespread, if not universal, acceptance. And even those who opposed what the church was doing acknowledged its right to chose its own course. The town council's goal of gearing a charitable endowment to civic purposes—in effect, to let the town limit what the trustees could do with their income—probably did not have widespread support. There was no easy formula to define the charitable purposes authorized by John Clarke. They could and did embrace uses covering a spectrum from building a Baptist meetinghouse to paying to support some of the town's paupers. If Rhode Island was dedicated to separation of church and state, it would have to let the Clarke trust be a nongovernmental entity and let it become closely attached to a single church if the trustees chose. The council's action under the statute of 1721 went as far as government might go with adequate support from the citizenry. The action amounted to enforcing legal regulation and giving up the attempt to set policy for the trustees. Sizable numbers of citizens in the colony held several different beliefs about how a church should be organized and financed, so no majority could coalesce behind any one; no majority wanted to legislate against the methods of a single church.

If the government concerned itself with form rather than content, procedure rather than purpose, the church was concerned with all these things. The result, as in earlier years, had much less to do with well-known matters of tenets and ritual than with style of religious fellowship. The church did not reverse the decisions made in the seventeenth century in favor of believer baptism and rejecting the seventh day sabbath and the mandatory laying on of hands for all members. Nor did it raise the doctrine of predestination from the optional category. William G. McLoughlin has written perceptively about the rise of an urban—and urbane—type of Baptist church in the years just before 1740. As he says, the phenomenon was distinctive and deserves attention.[5]

The Baptist church in Boston set the pattern and got its first college-bred pastor in Elisha Callender (or Callendar), and the First Baptist Church in Newport quickly followed. Its aspirations became tangible when it built its meetinghouse in the center of the commercial zone in 1708 and ordained Elder Peckham three years later. Its choice of Daniel White as associate pastor was a further step in the same direction. White was from London, where he had belonged to the sort of church that the Newport church became.[6]

After White's schism, the church turned in 1725 to John Comer, its first minister with some higher education since John Clarke. But Comer was an utterly different man than Clarke had been. His education did not make the difference: he had only one full year at Yale, although he had studied extensively with a few Congregationalist ministers.[7] Rather, he had radically different ideas about what a minister and a church should be. He had an odd, not very attractive personality. He had an inner drive to change people around him as well as intellectual ambitions that he did not live long enough to fulfill. A symptom of it came in his diary, where he rather incongruously adapted Livy's pattern of reserving a section in the report on each year for a list of uncommon events. Livy dwelt on freaks of nature, but Comer, apart from tremulous descriptions of the aurora borealis, told about people who met bizarre or violent deaths. Comer's diary also reveals a tendency to obsessive, morbid fears, a notion that others were cheating him, and an unshakable attachment to the First Baptist Church even after it had dismissed him.

In addition to these traits, Comer had a determination to collect historical materials about the Newport Baptist churches. Avowedly he wanted to write a history in order to make Baptists conscious of their past and feel a duty to follow their own traditions. Plainly, he liked collecting for its own sake. For that we should feel grateful, even if his sense of the past was such a reversal of what the past had been.

If Comer revealed his uglier traits in his diary, we should not assume that they appeared in his public deportment. Cotton Mather's well-known diary displayed a morbid spiritual egotism—or so it seems to a modern reader—that sometimes tainted his encounters with other people. Some could not abide him but others admired his facility at making moral instruction enjoyable. Just how Comer appeared to the First Baptist Church, unfortunately, has not been reported, but presumably he seemed to be a bright and energetic young minister who could hold the attention of his flock. He made quite a contrast with William Peckham.

Comer revealed his difference from John Clarke and Obadiah Holmes during the negotiations before he accepted the call at Newport. He asked advice from Elisha Callender and received a letter that devoted much more attention to worldly considerations than to religious ones. It was the sort of advice that clergymen often have given each other, possibly from the beginning of civilization, but as a rule they keep it among themselves rather than let the laity know they have any motive beyond serving God. Comer solemnly wrote it down in his diary. He also negotiated a salary.[8]

Comer wanted a fairly elaborate ordination, where he presented a long declaration of faith starting with basic Christian doctrines, proceeding into his Baptist versions of some of them, and reaching such specifics as his insistence on congregational singing. He got his way on the introduction of hymns. More revealing and more distinctive was his declaration on the ministry: "I Bel[ieve] yt Christ hath apointed an order of men to represent him as his Ambasadors yt they are to be Chosen by his people to be Set in office by fasting prayuer and Imposition of hands." He was to be Christ's ambassador, not just a preaching brother. Nevertheless, he did not question the procedure for elevating him.[9]

Here and elsewhere in the declaration he showed one side of his ambivalence on unity and precision in doctrine. He steered around some tenets on which the members had disagreed for generations. He did not even declare his belief in "free grace"—that is, predestination as the Antinomians had expounded it—which Obadiah Holmes had endorsed in a profession of faith written toward the end of his life. All the same he began to inject an emphasis on doctrinal unity that Clarke had opposed by resurrecting Clarke's treatise on predestination and copying it into the church records as a statement of what Comer thought the church had originally agreed upon and should return to.[10] In fact, Comer wrote it in when he was collecting whatever he could find about the church's past. Undoubtedly, he did not perceive the irony. There had been no systematic record preserved by the church.[11] One part of Comer wanted doctrinal uniformity; the other accepted the church's tradition of diversity, a tradition that had the support of the new cluster of educated urban pastors led by Elisha Callender.[12]

If neither Comer nor his church could take a strong stand for doctrinal unity, they did agree on improving appearances and using an orderly procedure for church government. Even before his arrival, the church had begun paying more attention to such matters. Especially in disciplinary actions, it took care to define the offenses and abide by the biblical rules on dealing with sinners—and to keep memos of these events. It took new care with the roster of members. The church chose deacons and ceremonially ordained them. It refurbished the new meetinghouse, with funds provided by the Clarke trustees. Two members contributed cloths for the communion table. The church firmly decided on providing the sacrament of communion once a month. Comer promoted these trends. He even persuaded the church to adopt a new covenant when he could not find the original one that he believed had been drawn up. The new covenant was a fairly long document, with much to say about church discipline, but it avoided endorsing any controversial tenets, such as predestination.[13]

More striking still, the church began to pay Comer a salary. This was a radical departure from the old aversion to a hired ministry. The church agreed to solicit a weekly contribution for this purpose,[14] and the Clarke trustees added more. Paying Comer was not a mockery of Clarke's convictions, but it was an abrupt rejection of established practice.

Comer eagerly made himself a part of the First Baptist Church. He married a daughter of John Rogers and borrowed money to build a house.[15] He also undertook to be a schoolmaster for the children of his flock. This may have been a rather uncontroversial addition to the pastor's duties, but he had further concerns. The weekly collection was not so generous as he could wish, and the supplement from the Clarke trust brought the total up to only a meager £35.[16] By teaching the children, however, Comer could legitimately claim more from the Clarke trust. He also wanted a better place for his pedagogy than the meetinghouse.[17]

The mercenary considerations are easy to see, but Comer's move into school teaching had more importance as another step away from the church's origins. Surely Baptist parents were as determined as any others to bring up their children properly, but they had not thought their church should provide a sectarian school. On the contrary, the church had never had a formal obligation to the children. By rejecting infant baptism and by focusing its concern on the vitality of the spiritual life among the adults, it had made any obligation to the children impossible. Quite likely, the members as part of their participation in the fellowship had felt a duty to help each other in rearing the young and preparing them for baptism when they grew up, and the elders may have assumed a stronger duty in this regard than other members. Still, the duty did not extend to holding classes to impart basic literacy.

Baptists hitherto had been satisfied with such schooling as was available. Their children could be educated along with the others in the neighborhood. They backed the town of Newport when it set aside land for schools and an endowment to provide money to build schoolhouses and pay masters. The Clarke trustees had contributed to this purpose. When Comer became a schoolmaster he pushed the church toward a new conception of what it should do. Taking this initiative probably was made easy by the growth of Newport's population, which called for more schools by one means or another, but in any case it was successful.

Comer shook up Clarke's old church but surely not against its will. Rather, he was the agent by which it explored new directions. He was vigorous and assertive, which suited the occasion well. He had a demanding concept of what a Baptist pastor should be and what a Baptist church should be, and he found a ready acquiescence. The church followed him as far as it wanted to be led. But that was not enough for John Comer: he had to make the congregation bend to his judgment. By 1728 he became convinced that the ceremony of laying on of hands should be performed on every member. This tenet had led to a schism in the mid-seventeenth century, and the church was not about to adopt what its ancestors had opposed. Hard feelings between Comer and his flock, possibly fomented by Edward Smith, led to a crisis.

Comer's report on the event is the only one that survives, and it arouses skepticism. He complained bitterly that the church "withheld wickedly" the stipend it had promised and asserted that the only reason was "because I preached up Imposition of Hands on Baptized believers," although without saying it was a prerequisite to communion.[18] He was so emphatic on this point as to suggest that there was more to the quarrel that he tried to blot out of his mind. Maybe the church sensed that he wanted to command as well as lead. He certainly alluded to more than he explained in a few passages where he mentioned Edward Smith, William Peckham, and unspecified others as his enemies and complained of their lack of repentance.[19] (Apparently he was reconciled with Peckham in 1731.)

Sometime in 1729 the First Baptist Church dismissed Comer, and he went over to the Six Principle church, where he filled the pulpit quite often without being ordained as an associate pastor. He continued to write in his diary about "my old church"—occasionally, even, "my church"—and its actions. Clearly remained emotionally tied to it. He fretted about whether he was properly forgiving, a theme that reached its climax around the time Edward Smith died.[20]

By then Comer had made himself unwelcome in the Six Principle church by advocating predestination. At his request they gave him a dismission.[21] He entered negotiations with a church at Rehoboth, Massachusetts, but before leaving Newport he achieved a reconciliation with the First Baptist Church. He acknowledged his mistakes—not just preaching the laying on of hands but also further offensive remarks in a later sermon—"and it was agreed that all papers that were written on both sides Relating to the difference might be produced, and burnt which was accordingly done [alas! for the historian] and the meeting finished in Love and peace with Prayer by mr Comer."[22]

After dismissing Comer, the First Baptist Church had some difficulty finding men to preach. (Comer reported its resort to various outsiders with a strong hint of satisfaction.) For a time the church seemed likely to fall back into old norms, but the appearance was deceptive. Although the church asked Deacon Samuel Maxwell to preach, it was not contented with another unlearned preaching brother. Besides, Maxwell took himself very seriously and embarked on a dizzying series of changes in affiliation, tenets, and locations. The old church knew what it really wanted. It invited several of the new breed of educated young Baptists for trial and negotiations and finally came to terms with John Callender, the nephew of Elisha. Uncle Elisha went down to assist at the ordination.[23] This time the Newport church had found a pastor with a full-fledged Harvard degree.

John Callender was steady, tactful, and ingratiating to a fault. Like his uncle, like Comer, and like others in this cluster, he cultivated the friendship and good will of leading Congregationalist ministers. He wanted to be like them and win acceptance as an equal. He followed through on Comer's initiatives to change the First Baptist Church. He made a reality of the idea that proper Baptists were just Puritans who had a special view of baptism. He was ecumenical and tolerant of diversity of convictions well beyond John Clarke. Callender was so tolerant, so determined to be congenial with leading Congregationalists, that he nearly precluded the possibility of attaining any intellectual eminence.[24] Conveniently for him, Elder Peckham died in 1734.

Callender's only literary attainment of any significance was his sermon on the history of his church, later expanded and published as a history of Rhode Island's first century. Its minor fame rests on its being the first—and for years, the only—history of the colony. Callender took care not to offend anybody, especially not his Congregationalist friends in Boston. So he left out anything that might revive bitter memories or provoke recrimination. Besides, he was not very well acquainted with the past of his new home. His tepid narrative was weak tea, indeed, and it washed away any flavor of the founding generation.[25]

John Callender may seem remarkably insipid in retrospect, because his achievement lay outside the standards commonly applied today. He brought to a culmination the transformation of the style of fellowship in the First Baptist Church. He all but ruled out any quarrels over faith or practice. If he did not openly put a stop to "prophesying," he surely made it highly unlikely. He wore robes like those of the most fashionable Congregationalist ministers in Boston. This fact is known because he had his portrait painted by the respected Robert Feke.[26] (He may well have been the first Rhode Island Baptist to sit for a good painter.) During his pastorate the church built him a new and more elegant meetinghouse. This had been under consideration since Comer's time and action was finally taken in 1737. Some members donated land on Spring Street, and the congregation raised money and chose committees to make all arrangements.[27] If not in principle, at least in practice, the church made Callender an exalted minister far beyond what John Clarke approved.

The new structure, once suitably adorned, completed the transformation of the church's appearance, but there were subtler changes, too. The church agreed on a regular rotation of ceremonies.[28] It received a badge of admission into the ranks of dignified urban Baptist churches when Thomas Hollis in distant London sent a donation, by way of uncle Elisha.[29] (This was an odd endorsement of Clarke's opposition to parochialism.) It showed its fraternal disposition by joining with the other Baptist churches in Newport to build a house for baptisms at Green End. More remarkable, a later William Weeden donated the land for this. There could hardly be stronger evidence of Callender's calming influence.[30] And First Baptist proposed to form an association with churches of its own sort in other places, provided they could "Guard against ye Disorders yt haue Attended som General Meetings," by which they referred to meetings held by the much less refined Six Principle churches.[31]

Elder Callender busily made himself a prominent figure in Newport in ways that comported with his sense of his place. He joined the Society for Promoting Virtue and Knowledge by a Free Conversation, a club of gentlemen with intellectual pretensions, which later sponsored the Redwood Library. He served on a committee to revise the colony's laws. And he served as a town schoolmaster for a short time before his death in 1748.[32]

After Callender's death, the church found a comparable successor in Edward Upham and thus could stabilize in its new style of fellowship. The practice of providing a salary had become routine, and the Clarke trustees contributed substantially.[33] The arrangement for Upham gave him the use of most of John Clarke's farm for a rent of £100 more than the trustees paid toward his salary. As the Rhode Island currency lost value, the salary and rent went up, so the £100 gap narrowed in practical terms. As a result, the trustees at the beginning of Upham's pastorate allocated about 35 percent of their income to educating children and supporting poor widows and a declining fraction as the years rolled by. The charitable expenditures went to people in the flock. So the Clarke trust had become an endowment for the church. Upham's successors got a smaller fraction of the income, but still well over half. After Upham left, the church called Erasmus Kelly and instituted a pew tax to pay two-thirds of his salary, with the Clarke trust paying the rest.³⁴ This decision took the church a long way from its origins.

So great was the transformation of Dr. John Clarke's church that Baptist chroniclers beginning with Isaac Backus, writing when Kelly filled the pulpit, could twist the record to tell a story they understood. To them, the church had been characterized by agreement on a creed, notably on the belief in predestination, and it had had a succession of pastors, one at a time, forming a chain from Clarke down to modern times. In this record, the dispute over the Clarke trust was an inexplicable if deplorable incident where, mysteriously, virtue (the opposition to Weeden) triumphed only with great difficulty. In addition, Comer merely served to make improvements in a fundamentally continuous institution and Callender to push them along.³⁵ This view of the record hides Clarke's convictions about what a Baptist church should be, trivializes the drama of the dispute over his estate, and overlooks the appealing style of religious fellowship that Clarke favored and the high-toned cosmopolitan style brought in by Callender. If John Clarke's legacy of leadership was abandoned, however, his legacy of property helped to bring about that result.

Like much else in the early history of New England, the story of John Clarke and his trust seems to descend from the grand events of the seventeenth century to end in local history. The increasingly parochial parts, however, had their importance. The last years of Clarke's life, the difficulties of his trustees after his death, the conflict over the trust in the early eighteenth century, and the denouement in the transformation of the Baptist church in Newport, all reveal how New England was proceeding from an offshoot of the Puritan movement into a society of its own. The legal battle over the trust illustrates how Rhode Island made adjustments to an imperial framework and assimilated English laws at a time and in a manner that paralleled events in other parts of New England. Comparable kinds of "anglicization" also occurred in the southern colonies. Exploring what happened on a small scale enables us to comprehend the larger pattern and its workings; the grand panorama needs sufficient detail to take on a realistic quality.

Appendix

Will of Dr. John Clarke

Whereas I John Clarke of Newport in the Colony of Rhode Island and Providence Plantations &c In New England Physician am att this present through the abundant goodness and mercy of my God (though weake in my body) yett sound in my memory, and understanding, and being Sensible of the inconveniences that may insue in case I should not sett my house in order, before this Spirit of mine be called by the Lord to remoue out of this Tabernacle Doe therfore make and declare this my Last Will and Testament in manner following, willingly and readily resigneing vp my Soule vnto my mercifull Redeemer thorough [sic] faith in whose death I firmly hope and belieue to Escape from that Second hurting death, and thorough his Resurrection and Life to bee glorified with him in Life Eternall; and my Spirit being returned out of this fraile body in which it hath conversed for about Sixty Six years my Will is that itt be decently interred (without any Vaine Ostentation) betweene my loueing wiues Elizabeth and Jane already deceased, in hopefull Expectation that the same Redeemer who hath laid downe a price both for my Soul and body will raise itt vp att the Last day a Spirituall one that they may together bee singing Hallelujah vnto him to all Eternity; And as touching my temporall Estate which the Lord of his goodness hath bestowed vpon mee my Will is that my funerall expences being discharged, and all my Just debts paid itt be disposed of in manner following; Imprimis my Will is that all my Land on the Island of Cononicutt and all my Land or interest in the Townes of Providence & Westerly bee Sould by my Executors hereafter named, for the best advantage, and the Produce thereof by them divided betweene my Brother Joseph Clarke and all his children by his first

---

The original copies of these documents are in the Newport Historical Society. Except for the signatures, the will and the subsidiary instructions are written in the hand of Richard Baily.

Wife (Except his son John, and betweene my cosin [blank] ffisk wife of Samuell ffisk and her children, and my cosin Mary Saunders wife of Tobias Saunders and her children, and in the said Division my said Brother Joseph and my said Cosins ffisk and Mary Saunders to haue each of them a double share; Item vnto each of my Brother Josephs children by his Second wife I giue and bequeath one Shilling in money; Item vnto my cosin John Clarke Son of my Brother Joseph by his first wife I giue, bequeath, and devise Six acres of Land to bee laid out vnto him by my Executors hereafter named, at that End of my Land in Towne next adjoyneing to the Land of Benedict Arnold Senior, the said Land hereby bequeathed vnto my said Cousin John Clarke to bee and remaine vnto him and his heires and assignes for Ever, hee and they being to fence against the Remainder of my Land; Item vnto my Loueing ffriends, William Weeden, Phillip Smith and Richard Baily I giue and devise a certaine piece of Land att the Southeast corner of my Orchard to bee, and remaine vnto them and their heires and assignes for ever for the vse and vses by mee declared in a Paper vnder my hand and Seale the said Land to containe in breadth next the streete three rodd, and in Length Six rodd; Item vnto my said Loueing ffriends William Weeden, Phillip Smith and Richard Baily I giue bequeath and devise all the remainder of my Land in the said Towne of Newport now in my owne Possession and my now dwelling house thereon being, containeing by Estimation thirty acres more or less; my farme now in Possession of George Browne or his Assignes containeing by Estimation One hundred and fifty acres, and all the Marshes to itt belonging, and my piece of Land lyeing and being in the Precints of the said Towne and called the neck containeing by Estimation tenn acres more or less to bee and remaine vnto the said William Weeden, Phillip Smith and Richard Baily for and dureing the naturall life of my deare and loueing Wife Sarah Clarke for her comfortable maintenance and Support, and if my said wife desire to dwell in my said house, then I will that she shall haue the improuement of the land to itt belonging and the Stock thereon being; Item vnto my said Loueing wife I giue and bequeath two bedds wch shee shall please to choose with bedsteads and all the furniture vnto them belonging and the biggest of my trunks; Item vnto my daughter in Law Sarah Davis I giue and bequeath forty pounds to bee paid vnto her att the age of eighteene yeares or att the day of her Marriage in money pay; Item vnto my Son in Law Simon Davis and his heires and Assignes for ever

I giue bequeath and devise all my Land lyeing att the waterside in the Towne of Newport aforesaid bounded on the South by Land which I sould vnto Sarah Reape and on the North by a highway; Item vnto my Son in Law Thomas Davis I giue and bequeath twenty pounds in the pay abouementioned to bee paid vnto him att the age of One and Twenty yeares; Item vnto my daughter in Law Mercy Davis I giue and bequeath twenty pounds in the pay abouementioned to bee paid vnto her att the age of eighteene yeares or att the day of her Marriage; Item vnto my daughter in Law Hannah Davis I giue and bequeath tenn pounds in like pay; Provided allwayes and my intent and will is that none of the Portions aboue by mee bequeathed vnto any of my wiues children shall bee paid vnto them dureing her life, Excepting only the Land vnto Simon Davis[;] Item vnto my Brother Carew Clarke I giue and bequeath his mainetainance for and dureing the terme of his naturall Life, and his being in my now dwelling house, to bee provided for in the same manner as hee now is if my wife shall keepe house in itt and they can in comfort remaine together; But in case of his remoueall from thence my Will is that hee bee paid for his mainetenance as aforesaid sixteene pounds a yeare in Provisions att Price currant out of the rent of the said farme; Item vnto Katharine Salmon wife of John Salmon I giue and bequeath six Ewe sheepe; Item vnto the said Richard Baily I giue and bequeath my Concordance and Lexicon to itt belonging written by my Selfe being the fruitt of Several yeares Study, my Hebrew Bibles, Buxtorffs, and Passors Lexicon, Cottons concordance and all the rest of my books; Item vnto my welbeloved friend Marke Lucar I giue and bequeath fifty Shillings a yeare in Provisions att Price currant for and dureing the terme of his naturall life; Item my Will is that after the decease of my said Wife my farme & Marsh abouementioned and my land abouesaid called the neck with all and Singular the houseing & appurtenences shall bee and remaine vnto the said William Weeden Phillip Smith and Richard Baily and their assignes qualified and chosen in manner following for Ever[;] that is to say that when it Shall happen that either of them three decease the two Surviving shall make choice of an Vnderstanding Person feareing the Lord to Succeed in the Roome or Place of him Soe deceased, and in case the two Surviveing differ in their choice of the person Soe to Succeed in the Roome or place of him Soe deceased, that then the choice Shall bee decided by Lott, which Person soe chosen Shall bee the assigne of the said Persons abouementioned and shall haue Equall power to act with them in all matters relateing to the disposall of the Proffitt or rent of the said Land and farme from time to time and Soe all Persons chosen as abouesaid to make good the said number of three Shall bee deemed and taken to bee the Assignes of the said William Weeden, Phillip Smith, and Richard Baily abouementioned and none other; wch Said Persons and their saide Assignes from time to time chosen and Succeeding as abouesaid Shall be seized of the said farme and Land called the neck to the vse and vses following for ever that is to say faithfully and truly[1] to distribute and dispose of the rent and Profitt of my Said farme and Land for the releife of the poore or bringing up of children vnto Learneing from time to time for ever, according to Such Instructions as I shall give vnto them beareing Even date with these presents[;] Item my Will is that after the decease of my Said Loueing wife my now dwelling house scituate and being in the Towne of Newport aforesaid, and the Land to itt belonging now in my Possession (Except what is aboue disposed off) containeing by Estimation thirty acres more or less shall bee and remaine vnto my said Cousin John Clarke and the heires males of his body Lawfully begotten for ever, but if hee decease without Such Issue then vnto John Clarke Son of my Co[torn—presumably ou]sin Joseph Clarke and his heires for Ever; Lastly of this my last will and Testament I constitute and appoint my said trusty and welbeloved ffriends, William Weeden, Phillip Smith and Richard Baily full Executors vnto whom and their Assignes Qualified & chosen as abouse[said?—off edge now] I giue and bequeath forty shillings a piece [torn—an]nually for ever, as Some part of recompence for their care and paines in discharge of that trust aboue reposed in them; In Wittness whereof I haue herevnto Sett my hand and Seale the twentieth day of Aprill 1676.

JOHN CLARKE [seal]

Signed, Sealed & Published
in the Presence of
    PHILLIP EDES
    THOMAS WARD
    WILLIAM HISCOX

1. This word is illegible in the original, so I have supplied the reading given in *Rhode Island Historical Magazine* 7 (1886–87): 132.

These[2] are to Signifie that on the 17th day of May 1676 Philip Edes & Thomas Ward two of the witnesses abouesaid before mee and vpon their engagement according to Law did affirm that they Saw the abouenamed John Clarke the Testator Signe & Seale the abouewritten and declare itt to bee his Last Will & Testament as witness my hand
                                                    Walter Clarke Govr

The aboue[3] Written will is Entred vpon Record in ye 158: 159; & 160 pages of ye Book of Record Belonging to ye Town of Newport p[er] Weston Clarke Town Clerk

William Hiscox the other of the witnesses abouenamed appeared before the Councill the 19th of May and affirmed vpon his ingagement that John Clarke deceased did declare this to bee his Last Will & Testament taken [torn—presumably be]ore ye Councill as attest
   [torn]   ye Concill

Subsidiary Instructions by Dr. John Clarke

Whereas I John Clarke of Newport on Rhode Island Physician did on ... the date hereof make & Publish my last Will and Testament and therein did giue grant and devise my farme in the Precincts of Newport aforesaid and a piece of Land in the Precincts of the said Towne called the neck vnto you William Weeden, Phillip Smith & Richard Baily and your assignes chosen and qualified as in my Said Will is Expressed for you and them faithfully to distrubute [sic] the Profitt thereof for the releif of the poore or bringing vp of children vnto Learneing according to Such Instructions as I should giue vnto you, I doe therfore in Pursuance thereof Now Signifie vnto you that In the disposall of that which the Lord hath bestowed on mee and I haue now betrusted you with; you and your Successors shall haue a Speciall regard and care to Provide for those that feare the Lord, and in all things and att all times Soe to discharge the trust which I haue reposed in you as may bee most for the glory of the Most high, and the good and benefitt of those for whom itt is by mee Expressly designed. In Wittness whreof I haue hereto sett my hand Seale the twentieth day of Aprill 1676
                                                    JOHN CLARKE [seal]

2. The ensuing caption is also in the handwriting of Richard Baily.
4. The following is in an unknown hand, probably that of Weston Clark.

Signed & Sealed in the presence of
  PHILLIP EDES
  THOMAS WARD

These are also to order you my Executors to vse your best endeavours for to Procure that debt which hath beene Soe long due vnto mee from the Collony and what of itt you shall receiue to pay vnto my deare & Loueing Wife Sarah Clarke for support of her Self and children

                                                JOHN CLARKE

The aboue Instrument Is Ordered to be Recorded by Ordr of Counll January the 5 1718

                    WM. CODDINGTON Clerke of Counll

Recorded in the town Councell book of Newport No 5 page 303 January the 24 1718/9

Attest   WM CODDINGTON clerke of Counll

Whereas I John Clarke of Newport on Rhode Island Physician did on the day of the date hereof by my last Will and Testament giue and bequeath a Small piece of Land att the South East Corner of my Orchard in the said Towne of Newport vnto William Weeden, Phillip Smith & Richard Baily and their heires and assignes for Ever for the vse and vses to bee by mee declared vnder my hand and Seale, Now bee itt knowne that I haue given the said Land to the said Persons and their heirs and Assignes as abouesaid, Soe that they shall bee Seized thereof only for the vse and behoofe of that Church of Christ on Rhode Island vnto which I am so neerly related for them and their Successors to emproue as a Place for buriall or for any other vse for the said Church as they shall haue occasion. In wittness whereof I haue herevnto Sett my hand and Seale the twentieth day of Aprill 1676

                                            JOHN CLARKE [seal]

Signed Sealed and Delivered
in the Presence of
  PHILIP EDES
  THOMAS WARD

The above Instrument is Rendered to be Recorded January the 5 1718 by the Counll attest

WM CODDINGTON Counll Clerke

Middletown September 18th 1809 Recd the within Instrument to record and the same is recorded in the 3d Book of Probate records page 254. Witness

ELISHA ALLEN, Probate Clerk

Notes

Introduction

1. Theodore Dwight Bozeman, *To Live Ancient Lives: The Primitivist Dimension in Puritanism* (Chapel Hill: University of North Carolina Press, 1988).

2. When he had the chance, Clarke chose not to imbed this point in the title of his book. There he preferred to emphasize that religious persecution in Massachusetts was a return to the oppressive past, whereas the direction taken in England during the Puritan Revolution and Interregnum was toward religious freedom. See John Clarke, *Ill Newes from New-England: Or a Narrative of New-Englands Persecution. Wherin is Declared that While Old England is Becoming New, New-England is Become Old. Also Four Proposals to the Honoured Parliament and Councel of State, Touching the Way to Propagate the Gospel of Christ (with Small Charge and Great Safety) Both in Old England and New. Also Christ out of His Last Will and Testament, Confirmed and Justified* (London: Henry Hills, 1652).

3. Richard S. Dunn, *Puritans and Yankees: The Winthrop Dynasty of New England, 1630–1717* (Princeton: Princeton University Press, 1962), esp. 131–47; Robert C. Black, III, *The Younger John Winthrop* (New York: Columbia University Press, 1966), esp. 221–31, 239–43. The case is nearly the same in Jack M. Sosin, *English America and the Restoration Monarchy of Charles II: Transatlantic Politics, Commerce, and Kinship* (Lincoln: University of Nebraska Press, 1980), 100–104, although Sosin provides a much wider context than the biography of John Winthrop, Jr.

1. Antinomian Storm to Rhode Island

1. John Callender started the argument—at least in print. See his *Historical Discourse on the Civil and Religious Affairs of the Colony of Rhode-Island and Providence Plantations in New-England in America. From the first Settlement in 1638 to the End of the First Century* (Boston: S. Kneeland and T. Green, 1739). It heated up more than a century later. See Samuel Adlam, *The First Church in Providence, Not the Oldest of the Baptists in America, Attempted to be Shown* (Newport, R.I.: Cranston and Norman's Power Press, 1850). A more strident version appeared in Thomas W. Bicknell, *Story of Dr. John Clarke, The Founder of the First Free Commonwealth of the World on the Basis of 'Full Liberty in Religious Concernments'* (Providence: published by the author, 1915). A gentler offering was Wilbur Nelson, *The Hero of Aquidneck: A Life of Dr. John Clarke* (New York: Fleming H. Revell, 1938). Edwin S. Gaustad, *Baptist Piety: The Last Will and Testimony of Obadiah Holmes* (New York: Arno Press, 1980), 140, writes that the argument "seems largely beside the point" because 1644 was "the critical date for Baptists in Rhode Island."

2. This Bible is at the Rhode Island Historical Society in Providence. Although considered Dr. John Clarke's Bible, it was originally his father's and became the property of his brother Joseph. The title page is missing, but the title page of the Concordance indicates that it was printed in London in 1608 by Robert Barker. Louis Franklin Asher, *John Clarke (1609–76): Pioneer in American Medicine, Democratic Ideals, and Champion of Religious Liberty* (University of Pittsburgh, 1997) appeared too late to cite in the present study.

3. According to G. Andrews Moriarty, "The Education of Dr. John Clarke," *Rhode Island History* 15, (April 1956): 42–43, he was probably the John Clarke who went to St. Catherine's College, Cambridge, but may have been the one who received a bachelor's degree from Brasenose College, Oxford, in 1628 and a master's degree in 1632. George Austin Morrison, *Clarke Genealogies: The "Clarke" Families of Rhode Island* (New York: Evening Post Job Printing House, 1902), 15, surmised that Clarke went to Cambridge.

4. Historical Records Survey, Division of Community Service Projects, Work Projects Administration, *Inventory of the Church Archives of Rhode Island; Baptist* (Providence: Historical Records Survey, 1941), 57; William G. McLoughlin, *New England Dissent, 1630–1833: The Baptists and the Separation of Church and State*, 2 vols. (Cambridge: Harvard University Press, 1971), I, 11; Bicknell, *Story of Dr. John Clarke*, 73–74.

5. This displacement of supposedly traditional family strategy was hardly unknown. Obadiah Holmes, of similar family origin, had two or three brothers who graduated from Brasenose College, Oxford. See Gaustad, *Baptist Piety*, 7, 136.

6. John Clarke, *Ill Newes from New-England: Or A Narrative of New-Englands Persecution. Wherin is Declared That while old England is Becoming New, New-England is Become Old. Also Four Proposals to the Honoured Parliament and Councel of State, Touching the Way to Propagate the Gospel of Christ (with Small Charge and Great Safety) both in Old England and New. Also Four Conclusions Touching the Faith and Order of the Gospel of Christ Out of his Last Will and Testament, Confirmed and Justified* (London: Henry Hills, 1652), [xvi–xvii]. This work has been reprinted in *Collections of the Massachusetts Historical Society*, ser. 4, II (Boston: Massachusetts Historical Society, 1854). The transcription was almost letter-perfect.

7. Clarke, *Ill Newes*, [xvii].

8. Ibid., [xvii].

9. William K. B. Stoever, *'A Faire and Easie Way to Heaven': Covenant Theology and Antinomianism in Early Massachusetts* (Middletown, Conn.: Wesleyan University Press, 1978), 10–11.

10. David D. Hall, "Introduction," in Hall, ed., *The Antinomian Controversy, 1636–1638, A Documentary History*, 2d ed. (Durham: Duke University Press, 1990), 6–7, 12–13, 16–20.

11. Stoever, *'Faire and Easie Way to Heaven,'* 161–62, 181–82.

12. Hall, ed., *Antinomian Controversy*, passim, esp. 202–8, 220, 222, 224, 227, 230, 232, 238, 245, 264–66, 275–76, 300–303, 342–44, 352, 358, 362, 372, 376, 378.

13. Nathaniel B. Shurtleff, ed., *Records of the Governor and Company of the Massachusetts Bay in New England*, 5 vols. (Boston: William White, 1853–54), I, 211.

14. Emery Battis, *Saints and Sectaries: Anne Hutchinson and the Antinomian Controversy in the Massachusetts Bay Colony* (Chapel Hill: University of North Carolina Press, 1962), 312, 323, mentioned two men named John Clarke. Battis put Dr. John Clarke in the middle of three categories of Antinomians, "the support group." Battis misleadingly said that this man went to Portsmouth, R.I., permanently. The other John Clarke, of Ipswich, was disarmed for signing a petition in support of Wheelwright but denied that he had done so. A Mr. Clarke of Boston was among those disarmed for backing Wheelwright, and no Clarke of Ipswich was on the list. See Shurtleff, ed., *Records of the Governor and Company of the Massachusetts Bay*, I, 212.

15. Clarke, *Ill Newes*, [xvii–xviii]; William Bradford to John Winthrop, 11 April 1638, in Samuel Eliot Morison, et al., eds., *Winthrop Papers*, 5 vols. (Boston: Massachusetts Historical Society, 1929–47), IV, 23.

16. Thomas Dudley to John Winthrop, 19 February 1637/38, *Winthrop Papers*, IV, 14; William Bradford to John Winthrop, 11 April 1638, *Winthrop Papers*, IV, 23; William Coddington to John Winthrop, 22 May 1640, *Winthrop Papers*, IV, 246. Clarke's narrative

gave a far from adequate story of what happened. Although no one else reported these events in such a complete sequence, he gave himself a greater role than is believable. He said he went north merely as a scout but he may have decided at first to join John Wheelwright, Anne Hutchinson's brother-in-law and the only prominent minister to stick with her, who went to Exeter, New Hampshire. He did not explain why he made this choice initially, and the explanation of his change of mind as based on harsh weather was misleading.

17. John Russell Bartlett, ed., *Records of the Colony of Rhode Island and Providence Plantations in New England*, 7 vols. (Providence: A. Crawford Greene and Bros., State Printers, 1856–62), I, 50–51. Battis, *Saints and Sectaries*, 229–31, gives Clarke no role whatsoever.

18. Roger Williams to the General Court of Commissioners of Providence Plantations(?), 25 August 1658, and Roger Williams to an Assembly of Royal Commissioners, 17 November 1677(?), in Glenn W. LaFantasie, ed., *The Correspondence of Roger Williams*, 2 vols. (Hanover, N.H.: University Press of New England for the Rhode Island Historical Society, 1988), II, 485, 752.

19. John Winthrop, *The History of New England from 1630 to 1649*, ed. James Savage, 2 vols. (Boston: Phelps and Farnham, 1825; rpt. New York, 1972), I 271, 273n.

20. Winthrop, *History of New England*, ed. Savage, I, 271, 273.

21. John Winthrop, "A Short Story of the Rise, reign, and ruine of the Antinomians, Familists & Libertines" (1644), in Hall, ed., *Antinomian Controversy*, 280–82; Winthrop, *History of New England*, ed. Savage, I, 261–62.

22. Winthrop, *History of New England*, ed. Savage, I, 271–73. Savage had Clarke's letter before him as well as the manuscript of Winthrop's history. The section of the manuscript containing this material burned in Savage's office in November 1825, and probably Clarke's letter with it. The letter is not in the Winthrop Papers at the Massachusetts Historical Society. An abbreviated and somewhat inaccurate version of Clarke's report as drawn from Savage's text is conveniently printed in Battis, *Saints and Sectaries*, 347–48. Battis, with advice from medical experts, concluded from Clarke's description that Hutchinson "had expelled an hydatidiform mole." See Battis, *Saints and Sectaries*, 346–47. The most widely available edition of John Winthrop's journal, James K. Hosmer, ed., *Winthrop's Journal "History of New England," 1630–1649*, 2 vols. (New York: Charles Scribner's Sons, 1908), I, 277, omitted the text rather than include the "repulsive details."

23. Winthrop, "Short Story," in Hall, ed., *Antinomian Controversy*, 214–15.

24. Bartlett, ed., *Records*, I, 53–56, 59, 73.

25. Winthrop, *History of New England*, ed. Savage, I, 280–81; II, 38.

26. Bartlett, ed., *Records*, I, 52.

27. As printed in Thomas Hutchinson, *The History of the Colony and Province of Massachusetts-Bay*, ed. Lawrence Shaw Mayo, 3 vols. (Cambridge: Harvard University Press, 1936; rpt. New York: Kraus Reprint, 1970), I, 415.

28. Larzer Ziff, *The Career of John Cotton: Puritanism and the American Experience* (Princeton: Princeton University Press, 1962), 97–98.

29. Dennis A. O'Toole, "Exiles, Refugees, and Rogues: The Quest for Civil Order in the Towns and Colony of Providence Plantations, 1636–1654" (Ph.D. diss., Brown University, 1973), 131–264, treats this period in great detail. See in particular, Bartlett, ed., *Records*, I, 52–53, 63–64.

30. Bartlett, ed., *Records*, I, 88–90, 99.

31. Antoinette F. Downing and Vincent J. Scully, Jr., *The Architectural Heritage of Newport Rhode Island 1640–1915*, 2d ed. (New York: Clarkson N. Potter, 1967), 17, 28, 31, plate 23.

32. Bartlett, ed., *Records*, I, 112.

33. Hutchinson, *History of the Colony and Province of Massachusetts-Bay*, I, 415.

34. Bartlett, ed., *Records*, I, 100.

35. The source commonly cited to show that Clarke did has been Thomas Lechford, "Plain Dealing: or, Newes from New-England: A Short View of New-Englands Present Government, both Ecclesiasticall and Civil, compared with the Anciently-received and Established Government of England, in some Materiall Points; Fit for the Gravest Consideration in these Times," *Collections of the Massachusetts Historical Society*, ser. 3, III (Cambridge, Mass.: E. W. Metcalf, 1833; originally London: W.E. and I.G. for Nath: Butter, 1642), 96 (orig. page 41), 402–3. In the published text, Lechford said that Clarke had been the Elder of the church at Newport, but that the church had dissolved. In a variant but incomplete text in manuscript at the Massachusetts Historical Society, Lechford said Clarke had been the pastor but said nothing about the church having dissolved. Lechford knew only what he picked up from reports in Boston, which were notoriously unreliable and prone to put the worst slant on news from Rhode Island. See also the brief remark in William Coddington to John Winthrop, 9 December 1639, *Winthrop Papers*, IV, 161.

36. Bartlett, ed., *Records*, I, 113.

37. Ibid., 88, 89.

38. Ibid., 94, 125.

39. Ibid., 53, 87, 106, 112, 156.

40. O'Toole, "Exiles, Refugees, and Rogues," 235–36.

41. William Coddington to John Winthrop, 5 August 1644, *Winthrop Papers*, IV, 490; William Coddington to John Winthrop, 11 November 1646, *Winthrop Papers*, V, 118.

42. Nathaniel B. Shurtleff and David Pulsifer, eds., *Records of the Colony of New Plymouth in New England*, 12 vols. (Boston: William White, 1855–61), IX, 23; Edward Winslow, *Hypocrisie Unmasked, A True Relation of the Governor and Company of the Massachusetts Against Samuel Gorton of Rhode Island* (London: Richard Cotes for John Bellamy, 1646; rpt. New York: Burt Franklin, 1968), 83.

43. In September 1648 the United Colonies said Rhode Island was in the jurisdiction of Plymouth Colony (although Plymouth had denied it ten years earlier) and ruled that Aquidneck must submit to Plymouth rather than be admitted to membership as an independent member. See Shurtleff et al., eds., *Records of the Colony of New Plymouth*, IX, 110.

44. William Coddington to John Winthrop, Jr., 31 [sic] September 1648, *Winthrop Papers*, V, 262–63; William Coddington to John Winthrop, Jr., 14 October 1648, *Winthrop Papers*, V, 270; Roger Williams to John Winthrop, Jr., March 1648/49, *Winthrop Papers*, V, 313; O'Toole, "Exiles, Refugees, and Rogues," 450–52.

45. Bartlett, ed., *Records*, I, 217, 221.

46. Ibid., 117.

47. Carl Bridenbaugh, *Fat Mutton and Liberty of Conscience: Society in Rhode Island, 1636–1690* (Providence: Brown University Press, 1974), 133.

48. Deed from Richard Tew to John Clarke, 27 February 1650/51; deed from John Price to John Clarke (represented by Thomas Clarke as attorney), 7 December 1652; both in box 36A, Newport Historical Society, Newport, R.I.

49. Bridenbaugh, *Fat Mutton and Liberty of Conscience*, 39–60.

2. "A Teacher: I will not say an Elder"

1. Christopher Hill, *The Collected Essays of Christopher Hill, Volume Two: Religion and Politics in 17th Century England* (Amherst: University of Massachusetts Press, 1986),

3–9, gives a wise caution against reading denominational history back beyond a time when it actually was justified.

2. Carla Gardina Pestana, *Quakers and Baptists in Colonial Massachusetts* (Cambridge: Cambridge University Press, 1991), 7.

3. J. W. Martin, *Religious Radicals in Tudor England* (London: Hambledon Press, 1989), esp. 2–4, 14–16, 23–35, 188–95; Irvin Buckwalter Horst, *The Radical Brethren: Anabaptism and the English Reformation to 1558* (Nieuwkoop, Neth.: B. de Graaf, 1972), 150 and passim.

4. Murray Tolmie, *The Triumph of the Saints: The Separate Churches of London, 1616–1649* (Cambridge: Cambridge University Press, 1977), 72–80.

5. Patrick Collinson, *The Religion of Protestants: The Church in English Society, 1559–1624* (Oxford: Oxford University Press, 1982), 266–67.

6. John Clarke, *Ill Newes from New-England: Or a Narrative of New-Englands Persecution. Wherin is Declared That while old England is Becoming New, New-England is Become Old. Also Four Proposals to the Honoured Parliament and Councel of State Touching the Way to Propagate the Gospel of Christ (with Small Charge and Great Safety) both in Old England and New. Also Four Conclusions Touching the Faith and Order of the Gospel of Christ Out of his Last Will and Testament, Confirmed and Justified* (London: Henry Hills, 1652).

7. William Coddington to John Winthrop, 9 December 1639, in Samuel Eliot Morison et al., eds., *Winthrop Papers*, 5 vols. (Boston: Massachusetts Historical Society, 1929–1947), IV, 161.

8. John Winthrop, *The History of New England from 1630 to 1649*, ed. James Savage, 2 vols. (Boston: Phelps and Farnham, 1825; rpt. New York: Arno Press, 1972), I, 287–89; Philip F. Gura, *A Glimpse of Sion's Glory: Puritan Radicalism in New England, 1620–1660* (Middletown: Wesleyan University Press, 1984), 64–67.

9. Winthrop, *History of New England*, II, 40–41; William Coddington to John Winthrop, 25 August 1640, 12 June 1643, 5 August 1643, *Winthrop Papers*, IV, 278, 393, 489–90; Dennis A. O'Toole, "Exiles, Refugees, and Rogues: The Quest for Civil Order in the Towns and Colony of Providence Plantations, 1636–1654" (Ph.D. diss., Brown University, 1973), 222, 260n96.

10. Winthrop, *History of New England*, II, 62.

11. Carl Bridenbaugh, *Fat Mutton and Liberty of Conscience: Society in Rhode Island, 1636–1690* (Providence: Brown University Press, 1974), 133–34.

12. Newport First Baptist Records, 129. This list came from Samuel Hubbard, who was not in Newport at the time. The list looks suspiciously short because it had twelve names and they included few women. The number may have been trimmed to equal the twelve Apostles of Christ.

13. Winthrop, *History of New England*, I, 293.

14. In his exposition of Christ's parable of the wheat and tares he argued against the use of governmental authority to punish religious error. See Clarke, *Ill Newes*, [viii–ix], 10, 70–76.

15. George Selement, ed., "John Cotton's Hidden Antinomianism: His Sermon on Revelation 4:1–2," *New England Historical and Genealogical Register*, 129 (1975): 285. Cotton actually did not go far beyond some other English Puritans of the early seventeenth century. See Geoffrey F. Nuttall, *The Holy Spirit in Puritan Faith and Experience* (Oxford: Basil Blackwell, 1947), 36 and passim.

16. Selement, ed., "John Cotton's Hidden Antinomianism," 286–88, 290.

17. Ibid., 288–89.

18. Samuel Hubbard's report of debates on the observance of the seventh day as the sabbath, in "The Book of Records belonging to the Church of Christ in New-port on Rhod-Island under the Pastoral Cear of mr William Peckam & mr John Comer . . ."

(manuscript, Newport Historical Society, Newport, R.I.; hereafter cited as Newport First Baptist Records), 139. In the passage where the quotation occurs, the idea contained in it was attributed both to Clarke and Mark Lucar, so exactly what Clarke thought on this point may be questioned. Cf. Clarke, *Ill Newes*, 49. That this conviction was orthodox has been shown by William K. B. Stoever, 'A *Faire and Easie Way to Heaven:*' *Covenant Theology and Antinomianism in Early Massachusetts* (Middletown, Conn.: Wesleyan University Press, 1978), 90.

19. Clarke, *Ill Newes*, [iv–v], 58, 68. Cf. Song of Solomon 4:15; Jeremiah 17:13; Revelation 7:17, 21:6, 22:1.

20. Clarke, *Ill Newes*, 46. Cf. Nuttall, *Holy Spirit*, 24–25.

21. Clarke, *Ill Newes*, 48.

22. Clarke, *Ill Newes*, [xiv], 57–58, 60–61. Some of the quoted words are in italics in the original.

23. Clarke, *Ill Newes*, 58.

24. E. Brooks Holifield, *The Covenant Sealed: The Development of Puritan Sacramental Theology in Old and New England, 1570–1720* (New Haven: Yale University Press, 1974), 2–3, 140–41; David D. Hall, ed., *The Antinomian Controversy: A Documentary History* (Middletown, Conn.: Wesleyan University Press, 1968), 16, 26, 30, 49, 84–85, 186–88, 230, 238–39, 340; Stoever, '*Faire and Easie Way to Heaven*,' 56, 62–63, 68–69, 82, 85, 90, 120–21.

25. Clarke, *Ill Newes*, [iv, xiv].

26. Clarke, *Ill Newes*, 49, 68.

27. Theodore Dwight Bozeman, *To Live Ancient Lives: The Primitivist Dimension in Puritanism* (Chapel Hill: University of North Carolina Press, 1988), dwells on the deep Puritan urge to restore the primitive church and on p. 137 remarks on how the urge led some Puritans to oppose infant baptism.

28. Edwin S. Gaustad, *Baptist Piety: The Last Will and Testimony of Obadiah Holmes* (New York: Arno Press, 1980), 17, 105–6; Roger Winthrop to John Winthrop, Jr., 10 November 1649, in Glenn W. LaFantasie, ed., *The Correspondence of Roger Williams*, 2 vols. (Hanover, N.H.: University Press of New England for the Rhode Island Historical Society, 1988), I, 302; Champlin Burrage, *The Early English Dissenters in the Light of Recent Research, 1550–1641* (Cambridge: Cambridge University Press, 1912), 302.

29. Pestana, *Quakers and Baptists*, 5.

30. David D. Hall, *Worlds of Wonder, Days of Judgment: Popular Belief in Early New England* (Cambridge: Harvard University Press, 1990), 153–56.

31. Stephen Foster, *The Long Argument: English Puritanism and the Shaping of New England Culture, 1570–1700* (Chapel Hill: University of North Carolina Press, 176–77, has insightful comments on this point. Some orthodox people in Massachusetts came to oppose infant baptism during the 1650s. See Pestana, *Quakers and Baptists*, 15, 47.

32. Charles E. Hambrick-Stowe, *The Practice of Piety: Puritan Devotional Disciplines in Seventeenth-Century New England* (Chapel Hill: University of North Carolina Press, 1982), 123–24.

33. Hambrick-Stowe, *Practice of Piety*, 124; Holifield, *Covenant Sealed*, 143–48.

34. E. Brooks Holifield, *Era of Persuasion: American Thought and Culture, 1521–1680* (Boston: Twayne Publishers, 1989), 42–49.

35. Hambrick-Stowe, *Practice of Piety*, 123–24; Holifield, *Covenant Sealed*, 152–58.

36. McLoughlin, *New England Dissent*, I, 27–43; Hambrick-Stowe, *Practice of Piety*, 123–24.

37. Clarke, *Ill Newes*, 47.

38. Ibid., 41.

39. Ibid., 65.

40. Ibid., 50–52. He cited 1 Corinthians 10:1, 2; Galatians 3:27; Romans 6:4, 5; 8:11; Colossians 2:12. Clarke's comparison of baptism to death and resurrection certainly was not new, but usually the comparison was merely one ingredient in the discourse. See Hambrick-Stowe, *Practice of Piety*, 123–24.

41. Clarke, *Ill Newes*, 51–52.

42. Bozeman, *To Live Ancient Lives*, passim, gives a powerful exposition of how reenactment of sacred precedents was not merely legalistic imitation but ritual identification.

43. Clarke, *Ill Newes*, [xiii].

44. Hambrick-Stowe, *Practice of Piety*, 94; Hall, *Worlds of Wonder, Days of Judgment*, 64.

45. Hambrick-Stowe, *Practice of Piety*, 96–126; Andrew Delbanco, *The Puritan Ordeal* (Cambridge: Harvard University Press, 1989), 230; Holifield, *Era of Persuasion*, 122–23.

46. Clarke, *Ill Newes*, 62. Cf. [ix–x]. On the place of prophesying in Separatist and other radical Puritan circles, as well as early New England, see David S. Lovejoy, *Religious Enthusiasm in the New World: Heresy to Revolution* (Cambridge: Harvard University Press, 1985), 50–61, 66.

47. Clarke, *Ill Newes*, 62.

48. For a summary of the record, see Nuttall, *Holy Spirit*, 77–81.

49. E.g., in Salem. See Richard P. Gildrie, *Salem, Massachusetts, 1626–1683, a Covenant Community* (Charlottesville: University of Virginia Press, 1975), 33; Darrett B. Rutman, *Winthrop's Boston: A Portrait of a Puritan Town, 1630–1649* (Chapel Hill: University of North Carolina Press, 1965), 267–68; Lechford, "Plain Dealing," *Collections of the Massachusetts Historical Society*, ser. 3, III, 75 (orig. pages 15–16); Hambrick-Stowe, *Practice of Piety*, 94.

50. Hambrick-Stowe, *Practice of Piety*, 103–26.

51. Clarke, *Ill Newes*, [ix].

52. The quotation is from a phrase written by Richard Baxter, quoted in Nuttall, *Holy Spirit*, 73. See also Nicholas Temperley, "Psalms, metrical, III," in Stanley Sadie, ed., *The New Grove Dictionary of Music and Musicians*, 20 vols. (London: MacMillan Publishers, 1980), XV, 366.

53. Nicholas Temperley, "The Old Way of Singing: Its Origin and Development," *Journal of the American Musicological Society* 34 (1981): 511–44, esp. 533; Irving Lowens, "The Bay Psalm Book in 17th-Century New England," *Journal of the American Musicological Society* 8 (1955): 22–29, esp. 25–26. The same material without annotations is in Irving Lowens, *Music and Musicians in Early America* (New York: W. W. Norton, 1964). See also Hambrick-Stowe, *Practice of Piety*, 111–15.

54. Temperley, "Psalms, metrical, III," 361–63.

55. Gildrie, *Salem, Massachusetts*, 86; Rutman, *Winthrop's Boston*, 131–32, 213–14; Delbanco, *Puritan Ordeal*, 205–6; Kenneth A. Lockridge, *A New England Town, the First Hundred Years: Dedham, Massachusetts, 1636–1736* (New York: W. W. Norton, 1970), 32.

56. Winthrop, *History of New England*, ed. Savage, I, 295.

57. Gaustad, *Baptist Piety*, 43.

58. Delbanco, *Puritan Ordeal*, 211–31, treats the subject of the style of piety and ecclesiastical practice in Massachusetts with great insight.

59. Isaac Backus, *A History of New England, with Particular Reference to the Denomination to Christians Called Baptists*, 2d ed. with notes by David Weston, 2 vols. (Newton, Mass.: Backus Historical Society, 1871), has this classification implicit or explicit throughout.

60. Gura, *Glimpse of Sion's Glory*, 98–116, 124–25, has a good discussion of General and Particular strands in Baptist mentality.

61. Clarke's treatise on the subject survives, either in its entirety or in a digest, in Newport First Baptist Records, 173, 175. In about 1725, John Comer copied it into the records from a manuscript held by a member of the church named Edward Smith. Comer wanted to persuade the people connected with the church that they should believe in this doctrine, too. It is doubtful that he influenced anybody.

62. McLoughlin, *New England Dissent*, I, 287–302.

3. "New Baptisme"

1. The quote in the chapter title is from Roger Williams to John Winthrop, Jr., 10 November 1649, in Glenn W. LaFantasie, ed., *The Correspondence of Roger Williams*, 2 vols. (Hanover, N.H.: University Press of New England for the Rhode Island Historical Society, 1988), I, 302.

2. Edwin S. Gaustad, *Baptist Piety: The Last Will and Testimony of Obadiah Holmes* (New York: Arno Press, 1980), 3. Letter to Plymouth Colony, 18 October 1649, in Nathaniel B. Shurtleff, ed., *Records of the Governor and Company of the Massachusetts Bay in New England*, 5 vols. (Boston: William White, 1853–1854), III, 173–74.

3.

4. Roger Williams to John Winthrop, Jr., 10 November 1649, in LaFantasie, ed., *Correspondence of Roger Williams*, I, 302.

5. Obadiah Homes to John Spilsbury et al., n.d., in John Clarke, *Ill Newes from New-England: or A Narrative of New-Englands Persecution. Wherin is Declared That While Old England is Becoming New, New-England is Become Old. Also Four Proposals to the Honoured Parliament and Councel of State, Touching the Way to Propagate the Gospel of Christ (with Small Charge and Great Safety) Both in Old England and New. Also Four Conclusions Touching the Faith and Order of the Gospel of Christ Out of His Last Will and Testament, Confirmed and Justified* (London: Henry Hills, 1652), 18. See also *Collections of the Massachusetts Historical Society*, ser. 4, II (Boston: Massachusetts Historical Society, 1854), 45–47.

6. Gaustad, *Baptist Piety*, 19–20.

7. Nathaniel B. Shurtleff, ed., *Records of the Governor and Company of the Massachusetts Bay in New England*, 5 vols. (Boston: William White, 1853–1854), III, 67; William G. McLoughlin, *New England Dissent, 1630–1833: The Baptists and the Separation of Church and State*, 2 vols. (Cambridge: Harvard University Press, 1971), I, 18–19.

8. Clarke, *Ill Newes*, 1–3.

9. Clarke, *Ill Newes*, 3; David S. Lovejoy, *Religious Enthusiasm in the New World: Heresy to Revolution* (Cambridge: Harvard University Press, 1985), 57–60.

10. Clarke, *Ill Newes*, 3–4.

11. Ibid., 4–6. Clarke's story was partly inaccurate on the dates, if nothing else. He said the sabbath was July 20 and then quoted the mittimus for his removal to prison as dated on July 22. He or his printer was wrong about the sabbath, which occurred on July 21 in 1651.

12. Clarke, *Ill Newes*, 5–6, 16.

13. Ibid., 6–14.

14. Ibid., 14–16.

15. Obadiah Holmes to John Spilsbury et al., in Clarke, *Ill Newes*, 22. Presumably Holmes had in mind beautiful flowers rather than thorns.

16. Clarke, *Ill Newes*, 16–34. McLoughlin, *New England Dissent*, I, 20n., points out the questionable parts of Clarke's report on the fines of Holmes and Crandall.

17. John Russell Bartlett, ed., *Records of the Colony of Rhode Island and Providence Plantations in New England*, 7 vols. (Providence: A. Crawford Greene and Bros., State

Printers, 1856–62), I, 234. Roger Williams to John Winthrop, Jr., 6 October 1651, in LaFantasie, ed., *Correspondence of Roger Williams*, I, 351.

18. Perry Miller made this point in *Roger Williams: His Contribution to the American Tradition* (Indianapolis: Bobbs-Merrill, 1953), 49, 78–79. The full title of Williams's book was *A Key into the Language of America: Or, An help to the Language of the Natives in that Part of America, called New-England. Together, with briefe Observations of the Customes, Manners and Worships, &c. of the aforesaid Natives, in Peace and Warre, in Life and Death. On all which are Added Spirituall Observations, Generall and Particular by the Authour, of chiefe and speciall use (upon all Occasions) to all the English Inhabiting those Parts; yet Pleasant and Profitable to the view of all men* (London: Gregory Dexter, 1643).

19. Samuel Gorton, *Simplicities Defence against Seven-Headed Policy* . . . (London: John Macock and Luke Fawne, 1646).

20. Shurtleff, ed., *Records of the Governor and Company of the Massachusetts Bay*, II, 52–54, 57; Gorton, *Simplicities Defence*, 74–78.

21. Shurtleff, ed., *Records of the Governor and Company of Massachusetts Bay*, III, 49.

22. Roger Williams to Gregory Dexter, 7 October 1652, in LaFantasie, ed., *Correspondence of Roger Williams*, I, 366, 370n. Governor of Massachusetts at the time of the Antinomian Controversy, Vane had returned to England late in 1637.

23. Bartlett, ed., *Records*, I, 283–84, 317, 346, 395.

24. W. Clark Gilpin, *The Millenarian Piety of Roger Williams* (Chicago: University of Chicago Press, 1979), 63, 74–78, 147–50, and passim.

25. Theodore Dwight Bozeman, *"To Live Ancient Lives:" The Primitivist Dimension in Puritanism* (Chapel Hill: University of North Carolina Press, 1988), 229–36, 243–62, deflates some extravagant interpretations of Puritan eschatology by earlier authors.

26. Roger Williams to John Winthrop, Jr., 10 November 1649, in LaFantasie, ed., *Correspondence of Roger Williams*, I, 302.

27. Clarke, *Ill Newes*, [xiv–xv], 46, 47, 57. (The quoted words are in italics in the original). There was no hint of the elaborate Puritan eschatology of the first half of the seventeenth century. See Bozeman, *"To Live Ancient Lives,"* 193–280.

28. Clarke, *Ill Newes*, 14.

29. Ibid., [viii], 47, 60, 76. Clarke was slightly clearer in a letter to Obadiah Holmes, 11 October 1652, where he said, "the promise of the glorious coming of our Lord doth quicken and freshen in my heart." Quoted in Isaac Backus, *A History of New England, with Particular Reference to the Denomination of Christians called Baptists*, 2d ed. with notes by David Weston, 2 vols. (Newton, Mass.: Backus Historical Society, 1871), II, 497–98.

30. Clarke, *Ill Newes*, 40, 41, 45.

31. Ibid., 48–49.

32. Ibid., 47–48, 58.

33. See, e.g., James Hallett Christian, "John Clarke: Baptist Statesman" (Th.D. diss., Eastern Baptist Theological Seminary, 1950), 85–95; Robert John Wilson, III, "A Lively Experiment: The Extraordinary Career of Dr. John Clarke of Newport, Rhode Island, 1609–1676" (Granville, Mass.: Pioneer Valley Baptist Association, 1983), 17.

34. Bernard S. Capp, *The Fifth Monarchy Men: A Study in Seventeenth-Century English Millenarianism* (London: Faber and Faber, 1972), 37–42, 76–98 (esp. 90–92), and passim.

35. [W. T. Whitley,] "The English Career of John Clarke, Rhode Island," *Baptist Quarterly* 1 (1922): 369.

36. [Whitley,] "English Career of John Clarke," 370.

37. Ibid.; Richard L. Greaves, "A Colonial Fifth Monarchist?: John Clarke of Rhode Island," *Rhode Island History* 40 (1981): 44–45; Christian, "John Clarke," 90–93; Capp, *Fifth Monarchy Men*, 121. In two letters written during these years, Clarke mentioned millennial expectations. See John Clarke to Robert Bennett, 25 August 1655 and 25

December 1658, in B. R. White, ed., "Early Baptist Letters (I)," *Baptist Quarterly* 27 (1977): 144, 145.

38. [Whitley,] "English Career of John Clarke," 371; Capp, *Fifth Monarchy Men*, 246.

39. Quoted in Gura, *Glimpse of Sion's Glory*, 138. See also Gilpin, *Millenarian Piety of Roger Williams*, 148–49; W. T. Whitley, *A History of British Baptists* (London: Kingsgate Press, 1932), 87–88; Murray Tolmie, *The Triumph of the Saints: The Separate Churches of London, 1616–1649* (Cambridge: Cambridge University Press, 1977), 76–78.

40. Clarke, *Ill Newes*, [xiii]. The quoted words are in italics in the original.

41. Greaves, "Colonial Fifth Monarchist?" 44–45; Capp, *Fifth Monarchy Men*, 246.

42. Tolmie, *Triumph of the Saints*, 39.

43. Gura, *Glimpse of Sion's Glory*, 66–67, 102, 103, 108, 116; Lovejoy, *Religious Enthusiasm*, 48, 72, 99–100; John Winthrop, *The History of New England from 1630 to 1649*, ed. James Savage, 2 vols. (Boston: Phelps and Farnham, 1825; rpt. New York: Arno Press, 1972), I, 291–92, 326; Tolmie, *Triumph of the Saints*, 25, 27, 58–60, 192.

44. Gura, *Glimpse of Sion's Glory*, 142; Greaves, "Colonial Fifth Monarchist?" 45.

45. Greaves, "Colonial Fifth Monarchist?" 43–44.

46. Bartlett, ed., *Records*, I, 485–91.

47. Mortgage in form of indenture, John Clarke to Richard Deane, 15 July 1663, box 36A, Newport Historical Society; receipt from Hanserd Knollys, 27 December 1661, box 36A, Newport Historical Society; receipt from Robert Osler, 2 April 1664, box 36A, Newport Historical Society.

48. Alice Osler to John Clarke, 12 August 1671, box 36A, Newport Historical Society.

49. It is necessary to say he might have tried because the colonial government of Rhode Island in 1666 promised to assume Clarke's obligations to Deane and to prevent Clarke from losing his land. The implication was that the colonial government would pay the redemption and its court would not uphold Deane's rights to a foreclosure. As to the colony's paying Deane, this was empty talk, but the obstruction in the court could have been effective because it cost nothing. See Bartlett, ed., *Records*, II, 175–79.

50. Letter of attorney by John and Elizabeth Clarke, 12 May 1656, box 36A, Newport Historical Society.

51. Alice Osler to John Clarke, 12 August 1671, box 36A, Newport Historical Society.

4. In Caesar's Court

1. John Russell Bartlett, ed., *Records of the Colony of Rhode Island and Providence Plantations in New England*, 7 vols. (Providence: A. Crawford Greene and Bros., State Printers, 1856–62), I, 433–34, 440–48.

2. Nathaniel B. Shurtleff, ed., *Records of the Governor and Company of the Massachusetts Bay in New England*, 5 vols. (Boston: William White, 1853–54), II, 26–27, 40, 41, 50–52.

3. Nathaniel B. Shurtleff and David Pulsifer, eds., *Records of the Colony of New Plymouth in New England*, 12 vols. (Boston: William White, 1855–61), IV, 33, 41, 50–53, 75, 86–89, 117; X, 98.

4. Shurtleff and Pulsifer, eds., *Records of the Colony of New Plymouth*, II, 158–59; IX, 218, 219, 221–22; Shurtleff, ed., *Records of the Governor and Company of the Massachusetts Bay*, III, 198–99, 216; IV, part 1, 17.

5. J. Hammond Trumbull and Charles J. Hoadly, eds., *The Public Records of the Colony of Connecticut*, 15 vols. (Hartford: Brown and Parsons, 1850–90), I, 204, 216,

234, 250, 292, 293, 298, 311, 335, 405, 570–72; Shurtleff, ed., *Records of the Governor and Company of the Massachusetts Bay*, II, 71; IV, part 1, 353; IV, part 2, 103; Simon Bradstreet et al., to Governor and Council of Connecticut, n.d. [after July 1661], *Collections of the Massachusetts Historical Society*, ser. 5, IX (Boston: Massachusetts Historical Society, 1885), 31–32.

    6. Elisha R. Potter, *The Early History of Narragansett, with an Appendix of Original Documents, Many of Which are Now for the First Time Published*, rev. ed. (Providence: Marshall, Brown, 1886), 53–57, 275–76; Bartlett, ed., *Records*, I, 418, 424; Land Evidence records of Warwick (manuscript, City Hall, Warwick), I, 205.

    7. Bartlett, ed., *Records*, I, 449. James N. Arnold, ed., *The Records of the Proprietors of the Narragansett, Otherwise Called the Fones Record* (Providence: Narragansett Historical Publishing Company, 1894) vol. 1 of "Rhode Island Colonial Gleanings," 1–16, 23–25; Potter, *Early History of Narragansett*, 61–62.

    8. Carl Bridenbaugh, *Fat Mutton and Liberty of Conscience: Society in Rhode Island, 1636–1690* (Providence: Brown University Press, 1974), 64–65.

    9. Bartlett, ed., *Records*, I, 448, 480, 482, 496, 505, 506.

    10. There are no surviving records for Newport. The Portsmouth Records show no action on this subject before July 1662 and disclose no results except delay until a mere £20 could be sent in December 1663 and £100 more than two years later. See Clarence S. Brigham, ed., *The Early Records of the Town of Portsmouth* (Providence: E. L. Freeman, 1901), 112, 114, 115, 117, 121–23, 131–32. Warwick records show nothing before plans for a tax in 1662. See Howard M. Chapin, ed., *The Early Records of the Town of Warwick* (Providence: E. A. Johnson, 1926), 131, 138. Providence records for these years are defective but show that a subscription was taken and the money collected was in unknown hands at the end of 1661, that the next year the town planned a tax of £76 2s. to send to the agent, with a tax of another £36 for the same purpose planned the following year. Unfortunately, the outcome of these plans was not reported in surviving documents. See Horatio Rogers et al., eds., *Early Records of the Town of Providence*, 21 vols. (Providence: Snow & Farnham, 1892–1915), III, 7, 28–30, 42–44.

    11. Bartlett, ed., *Records*, I, 143–45.

    12. Bartlett, ed., *Records*, I, 485–87; W. Noël Sainsbury et al., eds., *Calendar of State Papers, Colonial Series, 1574–1738*, 44 vols. (London: H.M. Stationery Office, 1860–1969), V, 4, 5, 20. The texts in Bartlett, ed., *Records*, are not letter-perfect but report the words correctly. Charles M. Andrews, *The Colonial Period of American History*, 4 vols. (New Haven: Yale University Press, 1934–38), II, 42n, pointed out a mystery in the date and may have made more of it than is warranted. The clerk in the office in London wrote endorsements saying the petition was presented on 29 January 1661 and the duplicate on 28 March 1661. Properly, January was the eleventh month in the royal calendar and March was the first, with the year number changing at 25 March. Someone was wrong on one year number or both, at least technically. Quite possibly the error merely illustrates the still-common tendency to forget to change the year number.

    13. Bartlet, ed., *Records*, 125.

    14. Ibid., 432–34.

    15. Ibid., 487.

    16. Ibid., 490–91.

    17. John Clarke, *Ill Newes from New-England* . . . (London: Henry Hills, 1652), 46.

    18. Andrews, *Colonial Period*, II, 42n.

    19. "The Declaration of Breda, 1660," in J. P. Kenyon, ed., *The Stuart Constitution* (Cambridge: Cambridge University Press, 1966), 358. It is generally believed that the text of the declaration was written by Edward Hyde, later earl of Clarendon. In any event, the wording carefully avoided any promise to grant full religious liberty or refrain

from restoring the Church of England to its old forms and episcopal government. See Anne Whiteman, "The Restoration of the Church of England," in Geoffrey F. Nuttal and Owen Chadwick, eds., *From Uniformity to Unity, 1662–1962* (London: Society for Promoting Christian Knowledge, 1962), 52; Godfrey Davies, *The Restoration of Charles II, 1658–1660* (San Marino, Calif.: Huntington Library, 1955), 340–41; R. W. Harris, *Clarendon and the English Revolution* (London: Chatto & Windus, 1983), 275.

20. Clarke was not the first Baptist to build his hopes on the Declaration of Breda and would not be the last of the dissenters to do so. See Mary Anne Everett Green et al., eds., *Calendar of State Papers, Domestic Series, of the Reign of Charles II*, 28 vols. (London: H.M. Stationers Office, 1860–1938), II, 218; Seaward, *Cavalier Parliament*, 168, 171.

21. Wesley Frank Craven, *The Colonies in Transition, 1660–1713* (New York: Harper & Row, 1968), 44–46, 48, 52–53; Harris, *Clarendon and the English Revolution*, 301–2, 306–10. Craven may have been unduly willing to see an easygoing approach to religion in New England on the part of the earl of Clarendon but expressed some undeniable realities well enough.

22. Mortgage in the form of indenture, 15 July 1663, between John Clarke and Richard Deane, box 36A, Newport Historical Society. Deane charged no interest.

23. Trumbull and Hoadly, eds., *Public Records of the Colony of Connecticut*, I, 369, 581.

24. "The Charter of the Colony of the Massachusetts Bay in New England, 1628–29," in Shurtleff, ed., *Records of the Governor and Company of the Massachusetts Bay*, I, 3–20.

25. Sainsbury et al., eds., *Calendar of State Papers, Colonial Series*, V, 74; Trumbull and Hoadly, eds., *Public Records of the Colony of Connecticut*, I, 581.

26. Richard S. Dunn, "John Winthrop, Jr., and the Narragansett Country," *William and Mary Quarterly*, 3d ser., 13 (1956): 77–78; undated and unsigned memorandum, c. July 1662, on "Expedients propounded to mr Clarke," Winthrop Papers (microfilm, Massachusetts Historical Society, Boston), reel 7.

27. Richard S. Dunn, *Puritans and Yankees: The Winthrop Dynasty of New England, 1630–1717* (Princeton: Princeton University Press, 1962), 120–21; Robert C. Black, III, *The Younger John Winthrop* (New York: Columbia University Press, 1966), 86–87, 137; Trumbull and Hoadly, eds., *Public Records of the Colony of Connecticut*, I, 568–70.

28. Trumbull and Hoadly, eds., *Public Records of the Colony of Connecticut*, II, 10; Arnold, ed., *Records of the Proprietors of the Narragansett*, 4, 12.

29. Arnold, ed., *Records of the Proprietors of the Narragansett*, 1–4, 6–8, 10–11, 13–16; Shurtleff and Pulsifer, eds., *Records of the Colony of New Plymouth*, X, 449.

30. Bartlett, ed., *Records*, I, 403–4, 420–21, 435–36, 438–39; Black, *Younger John Winthrop*, 195–98.

31. Black, *Younger John Winthrop*, 208–12; Andrews, *Colonial Period*, II, 43.

32. Black, *Younger John Winthrop*, 213–15, 221–24.

33. Ibid., 223.

34. Copy of John Clarke to the government of Rhode Island, August 8, 1662, Winthrop Papers, reel 7.

35. John Clarke to King Charles II, 14 May 1662, *Collections of the New-York Historical Society for 1869* (New York: New-York Historical Society, 1870), 44–45. This appeal began with the quaint salutation, "My Lord o King."

36. Black, *Younger John Winthrop*, 227.

37. Draft of John Winthrop, Jr., to Earl of Clarendon, 7 June 1662, *Collections of the Massachusetts Historical Society*, ser. 5, VIII (Boston: Massachusetts Historical Society, 1882), 75; John Winthrop, Jr., to Edward Hutchinson, 2 September 1662, *Collections of the Massachusetts Historical Society*, ser. 5, IX, 33–34.

38. Robert Emmet Wall, Jr., *Massachusetts Bay: The Crucial Decade, 1640–1650* (New Haven: Yale University Press, 1972), 164–69, 195, 202, 206, 209, 237; *Collections of the New-York Historical Society for 1869*, 36–43.

39. Roger Williams to John Winthrop, Jr., 6 February 1659/60, in Glenn W. LaFantasie, ed., *The Correspondence of Roger Williams*, 2 vols. (Hanover, N.H.: University Press of New England for the Rhode Island Historical Society, 1988), II, 495.

40. Copy of John Clarke to government of Rhode Island, 8 August 1662. A tailed *p* has been expanded into "per." The same practice will be followed in subsequent quotations.

41. Copy of John Clarke to government of Rhode Island, 8 August 1662.

42. Copy of John Clarke to government of Rhode Island, 8 August 1662.

43. E.g., John Winthrop, Jr., to Edward Hutchinson, 2 September 1662, and Edward Hutchinson to John Winthrop, Jr., 3 November 1662, *Collections of the Massachusetts Historical Society*, ser. 5, IX, 33–34, 41–43.

44. "Expedients propounded to mr Clarke in the business of suing out a charter for the Plantations of Providence & Rode Island," c. July 1662, Winthrop Papers, reel 7.

45. Trumbull and Hoadly, eds., *Public Records of the Colony of Connecticut*, II, 10.

46. Proposals by John Clarke, c. July 1662, Winthrop Papers, reel 7.

47. Copy (verified by Samuel Maverick) of statement by Robert Osler and John Scott, c. July or August 1662, Winthrop Papers, reel 7. The order of events here is debatable. The arbitrators may have proposed the line twelve miles west of Point Judith before Winthrop got the official copies of the charter. See Black, *Younger John Winthrop*, 228–30.

48. Copy of John Clarke to Earl of Clarendon, 8 August 1662, Winthrop Papers, reel 7.

49. See copy of statement by William Thirsby, n.d., and John Winthrop, Jr., to William Thirsby, August 1662, Winthrop Papers, reel 7.

50. Copy of John Clarke to government of Rhode Island, 8 August 1662; Black, *Younger John Winthrop*, 229.

51. Copy of John Clarke to Henry Hyde, Earl of Clarendon, n.d. but before 8 August 1662, Winthrop Papers, reel 7.

52. Copy of John Clarke to government of Rhode Island, 8 August 1662.

53. See draft of John Winthrop, Jr., to William Thirsby, [?] August 1662, Winthrop Papers, reel 7.

54. Memorandum, n.d. but c. August 1662 by John Winthrop, Jr., for William Thirsby on how to explain things to Clarendon, Winthrop Papers, reel 7; Black, *Younger John Winthrop*, 230.

55. William Thirsby to Sir Thomas Temple and Robert Boyle, c. July 1662, Winthrop Papers, reel 7.

56. Copy of John Clarke to the colonial government, 8 August 1662, Winthrop Papers, reel 7. Nothing on the copy tells who made it or when or how it got into the hands of John Winthrop, Jr. The copy may be inaccurate to some extent. The habits of spelling and punctuation in it were different from Clarke's, but such changes were ordinary in copies made during the seventeenth century. As will be explained below, there is reason to think that the last part of the letter was written directly or indirectly by Samuel Maverick rather than John Clarke.

57. Copy of John Clarke to the government of Rhode Island, 8 August 1662, Winthrop Papers, reel 7.

58. Copy of John Clarke to government of Rhode Island, 8 August 1662.

59. Samuel Maverick to Earl of Clarendon, n.d., *Collections of the New-York Historical Society for 1869*, 42–43.

60. Copy of petition by John Clarke to Charles II, 22 September 1662, Winthrop Papers, reel 7.

61. W. L. Grant et al., eds., *Acts of the Privy Council of England, Colonial Series*, 6 vols. (London and Hereford: H.M. Stationery Office, 1908–1912), I, 337; Sainsbury et al., eds., *Calendar of State Papers, Colonial Series*, V, 110 (#370); Black, *Younger John Winthrop*, 230–31.

62. John Clarke to John Winthrop, Jr., 7 October 1662, Winthrop Papers, reel 7.

63. John Clarke to John Winthrop, Jr., 16 October 1662, Winthrop Papers, reel 7.

64. John Clarke to John Winthrop, Jr., 21 October 1662, and memorandum of John Clarke for John Winthrop, Jr., n.d., unsigned, probably late October 1662, Winthrop Papers, reel 7.

65. Harris, *Clarendon and the English Revolution*, 313; Ronald Hutton, *Charles the Second, King of England, Scotland, and Ireland* (Oxford: Clarendon Press, 1989), 194.

66. Copy of proposal by Benjamin Worsley, William Brereton, and Robert Thomson, 19 December 1662, Winthrop Papers, reel 7.

67. Unsigned, undated memorandum by John Clarke, probably soon after 24 February 1662/63, Winthrop Papers, reel 7.

68. Memorandum from John Clarke to John Winthrop, Jr., c. October 1662 and memorandum from same to same, c. February or March 1662/63, Winthrop Papers, reel 7.

69. Unsigned, undated memoranda by John Clarke, late February or early March 1662/63; draft of "Representation" by John Winthrop, Jr., to Clarendon or the Privy Council, 17 March 1662/63, Winthrop Papers, reel 7.

70. Anne Whiteman, "The Restoration of the Church of England," in Geoffrey F. Nuttall and Owen Chadwick, eds., *From Uniformity to Unity, 1662–1962* (London: Society for Promoting Christian Knowledge, 1962), 81, 83; Harris, *Clarendon and the English Revolution*, 298–99, 310–13; Paul Seaward, *The Cavalier Parliament and the Reconstruction of the Old Regime, 1661–1667* (Cambridge: Cambridge University Press, 1988), 181, 186.

71. Edward Hutchinson to John Winthrop, Jr., 3 November 1662 and 18 November 1662, *Collections of the Massachusetts Historical Society*, ser. 5, IX, 41–44.

72. John Winthrop, Jr., to John Mason et al., 4 March 1662/3, *Collections of the Massachusetts Historical Society*, ser. 5, VIII, 79–80; Black, *Younger John Winthrop*, 236–39.

73. Bartlett, ed., *Records*, I, 518. Texts of the agreement differ in spelling and punctuation. There are two in Winthrop Papers, reel 7.

74. Bartlett, ed., *Records*, II, 18–20.

75. Black, *Younger John Winthrop*, 254–55; copy of John Scott to Edward Hutchinson, 29 April 1663, *Collections of the Massachusetts Historical Society*, ser. 5, IX, 53. The notion that Winthrop turned around and helped Clarke get the Rhode Island charter is romantic fantasy built on a short and equivocal statement in the instructions to the royal commission (1664) signed by Sir Henry Bennet. The author stated that the Rhode Island "charter ... passed the Great Seal rather upon the good opinion and confidence the King had in Winthrop than that the differences were composed on the boundaries." In the first place, the comment was on the subject of boundaries and not on the rest of the charter or the award of any charter at all. In the second place, it tells nothing of what the king thought Winthrop had done or would do, but rather suggests that the king (or whoever provided his opinions on this subject) took Winthrop's signature on the arbitration award as sufficient assurance that the conflict would be resolved. In the third place, Winthrop left well before the final text of the Rhode Island charter was written and approved. Black, *Younger John Winthrop*, 242–43, cautiously endorses the overly amiable view of C. M. Andrews that Winthrop not only was vital to Clarke's success but in particular to the clauses on religious liberty. See also Dunn, *Puritans and Yankees*, 141–42.

76. Charles II to governor and assistants of Massachusetts, Plymouth, New Haven, and Connecticut, 21 June 1663, in *Collections of the Massachusetts Historical Society*, ser. 5, IX, 54–55; or W. Noël Sainsbury et al., eds., *Calendar of State Papers, Colonial Series, America and West Indies, 1661–1668* (London: H.M Stationery Office, 1880), V, 143–44.

77. Bartlett, ed., *Records*, II, 6–7.

78. Trumbull and Hoadly, eds., *Public Records of the Colony of Connecticut*, II, 4–5; Shurtleff, ed., *Records of the Governor and Company of the Massachusetts Bay*, I, 9–10.

79. Trumbull and Hoadly, eds., *Public Records of the Colony of Connecticut*, I, 580.

80. The following comparison of the charters is based on Trumbull and Hoadly, eds., *Public Records of the Colony of Connecticut*, II, 3–11; Bartlett, ed., *Records*, II, 3–21. Both charters had many similarities to that of Massachusetts.

81. The inclusion of two passages on punishing wrongdoing came, more or less, from the Massachusetts model. See Shurtleff, ed., *Records of the Governor and Company of the Massachusetts Bay*, I, 16–17. That charter had been written on the assumption that the Massachusetts Bay Company and its members would be in England, where it might exercise only such judicial discipline as other corporations did, but would need a full jurisdiction over crimes, including felonies, committed by people in the colony to be sent to America. In this context, the duality of the clauses in the charter made perfect sense, but it did not in the charters to Connecticut and Rhode Island.

82. The Massachusetts charter had similar provisions, though it included a seven-year exemption from customs. See Shurtleff, ed., *Records of the Governor and Company of Massachusetts Bay*, I, 13–16.

83. The Massachusetts charter, for once, had the opposite provisions. The colony was forbidden to monopolize fishing off its territory and required to let any of the king's subjects use the unimproved coastal regions to dry and store fish. See Shurtleff, ed., *Records of the Governor and Company of Massachusetts Bay*, I, 18–19.

84. Trumbull and Hoadly, eds., *Public Records of the Colony of Connecticut*, II, 5; Shurtleff, ed., *Records of the Colony of Massachusetts Bay*, I, 12, 16–17.

85. Bartlett, ed., *Records*, II, 7, 14.

86. Bartlett, ed., *Records*, II, 8; Trumbull and Hoadly, eds., *Public Records of the Colony of Connecticut*, II, 5.

87. Bartlett, ed., *Records*, III, 7–11.

88. Ibid., I, 145–46.

89. Ibid., I, 485–86; II, 3–4.

90. Ibid., II, 4–5. Cf. I, 490–91.

91. Ibid., II, 5–6. Cf. "Declaration of Breda," in Kenyon, ed., *Stuart Constitution*, 358.

5. Waning Years in Newport

1. Copy of agreement between Richard Barnes and John Clarke, 29 March 1664, and release of claims by Richard Barnes, 15 November 1681, box 36A, Newport Historical Society; John Russell Bartlett, ed., *Records of the Colony of Rhode Island and Providence Plantations, in New England*, 7 vols. (Providence: A. Crawford Greene and Bros., State Printers, 1857–62), II, 588; copy of Thomas Olney to Town Council of Newport, 21 January 1718/19, Newport Town Council Records (manuscript, Newport Historical Society), V, 25.

2. Invoice, 21 March 1663/64, from Thomas Parsons for a consignment to John Clarke, box 36A, Newport Historical Society.

3. Bartlett, ed., *Records*, II, 23.

4. Carewe Clarke's accounts, 30 July 1663 to 20 April 1664, box 36A, Newport Historical Society.

5. Invoice from Thomas Parsons, 21 March 1663/64, box 36A, Newport Historical Society.

6. Invoice from Thomas Parsons, 21 March 1663/64, to John Clarke on consignment; inventory of the estate of John Clarke, 17 May 1676, box 36A, Newport Historical Society.

7. Sheet of accounts with Mr. Johnson, 1666, box 36A, Newport Historical Society.

8. John Clarke's accounts with tenants, 1669 and 1673, box 36A, Newport Historical Society.

9. Bartlett, ed., *Records*, II, 61, 90, 96, 130, 139, 146, 150, 180, 185, 220, 222.

10. Ibid., 242, 374.

11. Ibid., 63–64, 78–81, 433–34; Howard M. Chapin, ed., *The Early Records of the Town of Warwick* (Providence: E. A. Johnson, 1926), 146.

12. Bartlett, ed., *Records*, II, 78n–79n.

13. The quoted phrases are from the title of a pamphlet by Roger Williams, *The Hireling Ministry None of Christ's, or a Discourse Touching the Propagation of the Gospel of Christ Jesus* (London, 1652). As reprinted in Reuben A. Guild, et al., eds., *The Complete Writings of Roger Williams*, 7 vols. (New York: Russell and Russell, 1963), VII, 164, 166–67, it is clear that Williams did not oppose financial support for preachers, so long as it was voluntary, although he preferred that they earn their livings by secular work. Samuel Gorton of Warwick took an even more extreme position against monetary compensation. See Gorton, *Simplicities Defence Against Seven-Headed Policy* . . . (London: John Macock, 1646), 68–71; *An Antidote Against the Common Plague of the World* . . . (London: J. C. [John Macock?], 1657), [xxvi–xxvii], 212; *Saltmarsh Returned from the Dead, In Amico Philalethe. Or, The Resurrection of James the Apostle, out of the Grave of Carnall Glosses, for the Correction of the Universall Apostacy* . . . (London: Giles Calvert, 1655), 73; *An Incorruptible Key Composed of the CX: Psalme Wherewith You May Open the Rest of the Holy Scriptures* . . . (London: no printer specified, 1647), part 1 (second page series), 117.

14. Bartlett, ed., *Records*, II, 79n, 106–7, 143–44, 147, 176–79, 186–87, 204, 254, 337–38; General Assembly to town of Warwick, 27 March 1666, Rhode Island Historical Society Manuscripts, X, 141; Warwick town records, book A2 (manuscript at City Hall, Warwick, R.I., or on photostat or microfilm at Rhode Island Historical Society, Providence), 11–16, 31–33, 35–36, 42–45; Roger Williams to town of Warwick, 1 January 1665/66, and reply, 20 February 1665/66, in Glenn W. LaFantasie, ed. *The Correspondence of Roger Williams*, 2 vols. (Hanover, N.H.: University Press of New England for the Rhode Island Historical Society, 1988), II, 534–50.

15. Bartlett, ed., *Records*, II, 176–79.

16. Warwick town records, book A2, 11, 13–14, 31–33, 36.

17. Chapin, ed., *Early Records of the Town of Warwick*, 169–72.

18. Bartlett, ed., *Records*, II, 338, 358–60, 411–15, 438; Warwick town records book A2, 72, 79, 85–87; Rhode Island Historical Society Manuscripts, X, 143; William Harris to magistrates of Connecticut [February 1671/72], Rhode Island Historical Society *Collections*, X (Providence: Rhode Island Historical Society, 1902), 104–18, 118n.

19. Horatio Rogers et al., eds., *The Early Records of the Town of Providence*, 21 vols. (Providence: Snow and Farnham, 1892–1915), XV, 205.

20. William Brenton to John Green, 15 March 1668/69, Rhode Island Historical Society Manuscripts, X, 139. The document is printed in Rogers, et al., eds., *Early Records of the Town of Providence*, XV, 124–25.

21. J. Hammond Trumbull and Charles J. Hoadly, eds., *The Public Records of the Colony of Connecticut*, 15 vols. (Hartford: Brown and Parsons, 1850–90), I, 389–90 (October 1662).

22. Trumbull and Hoadly, eds., *Public Records of the Colony of Connecticut*, I, 407; II, 527.

23. Charles II to governor and assistants of Massachusetts, Plymouth, New Haven, and Connecticut, 21 June 1663, in *Collections of the Massachusetts Historical Society*, ser. 5, IX (Boston: Massachusetts Historical Society), 54–55; or W. Noël Sainsbury et al., eds., *Calendar of State Papers, Colonial Series, America and West Indies, 1661–1668* (London: H.M. Stationery Office, 1880), V, 143–44.

24. The refusal to honor the clause allowing the enclave is implicit in governor and deputy governor of Rhode Island to governor of Connecticut, 10 March 1663/64. See Bartlett, ed., *Records*, II, 34–36. See also letter to Richard Smith, 4 May 1664, Bartlett, ed., *Records*, II, 47–49; Richard Smith, Jr., to John Winthrop, Jr., 14 May 1665, 7 August 1665, 17 April 1666, in Winthrop Papers (microfilm, Massachusetts Historical Society), reel 8.

25. Bartlett, ed., *Records*, II, 71; Joseph Torrey (as general recorder) to Governor and Council of Connecticut, 26 October 1664; Joseph Torrey (as general recorder) to John Winthrop, Jr., (as governor), 30 November 1664, Winthrop Papers, reel 7.

26. *Samuel Gorton's Letter to Lord Hyde in Behalf of the Narragansett Sachems* (dated 4 April 1662) (Providence: Society of Colonial Wars in the State of Rhode Island and Providence Plantations, 1930). Gorton sent a copy of the sachems' submission and took the occasion to give a summary of what Massachusetts had done to him and his disciples. On the commissioners' instructions, see E. B. O'Callaghan, ed., *Documents Relative to the Colonial History of the State of New York*, 11 vols. (Albany: Weed, Parsons, 1853–61), III, 55–56.

27. Petition of governor and Company of Rhode Island and Providence Plantations to King, n.d., sent to royal commissioners, *Collections of the New-York Historical Society for 1869* (New York: New-York Historical Society, 1870), 140; Bartlett, ed., *Records*, I, 134–40..

28. Robert Carr et al. to Sir Henry Bennet, 27 May 1665, in O'Callaghan, ed., *Documents Relative to the Colonial History of the State of New York*, III, 97; W. Noël Sainsbury, et al., eds., *Calendar of State Papers, Colonial Series, 1574–1738*, 44 vols. (London: H.M. Stationery Office, 1860–1969), V, 300, 317, 342.

29. George Cartwright's reply to the "Briefe narrative" by the governor and Company of Massachusetts Bay, in *Collections of the New-York Historical Society for 1869* (New York: New-York Historical Society, 1870), 94. On Maverick being the guest of William Brenton, see Ibid., 128.

30. Bartlett, ed., *Records*, II, 90–92; *Collections of the New-York Historical Society for 1869*, 139–48.

31. Robert Carr et al. to Sir Henry Bennet, 27 May 1665, in O'Callaghan, ed., *Documents Relative to the Colonial History of the State of New York*, III, 97; *Collections of the New-York Historical Society for 1869*, 107.

32. Memorandum on Rhode Island by George Cartwright, *Collections of the New-York Historical Society for 1869*, 107–8.

33. Ibid., 149–56.

34. Bartlett, ed., *Records*, II, 110–18; Sainsbury et al., eds., *Calendar of State Papers, Colonial Series*, V, 373, 414–15.

35. Robert C. Black, III, *The Younger John Winthrop* (New York: Columbia University Press, 1966), 299–300.

36. Instructions to James Richards by the government of Connecticut, 1668, *Collections of the Massachusetts Historical Society*, ser. 5, IX (Boston: Massachusetts Historical Society, 1885), 76–77.

37. William Brenton to John Winthrop, Jr., 15 November 1666, Winthrop Papers, reel 8.

38. Trumbull and Hoadly, eds., *Public Records of the Colony of Connecticut*, II, 529. William Brenton to John Winthrop, Jr., 15 November 1666, 20 April 1667, Winthrop Papers, reel 8. Copy of John Winthrop, Jr., to William Brenton, 20 April 1667, Winthrop Papers, reel 8.

39. Trumbull and Hoadly, eds., *Public Records of the Colony of Connecticut*, II, 530–33.

40. John Clarke to John Winthrop, Jr., 11 December 1669, Winthrop Papers, reel 9.

41. John Clarke to John Winthrop, Jr., 8 May 1671, Winthrop Papers, reel 10.

42. Trumbull and Hoadly, eds., *Public Records of the Colony of Connecticut*, II, 533–39; Governor and Council of Rhode Island to governor and General Assembly of Connecticut, 23 May 1670, Winthrop Papers, reel 9.

43. John Clarke to John Winthrop, Jr., 8 May 1671, Winthrop Papers, reel 10.

44. Bartlett, ed., *Records*, II, 339, 411, 436, 454, 456, 458–61.

45. Ibid., 33.

46. The enumeration of Friends who were elected has to be conjectural in part because no firm record exists of when individuals became affiliated with the organization that served as the admission office, Rhode Island Monthly Meeting. The surviving records begin in 1676. Supposing that men who were participants in the monthly meeting usually had been members before 1671 and that some others were affiliated in a looser way if their families or descendants were associated with the monthly meeting at the time or shortly later, it is possible to estimate the number of Quakers in the Rhode Island General Assembly from year to year. For a careful estimate, see J. William Frost, "Quaker Versus Baptist: A Religious and Political Squabble in Rhode Island Three Hundred Years Ago," *Quaker History* 63 (1974): 3. For a similar assessment, see Arthur J. Worrall, *Quakers in the Colonial Northeast* (Hanover, N.H.: University Press of New England, 1980), 34–35.

47. Frost, "Quaker Versus Baptist," 39–46, and in the documents he published immediately following, presented the issue as one of a clash of two religions, but in his text he was much more judicious. Worrall, *Quakers in the Colonial Northeast*, 31–38, tried without entire success to put the religious opposition in the context of economic, personal, and other rivalries.

48. Bartlett, ed., *Records*, II, 266, 306, 371, 375, 386, 431.

49. Ibid., 477–78.

50. George Austin Morrison, *Clarke Genealogies: The "Clarke" Families of Rhode Island* (New York, 1902), 15.

51. Bartlett, ed., *Records*, I, 91; Emery Battis, *Saints and Sectaries: Anne Hutchinson and the Antinomian Controversy in the Massachusetts Bay Colony* (Chapel Hill, N.C.: Institute of Early American History and Culture, 1962), 318, 324; John Osborne Austin, *Genealogical Dictionary of Rhode Island, Comprising Three Generations of Settlers Who Came Before 1690*, rev. by G. Andrews Moriarty (Baltimore: Genealogical Publishing Company, 1969), 63.

52. Carl Bridenbaugh, *Fat Mutton and Liberty of Conscience: Society in Rhode Island, 1636–1690* (Providence: Brown University Press, 1974), 66–67, 117, 123.

53. John Noble and John F. Cronin, eds., *Records of the Court of Assistants of the Colony of Massachusetts Bay, 1630–1692*, 3 vols. (Boston: Suffolk County, 1904, 1928), III, 68, 69.

54. John L. Nickalls, ed., *The Journal of George Fox*, rev. ed. (Cambridge: Cambridge University Press, 1952), 625.

55. Bartlett, ed., *Records*, II, 507; Austin, *Genealogical Dictionary of Rhode Island*, 63.

56. Anonymous editor, "Samuel Hubbard's Journal Circa 1633–1686: Manuscripts Relating to Samuel Hubbard of Newport Rhode Island" (Providence: Rhode Island Historical Records Survey Project, Division of Professional and Service Projects, Work Projects Administration, 1940), 9.

57. John Comer, "The best, Most Correct, and Exact account of the first Settlement of the Baptist Churches in Newport on Rhode Island, together with their Progress Down to the Year 1730—to which is added the present State of those Churches—also Some brief account of the same Churches in Places adjacent," Backus Papers, ser. 1, no. 21, Rhode Island Historical Society. For the English background, see J. F. McGregor, "The Baptists: Fount of All Heresy," in *Radical Religion in the English Revolution*, J. F. McGregor and B. Reay, eds. (Oxford: Oxford University Press, 1984), 43; B. R. White, *The English Baptists of the Seventeenth Century* (Didcot, Eng.: Baptist Historical Society, 1996), 36–45.

58. Comer, "The best, Most Correct, and Exact account."

59. Several Fifth Monarchists took up the seventh day sabbath. See Bernard S. Capp, *The Fifth Monarchy Men: A Study in Seventeenth-Century English Millenarianism* (London: Faber and Faber, 1972), 245–55, 257, 258, 261–69.

60. Part of his obscurity stems from his going back to England, arriving at least by 1675. "Samuel Hubbard's Journal," 78.

61. The narrative written by John Comer in the Records of the First Baptist Church, complete with dramatic dialogue at a succession of church meetings (purportedly written down verbatim), was by Hubbard or William Hiscox. The report in "Samuel Hubbard's Journal," of course, was by Hubbard. Isaac Backus derived the passages on this episode in *A History of New England with Particular Reference to the Denomination of Christians called Baptists*, 2d ed., 2 vols. (Newton, Mass.: Backus Historical Society, 1871), I, 125, from the complete original of Hubbard's Journal, which Backus had consulted. See also Edwin S. Gaustad, *Baptist Piety: The Last Will and Testimony of Obadiah Holmes* (New York: Arno Press, 1980), 150–51.

62. Newport First Baptist Records, 137; Comer, "The best, Most Correct, and Exact account."

63. "Samuel Hubbard's Journal," 41. Hubbard referred to writings by Edward Stennett, Cowell, and B. Setlers. Gaustad, *Baptist Piety*, 51–52, contains quotations from a letter from Thomas Trenicke.

64. "Samuel Hubbard's Journal," 40–41, 50–55.

65. Ibid., 60–61.

66. Newport First Baptist Records, 139.

67. "Samuel Hubbard's Journal," 57–58.

68. Gaustad, *Baptist Piety*, 52–53; "Samuel Hubbard's Journal," 58.

69. Gaustad, *Baptist Piety*, 51.

70. Newport First Baptist Records, 143.

71. Ibid., 143, 145.

72. "Samuel Hubbard's Journal," 66.

73. Newport First Baptist Records, 145, 147.

74. Comer, "The best, Most Correct, and Exact account."

75. Newport First Baptists Records, 147, 149.

76. Ibid., 149, 151, 153.

77. Melchior Hoffman, "The Ordinance of God" (1530), in George Huntston Williams and Angel M. Mergal, eds., *Spiritual and Anabaptist Writers: Documents Illustrative of the Radical Reformation*, vol. 25 of the Library of Christian Classics (Philadelphia: Westminster Press, [1947]), 198; G. H. Williams, *The Radical Reformation* (Philadelphia: Westminster Press, 1962), 330–32; Hugh Barbour, *The Quakers in Puritan England* (New

Haven: Yale University Press, 1964), 146. Arthur G. Dickens called Hoffman "the evil genius of Anabaptism." See *Reformation and Society in Sixteenth-Century Europe* (New York: Harcourt, Brace & World, 1966), 130. I am grateful to Hugh Barbour for pointing out the connection of Fox to Hoffman.

78. Newport First Baptist Records, esp. 139, 141, 145, 147, 149, 151, 153.

79. Gaustad, *Baptist Piety*, 88.

80. Deed from John Price to Thomas Clarke as attorney for Dr. John Clarke, 7 December 1652, box 36A, Newport Historical Society; will of Thomas Clarke, 28 July 1674, as quoted in Morrison, *Clarke Genealogies*, 14–15.

81. Inventory of the estate of John Clarke made by James Barker, Thomas Ward, and Phillip Edes, 17 May 1676, box 36A, Newport Historical Society; Rogers et al., eds. *Early Records of the Town of Providence*, III, 22.

82. Bartlett, ed., *Records*, II, 175–79.

83. Morrison, *Clarke Genealogies*, 15.

84. Richard Baily to Sarah Clarke, 28 August 1676, box 36A, Newport Historical Society.

85. John Clarke Bible, Rhode Island Historical Society.

6. Clarke's Estate, His Church, and His Colony

1. John Russell Bartlett, ed., *Records of the Colony of Rhode Island and Providence Plantations in New England*, 7 vols. (Providence: A. Crawford Greene and Bros., State Printers, 1856–62), II, 580.

2. Bartlett, ed., *Records*, III, 5.

3. Letter of administration, 6 June 1676, box 36A, Newport Historical Society.

4. Deposition by Phillip Smith, 5 March 1693/94, box 36A, Newport Historical Society.

5. Horatio Rogers et al., eds. *Early Records of the Town of Providence*, 21 vols. (Providence: Snow and Farnham, 1892–1915), XV, 204–5.

6. Richard Baily to Sarah Clarke, 28 August 1676, box 36A, Newport Historical Society.

7. Originally, the Massachusetts standard was four to three against sterling, but by the latter part of the seventeenth century it was sliding toward three to two.

8. Draft of petition by Phillip Smith and Richard Baily, October 1676, box 36A, Newport Historical Society.

9. Bartlett, ed., *Records*, II, 558.

10. Ibid., III, 22–23.

11. Sydney V. James, *Colonial Rhode Island—A History* (New York: Charles Scribner's Sons, 1975), 93–146, 168–69, 171–72.

12. Rogers et al., eds., *Early Records of the Town of Providence*, XIV, 6.

13. The surviving sequence of acquittances or receipts for shares of this money show that it was paid beginning in August 1677 and not finished until January 1700/01. The payments included one double share to brother Joseph and nine single shares to children of John and Sarah Fiske of Watertown, Massachusetts. Presumably, John was the son of sister Margaret's daughter and probably had died before John Clarke. The documents are in box 36A, Newport Historical Society. John Clarke's will contained a blank for the first name of sister Margaret's daughter, identified only as the wife of Samuel Fiske. She was to get a double share, and her children were to get single shares. Either John misremembered the husband's first name (as he forgot the wife's) or both of them had died. There is no record of a double share to a Fiske.

14. The Providence right was sold for £5 to Thomas Olney, Jr., son of the recently deceased executor, Thomas Olney, and later a trustee himself. Rogers et al., eds., *Early Records of the Town of Providence*, XIV, 85–86. Olney claimed allocations in several divisions and, significantly, got the town's approval for at least one during the time when the town still required such approval. Olney still had rights to divisions when he died in 1721/22. See Rogers et al., eds., *Early Records of the Town of Providence*, IV, 65; VIII, 148; XIV, 43, 44, 117; XVI, 203. Mysteriously, a man named Thomas Kilton claimed the right, presumably contesting the Olney title. See Nathaniel Newdigate ledger of accounts and legal notes (manuscript, Rhode Island Historical Society), folio 82, s.v., "King & Queens Right to estates In land."

The right in Westerly fell afoul of the chronic turmoil in that town, which resulted from John Clarke's failure to get a decisive ruling on the boundary with Connecticut. Connecticut considered it part of Stonington, and the town of Stonington awarded lands in a pattern contradictory to the allocation by the syndicate of purchasers sponsored by Rhode Island. Phillip Smith and his fellow trustees offered John Clarke's share right to Joseph Clarke, son of brother Joseph, who said he would pay the asking price of £5 if the individual right could be converted to a specific tract speedily. A Mr. Turner, he reported, had "an Intent to make troble aboute it," and had—presumably under a Stonington grant—leased out the meadows that seemed to belong to the Clarke share. Joseph promised to do his best to thwart Turner until a division could be made. See Joseph Clarke to Phillip Smith, 1 July 1693, box 36A, Newport Historical Society.

By then, however, one of Joseph Clarke's cousins (or brothers-in-law) presented a claim. Phillip Smith told Joseph that he had offered a division to Mr. Turner, who refused it. So Smith hoped that Joseph would pay the £5 for John Clarke's right and defend it in court. See Phillip Smith to Joseph Clarke, 8 July 1693, box 36A, Newport Historical Society. At this time the town of Westerly was evading obligations to absentee shareholders and kept the process as obscure as possible. Any resolution of the boundary was unlikely to disturb individual holdings, especially tracts actually used by residents. As a result, the John Clarke right may well have been thrown into oblivion.

15. Thomas Olney to the Newport Town Council, 2 January 1718/19, Newport Town Council Records (manuscript, Newport Historical Society), V, 25.

16. Letter of attorney from Sarah Walley (or Mallens?) to William Hedge, 13 August 1678, box 36A, Newport Historical Society.

17. Receipt for rents by Sarah Mallens, 16 June 1691, box 36A, Newport Historical Society. That this was written in Rhode Island is shown by the names of the witnesses.

18. Acquittance or receipt by Sarah Myles, executrix to Sarah Mallens, 14 March 1691/92, box 36A, Newport Historical Society. After the widow's death, the trustees paid the sums given to her children. See Rogers et al., eds., *Early Records of the Town of Providence*, IV, 88–91, 94–95.

19. Lease in articles of agreement between George Brown and Phillip Smith, Richard Baily, and Thomas Olney Jr., 1 January 1676/77, box 36A, Newport Historical Society.

20. Inventory of the estate of Dr. John Clarke by James Barker, Thomas Ward, and Phillip Edes, 17 May 1676, box 36A, Newport Historical Society. On the back of the lease with Brown, under date of 5 April 1677 was a new inventory of livestock and utensils. At that time the numbers were the same, though the sheep were subdivided into 106 ewes, 22 ewe lambs, 43 wethers, 5 old rams, and 4 young rams.

21. Lease or agreement between Edward Wolley and Phillip Smith, Thomas Olney, Jr., and James Weeden 18 July 1695, box 36A, Newport Historical Society. The rent was lowered to £2 in 1702 when Jahleel Brenton took the lease. See Newport Town Council Records, V, 35.

22. Rogers et al., eds., *Early Records of the Town of Providence*, VIII, 89–91; Clarence S. Brigham, ed., *The Early Records of the Town of Portsmouth* (Providence: E. L. Freeman & Sons, 1901), 207.

23. Copy of Phillip Smith, Thomas Olney, and James Weeden, to Richard Deane, 11 November 1693, box 36A, Newport Historical Society.

24. On William Brenton, see John Frederick Martin, *Profits in the Wilderness: Entrepreneurship and the Founding of New England Towns in the Seventeenth Century* (Chapel Hill: University of North Carolina Press, 1991), 74–75. On Jahleel Brenton, see Thomas C. Barrow, *Trade and Empire: The British Customs Service in Colonial America, 1660–1775* (Cambridge: Harvard University Press, 1967), 40, 292n.

25. Indenture between Jahleel Brenton and Joseph Bamford and wife Mary, administratrix to Richard Deane and his daughter Elizabeth, 5 September 1699, box 36A, Newport Historical Society.

26. Thomas Olney to the Newport Town Council, 2 January 1718/19, Newport Town Council Records, V, 25; accounts in Newport Town Council Records, V, 34.

27. Undated narrative about the founding of the First Congregational Church in Newport, probably by Nathaniel Clap but in the handwriting of Thomas Brown (manuscript, Newport Historical Society), box 40, folder 6; Bartlett, ed., *Records*, III, 302.

28. George Champlin Mason, ed., *Annals of Trinity Church, Newport, Rhode Island, 1698–1821* (Newport: privately printed, 1890), 26–27; Raymond W. Albright, *A History of the Protestant Episcopal Church* (New York: Macmillan, 1964), 57.

29. Bartlett, ed., *Records*, IV, 206. William G. McLoughlin, *New England Dissent, 1630–1833: The Baptists and the Separation of Church and State*, 2 vols. (Cambridge: Harvard University Press, 1971), I, 198n, interpreted the law as one aimed at certain unnamed Baptist churches that were planning to make payments to support a minister by contractual obligations, enforceable in the courts. I have found no evidence to support this view. No Baptist church in Rhode Island began to plan a regular salary for a pastor until a decade later. McLoughlin's interpretation may have been influenced by the views of John Leland more than seventy years later in quite a different context. See *New England Dissent*, II, 934, 942n.

30. Edwin S. Gaustad, ed., *Baptist Piety: The Last Will and Testimony of Obadiah Holmes* (New York: Arno Press, 1980), 61–64.

31. Copy by B. B. Howland of diverse documents, including a history of the First Baptist Church in Newport (manuscript, Newport Historical Society), 9–11.

32. John Comer, "The best, Most Correct, and Exact account of . . . the Baptist Churches in Newport," Backus Papers, ser. 1, no. 21, Rhode Island Historical Society.

33. Copy of warrant for arrest of Joshua, Thomas, and Kery Clarke, signed by Governor John Easton, 15 February 1692/93, box 36A, Newport Historical Society.

34. Newport Town Meeting Records (manuscript, Newport Historical Society), I, 47.

35. Copy of town council order, 1 May 1693, box 36A, Newport Historical Society.

36. The subsidiary instructions were not formally recorded in the town council's records until 5 January 1718/19. See Newport Town Council Records, III, 238. See also 241, where the record is almost illegible.

37. Lease or agreement between Jeremiah Weeden and Phillip Smith, Thomas Olney, and James Weeden, 3 March 1693/94, box 36A, Newport Historical Society.

38. W. Perry Bentley et al., "Genealogy of the Peckham Family of Newport and Westerly, R.I., and Its Allied Families" (typewritten, 1957, Rhode Island Historical Society), 161, 163–64.

39. On Jeremiah's affiliation, see Newport Land Evidence Records, post-revolutionary series (manuscript, Newport City Hall), XXIV, 478–84.

40. Gareth Jones, *History of the Law of Charity, 1532–1827* (Cambridge: Cambridge University Press, 1969), 11–15, 32–36, 76–87, 141.

41. Jones, *History of the Law of Charity*, 22–39.

42. Bartlett, ed., *Records*, II, 9.

43. Lyndon's statement is quoted in Isaac Backus, *A History of New-England, With Particular Reference to the Denomination of Christians called Baptists*, 2d ed., 2 vols. (Newton, Mass.: Backus Historical Society, 1871), I, 353n.

44. Bartlett, ed., *Records*, II, 4–6. Church courts—the bishop's court or ordinary—had at various times exercised a variety of jurisdictions over inheritance, even over land devised to noncharitable uses, but mainly over personalty bequeathed by will. See Jones, *History of the Law of Charity*, 17–18; Stephen W. Devine, "Ecclesiastical Antecedents to Secular Jurisdiction Over the Feoffment to the Uses to be Declared in Testamentary Instructions," *American Journal of Legal History* 30 (1986): 308–14.

45. Jones, *History of the Law of Charity*, 40–48, 224–28.

46. Ibid., 36, 69–70.

47. Document by Phillip Smith and Thomas Olney appointing William Weeden, 12 September 1695, box 36A, Newport Historical Society.

48. Bentley et al., *Genealogy of the Peckham Family*, 3, 163.

49. Newport Town Meeting Records, I, 71.

50. Newport Town Council Records, V, 34–49. See also deed exchanging property between Thomas Cornell and the trustees (Henry Tew, William Weeden, and Thomas Olney), 5 March 1704/05, box 36A, Newport Historical Society.

51. For an unsubstantiated claim that it was built in 1639, see Historical Records Survey, Division of Community Service Projects, Work Projects Administration, *Inventory of the Church Archives of Rhode Island; Baptist* (Providence, 1941), 57.

52. Newport First Baptist Church Records, 236.

53. Bentley et al., *Genealogy of the Peckham Family*, 3, 164; Stephen Farnum Peckham et al., *Peckham Genealogy; The English Ancestors and American Descendants of John Peckham of Newport, Rhode Island, 1630* (New York, [1922]), 220–21.

54. Comer, "The best, Most Correct, and Exact account."

7. The Dispute over the Clarke Trust

1. John Comer, "The best, Most Correct, and Exact account of . . . the Baptist Churches in Newport," in Backus Papers, ser. 1, no. 21, Rhode Island Historical Society; "The Book of Records belonging to the Church of Christ in New-port on Rhod-Island under the Pastoral Cear of mr William Peckam & mr John Comer 1725" (manuscript, Newport Historical Society; hereafter cited as Newport First Baptist Church Records), 237.

2. Newport Town Council Records (manuscript, Newport Historical Society), V, 34–49. The council's lawyer, Nathaniel Newdigate, had a book that told him what charitable uses were permissible. They included maintaining the old or poor or physically impaired, building or repairing churches, maintaining a preaching minister, and supporting education in virtually every form except at dancing or fencing schools. See Nathaniel Newdigate's ledger of accounts and legal notes (manuscript, Rhode Island Historical Society), legal notes section, folio 149, s.v., "Uses Trust & Confidence"; William B. Nelson, *Lex Testamentaria: Or, a Compendious System of all the Laws of England, As well before that Statute of Henry VIII. as since, concerning Last Wills and Testaments, . . .* (London: J. Nutt, 1714), 121–22.

3. Newport Town Council Records, V, 25.

4. Ibid., V, 5.
5. Ibid., III, 242.
6. Ibid., V, 4.
7. Ibid., V, 5, 92.
8. Read by origin was a Connecticut man who had graduated from Harvard, served as a minister in a few Connecticut towns until his conversion to the Church of England in 1707, then found himself at loose ends except for some disputes over land, which prompted him to study law on his own and set up as an attorney the next year. After a slow and somewhat clouded early phase, his career began to prosper. Comments on him often hinted at chronic failures to meet Puritan standards of rectitude. Possibly these strictures merely referred to his religious defection. Connecticut officials trusted him to represent the colony on a few occasions, and his success in these episodes led him to move to Boston in 1721. See Clifford K. Shipton, "John Read," in *Sibley's Harvard Graduates: Biographical Sketches of Those Who Attended Harvard College*, vol. 4 (Cambridge: Harvard University Press, 1933), 369–77; David H. Flaherty, "Criminal Practice in Provincial Massachusetts," in Daniel R. Coquillette, ed., *Law in Colonial Massachusetts, 1630–1800*, vol. 62 of Publications of the Colonial Society of Massachusetts (Boston: Colonial Society of Massachusetts, 1984), esp. 197–98.

9. The best information on Newdigate's life appears to be in the manuscript notebook of Dr. Henry Turner, which is book 218 in vault A of the Newport Historical Society. See also Nathaniel Newdigate's ledger of accounts and legal notes, passim; John Russell Bartlett, ed., *Records of the Colony of Rhode Island and Providence Plantations in New England*, 7 vols. (Providence: A. Crawford Greene and Bros., State Printers, 1856–62), IV, 26. A large number of Newdigate's legal documents survive in court records and various collections at the Rhode Island Historical Society and the Newport Historical Society.

10. The time of the move is evident from the page headings in Newdigate's ledger of accounts and legal notes, accounts section, no page no.

11. Bartlett, ed., *Records*, IV, 226, 289.

12. Newport Town Council Records, V, 92, 93.

13. Comer, "The best., Most Correct, and Exact account."

14. Copy of letter from the church at Newport to the church at Swansea, 26 April 1719, in Newport First Baptist Church Records, 230. The copy was made by John Comer from the records of the church in Swansea.

15. Newport First Baptist Church Records, 230, 232, 242.

16. A Massachusetts law of 1672 or earlier had given jurisdiction over all gifts and legacies to support education "or any other Publick use" to the county courts, which like town councils in Rhode Island were the probate courts. The Massachusetts county courts were empowered to make sure that such donations were used according to the intent of the donors. To do this, the courts could require persons who were entrusted with the property "from time to time to give account of their disposl and management thereof to the County Court of that Shire where they dwell, and where such Estate shall lye." The law also empowered the county courts, when they saw cause, "to appoint Feoffees of trust, to settle and manage the same according to the will of the Donors." See *The General Laws and Liberties of the Massachusetts Colony: Revised & Re-printed* (Cambridge, Mass.: Samuel Green for John Usher, 1672), 9. This law contemplated appointing feoffees where none had been provided for but not removing some and replacing them with others. Nor did it provide remedies for mismanagement once it had taken place. Besides, the law may have gone out of force after 1692. The first act of the government organized that year under the second charter continued all earlier laws "not repugnant to the laws of England nor inconsistent with the present constitution and settlement" under the new charter. Quite likely there had been no occasion before 1719

to ponder whether the old law conformed sufficiently to the laws of England. See *The Acts and Resolves, Public and Private, of the Province of Massachusetts Bay. To which are Prefixed the Charters of the Province, with Historical and Explanatory Notes, and an Appendix*, 21 vols. (Boston: Wright & Potter, State Printers, 1869–1922), I, 27. Connecticut had no law on charitable donations before 1719.

17. Records of the Colony of Rhode Island and Providence Plantations (often untitled; manuscript, State Archives, Providence), IV, 207–8.

18. Ibid., 208–9.

19. Ibid.

20. Newdigate was emphatic on the point that English law and statutes applied to the colonies, although he recognized that colonial law might vary from English. See the legal notes section of his ledger of accounts and legal notes, folio 89, s.v. "Law"; folio 96, s.v. "Maxims & rules of law"; folio 117, s.v. "Plantations in America." Newdigate was acquainted with the Statue of Charitable Uses. See the legal notes of his ledger, folio 133, s.v. "Statutes."

21. "Cases Argued and Decreed in the High Court of Chancery, from the 12th year of King Charles II. to the 31st [First Part, 1649–1679]," in *English Reports*, XXII (Edinburgh: William Green & Sons, 1902), 825–26 (orig. pages 18–19); legal notes section of Newdigate ledger, folio 36, s.v. "Devises."

22. Records of the Colony of Rhode Island, IV, 209; Gareth Jones, *History of the Law of Charity, 1532–1827* (Cambridge: Cambridge University Press, 1969), 47–48, 51–52, 224–28.

23. Records of the Colony of Rhode Island, IV, 209–10; Jones, *History of the Law of Charity*, 45–46, 50, 227–28.

24. Newport Town Council Records, V, 13.

25. Ibid., 92.

26. Ibid., 17.

27. Newdigate's ledger of accounts and legal notes, accounts for 3 October 1719. In the list, the item identified as "Hardresses Reports," had a purpose in connection with the wrangle over the Clarke estate. This book was Hardres's reports of Exchequer decrees. The others did not, unless "Keling Reports" was not Kelyng's reports on criminal justice but rather a set that included reports by Keeling. Possibly Newdigate referred to a rather instructive item in pages 201–2 of "A *General Abridgment of Cases in Equity, Argued and Adjudged in the High Court of Chancery*, etc., Vol. II," now most readily consulted in the *English Reports*, XXII, 172–73 (orig. pages 201–2). There an order from the chancellor to Lord Chief Justice Keeling (and the summary of the transaction was attributed to a manuscript by Keeling) told of an inquisition by "Commissioners of charitable Uses" in 1668. The commissioners found that a panel of trustees for charitable uses had failed to employ the profits of land they held for the charitable uses for twenty-two years and so ran up arrears of £3,847 10s. So the commissioners decreed that the trustees who disputed this allegation (the "Exceptants") must *"every of them, being five of the said thirteen* [trustees] . . . *pay the said £ 3847 10s."* Moreover, the commissioners insisted that the feoffees (i.e., trustees) who held the property be changed. Keeling and other judges found several faults in the commissioners' actions and decrees—notably, that some of the Exceptants had not been heard by the jury until after the decrees had been framed, and that the commissioners had misjudged the accounts and had ignored the traditional procedures for an audit in the parish. So Keeling rejected the commissioners' decree. But he and his brethren on the bench added a concluding judgment that might have seemed vital to Newdigate: "and for an *Expedient to prevent the Frustrations of Commissions upon the Statute* for charitable Uses *by the Wilfulness of any Person* . . . [that] *the Persons*

who are complained of for divesting the charity be heard before the Jury" before the inquisition be "found" (i.e., a conclusion reached and the decrees drafted to implement it).

28. Newport Town Council Records, V, 18.

29. Newdigate consulted his law books and found that one assign in trust was not responsible for the acts of another. See legal notes section of his ledger, folio 146, s.v. "Uses Trust & confidence."

30. Newport Town Council Records, V, 27, 92.

31. The business was still pending in March 1719/20 when Governor Samuel Cranston, who was ill, asked the town council to put off for further consideration the execution of its order against the assigns of John Clarke. See Newport Town Council Records, V, 53.

32. Ibid., V, 90, 93.

33. Records of Newport First Baptist Church, 232, 234.

34. Ibid., 232, 234.

35. Newport Town Council Records, V, 4, 88. The council's suspicion on this point may have been stimulated by Newdigate, who had read two texts that together implied a conclusion. One was Nelson, *Lex Testamentaria*, 129–30, where a case was discussed concerning trustees who had leased tithes for less than their true value and let the lessee pocket the difference. The trustees were ordered to lease the tithes at proper rent. The other was in "Cases Argued and Decreed in the High Court of Chancery," first part, 759 (orig. page 195), where the chancellor ruled that trustees for charitable uses who had leased property for below its real worth should make up the difference out of their own estates for the benefit of the poor.

36. Papers of *John Wanton et al. v. Jeremiah Weeden*, in papers of the General Court of Trials (manuscript, Providence College Library or subsequent relocation). The council's order is not complete or entirely legible in what exists of the council's books. Parts of it are in Newport Town Council Records, V, 88–89.

37. Newport Town Meeting Records (manuscript, Newport Historical Society), I, 185, 190, 194.

38. Newport Town Council Records, V, 88–94. Weeden claimed that the Clarke estate owed him reimbursement for his expenses in opposing the town council.

39. Ibid., V, 109. This was in April 1721.

40. Ibid., V, 93.

41. Ibid., V, 123, 124.

42. Ibid., V, 133.

43. Benoni Perham, *American Precedents of Declarations, Collected Chiefly from Manuscripts of Accomplished Pleaders, Digested and Arranged under Distinct Titles and Divisions and Adapted to the Most Modern Practice* (Salem, Mass.: Bernard B. Macanulty, 1802), 288.

44. On the names for the action, see citations in next note. For examples of its use in Massachusetts in these years, see David T. Konig, ed., *Plymouth Court Records, 1686–1859*, 16 vols. (Wilmington, Del.: Michael Glazier, 1978–81), V, 24, 61, 85; VI, 14–15. By 1737, the name was cut down to ejectment and a few signs of English contrivances were in view.

45. David T. Konig, "Editor's Introduction: A Guide to the Use of the Plymouth County Court Records," in *Plymouth Court Records*, I, 163–64; William E. Nelson, *Americanization of the Common Law: The Impact of Legal Change on Massachusetts Society, 1760–1830* (Cambridge: Harvard University Press, 1975), 74; Asahel Stearns, *A Summary of the Law and Practice of Real Actions, with an Appendix of Practical Forms* (Boston: Cummings, Hilliard, 1824), 146, 397n, 398n; Zephaniah Swift, *A System of the Laws of the State of Connecticut*, 2 vols. (New York: Arno Press, 1972; facsimile of Windham, Conn.: John Byrne, printer, 1795), 67–68. Stearns remarked that there were only two times when the fictional ejectment was used, both in quite special circumstances, when

the plaintiff expected that the case would be appealed to the Privy Council. See Stearns, *Summary*, 397n. He missed some examples. See L. Kinvin Wroth and Hiller B. Zobel, eds., *Legal Papers of John Adams*, 3 vols. (Cambridge: Harvard University Press, 1965), I, 261. Nevertheless, William E. Nelson, "Court Records as Sources for Historical Writing," in Daniel R. Coquillette, ed., *Law in Colonial Massachusetts, 1630-1800*, vol. 62 of Publications of the Colonial Society of Massachusetts (Boston: Colonial Society of Massachusetts, 1984), 506-7, tells us that Massachusetts used the English form of ejectment. Stearns also included an example of a colonial type of action of trespass and ejectment in 1694 but did not comment on it. See Stearns, *Summary*, 502. He added that the improvement in real actions during the eighteenth century was "chiefly ascribed to the efforts and influence of John Read." See Stearns, *Summary*, 507.

The use of the term "plea of land" appeared in Rhode Island as early as 1677, when it was treated as a novelty. (Defendants responded to "a plea of Land [As they say].") Previously, disputes over land had taken the name of trespass, trespass upon the case, or trespass of a plea of land. See Irving B. Richman and Clarence S. Brigham, eds., *Harris Papers*, Rhode Island Historical Society *Collections*, X (Providence: Rhode Island Historical Society, 1902), 54, 60, 193, 198, 205, 216, 221. See also Bruce H. Mann, *Neighbors and Strangers: Law and Community in Early Connecticut* (Chapel Hill: University of North Carolina Press, 1987), 87-88. On the English actions, see A. W. B. Simpson, *An Introduction to the History of the Land Law* (Oxford: Oxford University Press, 1961: rpt. 1979), 42, 136-39, 152; William Holdsworth, *A History of English Law*, VII (London: Methuen, 1966; orig. published 1925), 12-18. Newdigate read about ejectment in *The Law of Ejectments* . . . (London: J. Nutt, 1713), especially 7-12.

46. According to Perham, *American Precedents of Declarations*, 288, the claim for damages was a "mere matter of form."

47. Records of the General Court of Trials (manuscript, Providence College Library), I, 348; Declaration and Complaint on behalf of the plaintiffs by Nathaniel Newdigate, in papers of *John Wanton et al., v. Jeremiah Weeden*, in papers of the General Court of Trials. The Newport town meeting probably (the record is defective) had voted in July that no town money should be used to press action on the Clarke estate without permission from a future town meeting. See Newport Town Meeting Records, I, 195; cf. the nineteenth-century transcript, 213.

48. "Cases Argued and Decreed in the High Court of Chancery, from the 12th year of King Charles II. to the 31st [First Part, 1649-1679]," in *English Reports*, XXII, 825-26 (orig. pages 18-19).

49. Newdigate was looking at Thomas Hardres, *Reports of Cases Adjudged in the Court of Exchequer. In the Years 1655, 1656, 1657, 1658, 1659, and 1660. And from thence continued to the 21st Year of the Reign of his late Majesty king Charles II* (London: Assigns of Rich. and Edw. Atkins, 1693), 104. See legal notes section of Newdigate ledger, folio 148, s.v. "Uses Trusts & confidence."

50. *Law of Ejectments*, 8.

51. Newdigate ledger of accounts and legal notes, folio 35, s.v., "Devises"; folio 72, s.v., "Intent"; folio 95, s.v., "Mortmaine"; folio 149, s.v. "Uses Trusts & confidence."

52. Newdigate ledger of accounts and legal notes, folios 86 and 87, s.v., "Leases"; folio 97, s.v. "Misfeasance & Malefeasance."

53. Newdigate ledger of accounts and legal notes, folio 110, s.v. "Ordnary or Judge probatts."

54. Newdigate ledger of accounts and legal notes, folio 143, s.v. "Trespass." These citations had nothing directly applicable to the case against Jeremiah Weeden, but Newdigate picked out parts that he thought useful without regard to context.

55. Newdigate ledger of accounts and legal notes, folio 113, s.v., "Possession & Seisin."

56. Newdigate had anticipated something of this sort. He had studied the Duke of Norfolk's case, which was settled definitively in 1685. Once again, Newdigate was studying noncharitable transfers of land to trustees. The Duke of Norfolk's case has attained renown as the occasion when Lord Nottingham, the lord keeper (chancellor in later terminology), launched a durable rule against perpetuities into English land law. Actually, Nottingham's arguments, which Newdigate noted (rather than the advisory views of the king's judges of the common law), concluded in *denying* the applicability of existing precedents against perpetuities in the case under consideration and affirming the claims of a plaintiff who had been unsuccessful before another tribunal. Lord Nottingham's decree was sustained on appeal by the House of Lords. See "Select Cases in the High Court of Chancery, solemnly Argued and Decreed by the Lord Chancellor With the Assistance of the Judges [Also known as 3 Chancery Cases] [1681–1698]," *English Reports*, XXII, 931–63 (orig. pages 26–54.) Newdigate's interest in this case may have been aroused by more than the dispute over the Clarke donation—he had two sets of cases pertaining to entails to worry about—but he may have been anticipating an assertion by Read that Clarke's will and instructions attempted to create an illegal perpetuity. No such assertion could last long, because the basic concept of an illegal perpetuity was an unbreakable entail, but possibly Newdigate was unaware that charitable trusts were not considered impermissible perpetuities. But he was ready with knowledge of a case that dealt with the subject. On the concept of a perpetuity, see Simpson, *Introduction to the History of the Land Law*, 216. Or Newdigate may have been preparing a defense against Read's argument that any departure from Clarke's will as to the choice of assigns to the original executors would destroy the trust and give the natural heir a right to the estate. The Duke of Norfolk's case was applicable after a fashion. It also could have been helpful on the chancellor's power to protect trusts and hold trustees to their instructions. Newdigate probably was learning what he could about the chancellor's treatment of trustees who committed a breach of trust.

57. Plea and Answer by John Read for Jeremiah Weeden, in papers of *John Wanton et al., v. Jeremiah Weeden*, papers of General Court of Trials.

58. The entry in the Records of the General Court of Trials, I, 348, reported only that a continuation had been requested and granted. These records report nothing further. On the subsequent agreement out of court, see Newport Town Council Records, V, 136.

59. Newport Town Council Records, V, 137, 146. The council's choice of Nathaniel Byfield was an odd one. Byfield at that time lived in Bristol and was a judge of the county Court of Common Pleas and the Probate Court and had served intermittently as judge of vice admiralty. In that position he had been given jurisdiction in Rhode Island, which he used in a characteristic way. In 1705 he had belligerently opposed an effort by the Governor and Council of Rhode Island to declare a lawful prize when Captain John Halsey, acting under a commission from the governor, brought a captured Spanish vessel into Newport. Governor Samuel Cranston vigorously protested, and Byfield just as vigorously held his ground until one of the owners of Halsey's privateer revealed that he had an appointment as agent for the lord high admiral and as "one of the Commissioners for Prizes." This man, named John Coleman, also revealed that he had urged Governor Cranston and his legislature to adopt the law under which Cranston and his council had presumed to declare the captured vessel a lawful prize. Byfield's truculence turned to treacle when confronted with a strong show of authority derived from a high English official. Byfield was a bully, always willing to be chummy with those he thought most powerful. He was often successful, always willing to change sides when he saw the value

of doing so, always willing to take advantage of his eminence to gain something for himself. Wily and cunning, he must have had conspicuous ability to keep himself in prominence. As Barbara Black has remarked, "Byfield was where the action was," even if he had a minor part in it.

Why, then, did the Newport council pick this repellent man to be an arbitrator? Maybe the motives were simple and well-meaning: Byfield was an outsider, a judge with experience in fields of law outside the common law, a person without friends in Rhode Island, and no Baptist. Or maybe Byfield had let key men in the town council think he favored their side. Newdigate had lived in Bristol and surely knew Byfield, if only as the local big shot who had carried on a nasty judicial contest with Nathaniel Blagrove, who was the first approximation of a true lawyer to practice in Rhode Island and Newdigate's opposing counsel in countless cases when Newdigate became the second. On the whole it is unlikely that Newdigate's professional rivalry with Blagrove extended to a personal hostility, however, so it is more plausible to think that Newdigate had an appreciation of Byfield's sycophancy and bullying. Possibly a reason for the choice was to have a man serve as arbitrator who had upheld English law and denounced Rhode Island's actions as violations of it, so he could see how the council had tried to follow English law and would not denounce the colony again for disregarding it. On the dispute over Halsey's prize, see Bartlett, ed., *Records*, III, 537–39; Howard M. Chapin, *Privateer Ships and Sailors; The First Century of American Colonial Privateering, 1625–1725* (Toulon, France, 1926), 179–88. On Byfield's character and contest with Blagrove, see Barbara A. Black, "Nathaniel Byfield, 1653–1733," in Daniel R. Coquillette, ed., *Law in Colonial Massachusetts, 1630–1800*, vol. 62 of Publications of the Colonial Society of Massachusetts (Boston: Colonial Society of Massachusetts, 1984), 57–105 (the quotation is at 57).

60. Records of the Colony of Rhode Island, IV, 277.
61. Ibid., 273.
62. Ibid., 273; Jones, *History of the Law of Charity*, 225.
63. Records of the Colony of Rhode Island, IV, 272–74.
64. Newport Town Council Records, V, 144.
65. Ibid., V, 146.
66. Ibid., IV, 27.
67. Ibid., IV, 28.
68. Ibid., IV, 28–29.
69. Ibid., IV, 29–30.
70. Ibid., IV, 31.
71. Report by committee of five messengers from Baptist church in Swansea to church in Newport, c. April 1722, Backus Papers, ser. 1, no. 5, Rhode Island Historical Society; Comer, "The best, Most Correct, and Exact account."
72. Newport First Baptist Church Records, 238.
73. Ibid.; Daniel White's statement justifying sale of the meetinghouse, Newport 25 June 1728, in Backus Papers, ser. 1, no. 8, Rhode Island Historical Society; Backus Papers, ser. 1, no. 1, p. 31, Rhode Island Historical Society.
74. Document a in folder no. 4, box 103, Newport Historical Society.
75. Newport Town Council Records, IV, 41.
76. Ibid., IV, 45, 46.
77. Ibid., V, 150.
78. Newport First Baptist Church Records, 23.
79. Newport Town Council Records, V, 174.
80. Ibid., V, 192; VI, 237; VII, 72; VIII, 111, 190; IV, 85. The surviving town books do not show what the trustees did about leases to specific individuals, notably the lease to Jeremiah Weeden.

81. Newport Town Council Records, V, 25.

82. The next endowment for the First Baptist Church came in 1748, and then it was a bequest of £150 to be lent at interest by such trustees as the church would choose with the interest devoted to support the pastor or in any interval when the pulpit was empty for "The poor of said Church." (See Newport Town Council Records, IX, 320.) There had been conveyances of land into the control of trustees since John Clarke's death and before the altercations over Weeden's misconduct, but all but one of these—a large endowment for the Newport Quaker meeting—were for simple ecclesiastical purposes: they gave land for a meetinghouse or a graveyard. Such conveyances had been pioneered by Quakers, who developed a standard routine for the formalities and the appointment of new trustees by the church that benefited. The trustees merely held title; the church used and improved the land as it saw fit. The First Baptist Church used this device when Josias Lyndon, Hezekiah Carpenter, and their wives gave land for a new meetinghouse in 1737. (See deed in trust, 6 September 1737, box 103, folder 3, Newport Historical Society; Newport First Baptist Church Records, 39–40.) The first donation to charitable uses that was like Clarke's occurred in 1734, when Nathaniel Kay died, leaving (after the death of his widow) his real estate in Newport and £400 in Rhode Island currency to the minister, wardens, and vestry of Trinity Church (for the time being) to support an Anglican schoolmaster and provide tuition at his school for ten poor boys. See George Champlin Mason, *Annals of Trinity Church, Newport, Rhode Island, 1698–1821* (Newport: privately printed, 1890), 28n.

Epilogue

1. Newport Town Council Records (manuscript, Newport Historical Society), V, 192; VI, 237; VII, 72; VIII, 111, 190; IV, 85. The surviving town books do not show what the trustees did about leases to specific individuals.

2. Ibid.,, V, 25.

3. Middletown Town Council Records (manuscript, town hall, Middletown, R.I.), passim and loose documents at the end of vol. 1; attested copy of the General Council's decrees, October 1813, in account book of John Clarke charity farm, 1753–1835, box 36A, Newport Historical Society.

4. In 1781 the trustees (another William Peckham, Benjamin Hall, and Joseph Pike) decided that to prevent a recurrence of the dispute they would act by majority rule but would first hear the views of a dissenting member. They referred to the old controversy, "which we feel the sad effects of to this day," and feared trouble ahead. See agreement, 12 April 1781, box 36A, Newport Historical Society.

5. William G. McLoughlin, *New England Dissent, 1630–1833: The Baptists and the Separation of Church and State*, 2 vols. (Cambridge: Harvard University Press, 1971), I, 282–317.

6. "The Diary of John Comer," ed. C. Edwin Barrows and J. W. Willmarth, in Rhode Island Historical Society *Collections*, VIII (Providence, 1893), 41n; McLoughlin, *New England Dissent*, I, 294–95.

7. "Diary of John Comer," 25–32.

8. "Diary of John Comer," 35–36, which includes Elisha Callender to John Comer, 13 September 1725 on p. 36.

9. Newport First Baptist Church Records (manuscript, Newport Historical Society), 7, 9, 11, 13.

10. Presumably among the papers that John Clarke left to Richard Baily, this treatise reached Comer from Edward Smith. The likeliest explanation is that it came to Smith through his father, Phillip, who got it after Baily's death.

11. Newport First Baptist Church Records (manuscript, Newport Historical Society), 7, 9, 11, 13.
12. McLoughlin, *New England Dissent*, I, 304.
13. Newport First Baptist Church Records, 5, 13, 23, 25, 27, 29, 43, 101, 103, 179.
14. Newport First Baptist Church Records, 43.
15. "Diary of John Comer," 37, 45, 54, 55, 59, 91, 98.
16. When he left the First Baptist Church, Comer summarized what he had received: £85 14s. 6d. in 1726, £93 12s. 4d. in 1727, £38 in 1728; £43 11s. toward building his house (out of £302 3s. 6d. total cost), and £26 14s. in "Small gifts," for a grand total of £287 11s. 10d. He also listed the debts (and interest) he incurred in building the house. See "Diary of John Comer," 55, 58, 59.
17. John Comer to the First Baptist Church, 10 October 1728, in Backus Papers, ser. 1, no. 20, Rhode Island Historical Society.
18. "Diary of John Comer," 58.
19. Ibid., 94, 100–102.
20. Ibid., 109, 110, 111, 113.
21. Ibid., 119.
22. Ibid., 118; Newport First Baptist Records, 35.
23. Newport First Baptist Records, 33, 35; Clifford K. Shipton, "John Callender," in *Sibley's Harvard Graduates: Biographical Sketches of Those Who Attended Harvard College in the Classes 1722–1725*, vol. 7 (Boston: Massachusetts Historical Society, 1945), 151.
24. McLoughlin, *New England Dissent*, I, 293, 298; Shipton, "John Callender," 152.
25. John Callender, *An Historical Discourse on the Civil and Religious Affairs of the Colony of Rhode-Island and Providence Plantations in America. from the first Settlement 1638, to the End of first Century* (Boston: S. Kneeland and T. Green, 1739). Oddly enough, it was dedicated to William Coddington, a man probably of the Congregationalist persuasion, whose chief distinction was being the grandson and bearing the name of the founder of Newport. See also, Shipton, "John Callender," 153–54.
26. Henry Wilder Foote, *Robert Feke* (Cambridge: Harvard University Press, 1930), 64.
27. Newport First Baptist Records, 39–40, 43.
28. Ibid., 35, 38.
29. Ibid., 38.
30. Deed of land in trust by William Weeden to committee of the three Baptist churches, 22 July 1738 (mentioning earlier gift of 15 May 1734), box 104, Newport Historical Society.
31. Newport First Baptist Records, 37–38.
32. Shipton, "John Callender," 154.
33. Account book of John Clarke charity farm.
34. Newport First Baptist Church Records, 52–54.
35. Isaac Backus, *A History of New England, with Particular Reference to the Denomination of Christians called Baptists*, 2d ed. with notes by David Weston, 2 vols. (Newton, Mass.: Backus Historical Society, 1871), II, 17–19, 497–98.

About the Author

Sydney V. James (1929–93) received his bachelor's, master's, and doctoral degrees from Harvard University. He taught at Kent State University, Brown University, and the University of Oregon before coming to the Department of History at the University of Iowa in 1965. He took pride in the department's democratic tradition and its rigorous approach to faculty recruitment and promotion, serving as chairperson in 1970–74 and 1992–93. Much sought after at the University of Iowa for his keenness and wisdom in educational administration, he served on twenty-five departmental search committees as well as numerous dean's and president's committees to recruit and review university executives and performed many other selfless services.

His specialty was American colonial history. His scholarship was driven by a need to understand the complex conditions that might sustain religious liberty and secular toleration, values he himself cherished; and—as readers of this volume will note—it expressed a particular fascination with religious and legal issues. He brought strong skeptical instincts to his work, together with a delight in precise and thorough archival research. *A People Among Peoples: Quaker Benevolence in Eighteenth-Century America* (1963) explored the tension between Quaker asceticism and attraction to public authority. *Colonial Rhode Island: A History* (1967) is at once a compendium of existing scholarship in the field and a creative synthesis with many original features based on a formidable knowledge of manuscript sources. After 1976 he continue his scrutiny of Rhode Island records and drafted a massive institutional history of the colony. The manuscript, which is not yet published, is available to researchers at the Rhode Island Historical Society. At his death he had virtually completed the present biography of John Clarke and his colony.

James's honors include the Walter Muir Whitehill prize in colonial history (1984) and fellowships from the National Endowment for the

Humanities, American Council of Learned Societies, and the Charles Warren Center for Studies in American History at Harvard University. He served on the council for the Institute of Early American History and Culture and the board of editors of the *William and Mary Quarterly*, and he was a fellow of the Rhode Island Historical Society. He took great pride in his service on the American Historical Association's Committee on Women Historians in 1976–79 and was principal author of the second edition of the association's *A Survival Manual for Women (and Other) Historians* (1980).

Index

Antinomian doctrine and controversy, 4–7, 28, 30, 38
Antinomians in Rhode Island, 10, 12–13, 26, 94
   return to Boston, 27
Atherton Company (or Narragansett Proprietors), 65–66, 70–72, 74, 76–78, 89, 91–93, 95–96

Baptists and baptism, xii, 21, 23–24, 27–28, 32–36, 119
   association with Anabaptists, 23, 27
   and biblical typology, 33–34
   dipping or immersion, 32–33, 35
   in England, 23–25, 40, 53–55
   General Baptists, xii, 24, 40, 53–54
   in Massachusetts, 32, 45–48
   in New Plymouth, 43–45
   Particular Baptists, 25, 40, 53–54
Brenton, William, 26–27, 88, 91–92, 94–95
Brereton, William, 76, 94

church and state, xiii–xiv, 15–16, 22, 26, 39, 50–51, 62–64, 111–12, 124–25, 143–44
Clarendon, Sir Edward Hyde, Earl of, 67, 69, 70, 72–73
Clarke, Elizabeth Harges, 4, 17–18, 56–57, 96
Clarke, Jane Fletcher, 96
Clarke, John
   and Anne Hutchinson's "monstrous birth," 10–12
   and antinomian controversy, 5
   arrested in London, 53
   arrested in Lynn, Massachusetts, 46
   arrival in Boston, 4
   education, 3–4
   English Puritan background, 3–4, 24
   Ill Newes from New England, 25, 50–51, 54, 67, 102
   livelihood, 17–18
   marriages, 4, 96–97
   negotiating Rhode Island's charter, 66–78
   physician, 3, 17–18
   will and trust. *See* Clarke's will and trust
Clarke, John, views regarding
   baptism, 28, 35–36
   church attendance and taxes, 39
   church hierarchy, 22
   church music, 38–39
   direct revelation, 30–32
   prophecy, 37
   sabbatarianism, 102
   Second Advent, 51–53, 55–57
   separation of church and state, 52
   women in church, 37, 54
Clarke, Sarah Davis, 90–97, 105, 109–11
Clarke's will and trust, xiii–xiv, 55, 103–19, 123–45, 147–50, 152
   attempts to control trust by Newport town, 115, 124, 148–49
   and First Baptist Church, Newport, 106, 113–15, 118–20, 124–27, 131, 140–45, 152, 156–57
Coddington, William, 10, 12–16, 51, 94–95
Connecticut
   boundary disputes with Rhode Island, 64–81, 86, 89, 92–93, 95–96
   charter of 1632, 65, 68–69, 73
   charter of 1662, 66–73, 77, 79–80, 89, 91
Cotton, John, 11, 13, 28–32, 51
covenants of grace and works, 6–7

Davis, Sarah, 96
Deane, Richard, 55–56, 64, 76, 87–88, 104, 108–11

Easton, Nicholas, 21, 26, 94–95
eschatology, xii, 51–53, 55–56

First Baptist Church, Newport
   antinomian elements. *See* antinomian doctrine and controversy; antinomians in Rhode Island
   Arian heresy in, 102–3
   baptismal issues. *See* Baptists and baptism
   changing relationship to the state, 143–44
   and Clarke's trust. *See* Clarke's will and trust
   consociational trends, 127, 131, 140, 142–43, 156

dispute over laying on of hands, 97–98,
    153–54
founding, 15, 26
laic emphasis, 22, 37
lay prophesying, 29, 37–38, 155
new meetinghouses, 119–20, 155–56
order of worship, 38
psalmody, 38–39
rejection of fixed creeds, 25, 29, 39–40
resurgent clericalism, 120–21, 145, 151–56
schism, 26–27, 98, 100–101, 140–41
seventh-day sabbatarianism, 98–102
style of fellowship, xii, 22, 25, 41, 124
tithes, 39
trends toward orthodoxy, 97, 103, 152
trends toward urbanity, 144–45, 147,
    150–57
women, role of, 41
Fletcher, Jane, 96
freedom of religion, xiii, 2, 15, 51, 62–64, 74,
    82–83, 143, 167 n. 2

Geneva Bible, 3–4

Holmes, Obadiah, 43–45, 47–48, 50,
    100–102, 112
Holy Spirit, 6–8, 28–31, 54
Hutchinson, Anne, 4–12, 21, 24, 29

Indians, Narragansett, 90, 103

law
  biblical, 6–8
  biblical law as a basis of government, 5,
      13–15
  English law in Rhode Island, xiv, 13–14,
      61–62, 80, 127–28, 130, 133, 136–37
  English law on trusts and the Charitable
      Uses Act of 1601, xiv, 113–14, 116,
      127–28, 138–39
  Rhode Island acts regulating trusts of 1719
      and 1721, xiv, 128, 138
  seisin, 135–36
  trespass and ejectment, 134

Lucar, Mark, 32, 43–44, 79, 87, 99, 105–6,
    109
Lynn, Massachusetts, church in, 45–46

Newport, Rhode Island
  early government, 14–15
  founding, 14
  land allotments, 12–14, 18
  relations to Clarke's trust. See Clarke's will
      and trust
  town council, 112–13, 115–18, 124–44,
      147–50

Portsmouth, Rhode Island, 12–14
  early government, 13
predestination, 5–8, 40, 54, 150, 154, 157
primitive Christianity, xii, 3, 22, 32–33, 44

Quakerism, 26, 93–97

Rhode Island
  boundary disputes with Connecticut. See
      Connecticut
      boundary disputes with Rhode Island
  charter of 1643/44, 2, 16, 49, 51, 59, 61,
      65, 69–70, 79
  charter of 1663, xiii, 59–83, 86, 91
  form of government laid down by charter
      of 1663, 79–83
  General Assembly, 81, 86, 88, 116, 127–28,
      138–39
  patent of 1651, 17, 49
  town councils, 115–17
  visited by royal commission in 1664, 75,
      90–91

sanctification, 5–7, 28
Seekonk, New Plymouth
  church in, 43, 97
Swansea, Massachusetts
  church in, 127, 131, 140

Williams, Roger, 1–2, 16, 44, 49, 51, 54, 68,
    87, 92–93
Winthrop, John, 10–12, 26, 44, 91–93

www.ingramcontent.com/pod-product-compliance
Lightning Source LLC
Chambersburg PA
CBHW031550300426
44111CB00006BA/252